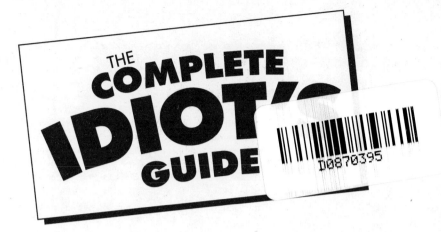

THE **COMPLETE IDIOT'S GUIDE**

Starting a Band

by Mark Bliesener and Steve Knopper

ALPHA

A member of Penguin Group (USA) Inc.

To Nilda, Emma, Pepper, Melissa, and Rose for everything and more. And to Mr. Richard Penniman, Sir Charles Comer, Peter Townshend's nose, and all young bands everywhere.

International Standard Book Number: 1-59257-181-6
Library of Congress Catalog Card Number: 2003116928

06 05 04   8 7 6 5 4 3 2 1

Interpretation of the printing code: The rightmost number of the first series of numbers is the year of the book's printing; the rightmost number of the second series of numbers is the number of the book's printing. For example, a printing code of 04-1 shows that the first printing occurred in 2004.

Printed in the United States of America

Note: This publication contains the opinions and ideas of its authors. It is intended to provide helpful and informative material on the subject matter covered. It is sold with the understanding that the authors and publisher are not engaged in rendering professional services in the book. If the reader requires personal assistance or advice, a competent professional should be consulted.

The authors and publisher specifically disclaim any responsibility for any liability, loss, or risk, personal or otherwise, which is incurred as a consequence, directly or indirectly, of the use and application of any of the contents of this book.

Most Alpha books are available at special quantity discounts for bulk purchases for sales promotions, premiums, fund-raising, or educational use. Special books, or book excerpts, can also be created to fit specific needs.

For details, write: Special Markets, Alpha Books, 375 Hudson Street, New York, NY 10014.

Publisher: *Marie Butler-Knight*
Product Manager: *Phil Kitchel*
Senior Managing Editor: *Jennifer Chisholm*
Senior Acquisitions Editor: *Renee Wilmeth*
Development Editor: *Jennifer Moore*
Senior Production Editor: *Christy Wagner*
Copy Editor: *Michael Dietsch*
Illustrator: *Chris Eliopoulos*
Cover/Book Designer: *Trina Wurst*
Indexer: *Tonya Heard*
Layout/Proofreading: *John Etchison, Ayanna Lacey*

Contents at a Glance

Contents

Appendixes

Foreword

I am writing this foreword for two reasons. First, I was asked to by Mr. Knopper, whom I've spoken to in the past and found to be a wonderful music enthusiast. And second, I am an idiot who started my own band. That said, I do not believe my wisdom, knowledge, or experience can actually be of any assistance to anyone who wishes to be a "rock star." If you love music, love playing music, love recording, and don't mind public humiliation, perhaps some of my advice might prove helpful, insightful, or at least entertaining. But if your desire is to be a "rock star," I am not your man. Or should I say, this is not your book. I make a reasonably good living. But I am not rich by "rock star" standards. I am not famous, and I am not idolized by teenagers. But I am very lucky. I do, pretty much, as I please and live a colorful, unpredictable existence.

The Flaming Lips started in 1983 when I was just 22 years old. I am now 42, and the band has been going, I guess, for 20 years. We did not think we would still be here. We did not think ahead too much. We simply played the kind of music we were interested in.

Question: How did you find other musicians to play with?

Answer: At first I just went to the local music stores and got phone numbers off the notice board. Most of these guys were way out of my league. They could actually play very well and were looking to hook up with some other professionally minded players and do Led Zeppelin covers for a hundred bucks a night. I was more interested in doing my own songs (I couldn't play Led Zeppelin covers), which they thought was kind of a dead end. But eventually I found more compatible musicians within the underground social scene. My brother knew of a "punk rock"–looking guy who played bass. I asked him if he wanted to be in a band, he said okay, and Michael Ivins is still playing bass 20 years later. None of us played very well and, for that matter, still don't (well, me and Michael, anyway). But we thought, "This will be fun. We'll have some adventures together and that will be all we demand of this thing of being in a band."

But one must remember that we were inspired by the times we lived in, and in the late 1970s/early 1980s, the trend was more toward art than musicianship. Sad to say, but if you played with some amount of skill, you were dismissed as being a fake. It seemed the more of a disaster you were, the more genuine you were perceived. Folks would flock to see a dominatrix with electrical tape on her nipples destroy a television using a chainsaw, but the guy who just plays piano—who has time for that? There was a local band called the Hostages that had a woman singer. She wore a beekeeper's mask and shrieked like the worst of Yoko Ono's primal scream therapy. They had two gay guys, and I mention it only to point out how radical it was. This was Oklahoma in 1983—long before the *Queer Eye for the Straight Guy* days. To be openly gay was quite freaky and confrontational, and it added to their identity. Anyway, one played distortion bass, the other amateur drums. They were an onslaught of feedback brutality! And for about 20 minutes, they were the greatest thing you could ever witness. We'd stand there and think, "This is not The Beatles or Stravinsky, but this, in its own way, is just as powerful." We were lucky that we could appreciate a wide range of music.

Question: How did you make records?

Answer: Little by little, we would run into people who made their own records and we'd ask them, "What do you do?" I remember Mike Watt of the Minutemen would say, "Just do it your own way." If your mother tells you that you say, "Ma, you don't know." But if Mike Watt says it, you think, "Well maybe he knows." What he meant was: You can find your niche. And for us, at the time, the trends and the culture would allow it. We wanted to do something weird, and the audience wanted weird bands. We got lucky.

The main thing bands should always be doing is making sure they're interesting and entertaining. Record companies want great, unique artists. They really want to stumble upon a Jimi Hendrix or a White Stripes. A lot of bands think it's the other way around, and perhaps it is. If they want to be "rock stars," they think, "If we sound more like Matchbox Twenty, we'll get signed." I tell people, "Record companies just help you make records. They don't make you interesting. You have to make yourself interesting."

The Complete Idiot's Guide to Starting a Band is a great resource for bands who consider themselves interesting and just need some advice and resources to go a little bit farther. But if you are reading these things and wondering, "Is this true?" the only thing you can do is *try it*. Experience is all there is. Do it and you'll know. You'll see if playing to five people in Bozeman, Montana, in a blizzard on Christmas Eve is tolerable or if you'd rather be warm and cozy sitting at home around the fire with your family. You have to enjoy the uncertainty of it. You have to be a little bit of a daredevil, a little bit of a pirate.

Wayne Coyne
Oklahoma City, Oklahoma
December 2003

Wayne Coyne has been the voice and philosophy of The Flaming Lips, his first and only band, since 1983. The Lips' first big break came when they stumbled upon some very expensive, high-quality music reinforcement equipment on the Oklahoma City black market—which means it was most likely stolen from a church or a country-and-western bar. In 1984, they released their first recording, titled *The Flaming Lips*, on their own Lovely Sorts Of Death record label. Slowly, through relentless touring and playing with the likes of The Butthole Surfers and Meat Puppets, they became one of the more significant "experimental freak rock" outfits of the late 1980s. They signed to Warner Bros. Records in 1990 and consistently released sonically adventurous recordings, culminating with 1997's *Zaireeka*, a challenging, four-disc behemoth. Later albums *The Soft Bulletin* and *Yoshimi Battles the Pink Robots* have become space bible favorites and reveal a vivid and intense psychic life.

Introduction

Mark's first band, The Prophets, had a guitarist so obsessed with The Rolling Stones' Brian Jones that he styled his hair exactly the same way. Once, before going on stage, he squeezed lemons into his hair in a last-ditch attempt to make it more blonde. The band formed in 1965, a time when American teenagers were just starting to imitate The Ventures, The Beach Boys, The Byrds, The Stones, and, of course, The Beatles.

In today's post-peroxide world, few members of bands squeeze lemons into their hair. But the infatuation remains the same. For people in bands, then as now, music is the overriding concern of their lives. The payoff is incredible. Mark remembers playing drums on The Prophets' version of "All Day and All of the Night," by The Kinks. "The band was making a thunderous noise and it sounded all right," Mark recalls. "Suddenly we all realized, 'We can do this!'" No matter how things have changed since 1964, the feeling when the band clicks is just as exhilarating.

Another thing that hasn't changed: Playing in a band is a free ticket to a sort of underground social network. "When I was growing up, there was a burgeoning band on every block. You practiced in the basement and invited your friends over. Or you played in the garage with the door open with hopes of attracting other kids," Mark recalls. "You were getting attention, which is part of what we were after."

Since The Prophets, Mark has played drums in a slew of bands—Humpback Whale, the W.C. Fields Memorial Electric Blues Band, the Pffft, the Fabulous Dogs, and ? and the Mysterians, to name a few. While he has since moved on to managing and counseling bands, the rush comes back when he sits in with friends.

The most significant change from Mark's time with The Prophets is technological. In the seminal days of rock bands, not to mention country, R&B, blues, jazz and pop, gear was primitive and minimal. The PA system The Prophets brought to a gig in 1965 would be laughable today.

Today, guitars and amplifiers are inexpensive enough for most band members to buy. You can make a decent demo at home using cheap microphones, recorders, and mixers. The venues have expanded, too: In the 1960s, clubs catered to lounge singers and jazz combos, but now almost every town has a club that puts on rock or country at least one night a week.

It's so easy that even Steve, who shares Mark's love of bands but is limited to repeating the same blues-piano run in the key of F, is able to join one now and then. A drummer friend recently bought a beat-up Farfisa organ for $100 on eBay and invited Steve to sit in on Velvet Underground and Modern Lovers classics. The friend rented a warehouse room, the band rehearsed once a week for months, and they performed one night at a miraculously packed Chicago club. Although Steve forgot to turn up his amp on the solo for the Seeds' "Pushin' Too Hard," it was one of the greatest nights of his life. That's what bands can do for you.

But don't stop at one night. In *The Complete Idiot's Guide to Starting a Band*, Mark and Steve give the basics of buying and learning instruments, finding band members, setting collective goals, getting gigs, building a fan base, road-tripping, shooting videos, approaching record labels and, most importantly, getting along as a group.

"You can do it," Mark says. "Aside from getting your musical rocks off, you will also gain valuable small-business experience and, maybe most importantly, you can accomplish something. Playing in bands taught me valuable life lessons on how to work with people and do something creative. Plus, it provided a sense of accomplishment in my teen years that set me on a definite career path."

How to Use This Book

This book is divided into six parts, as follows:

Part 1, "So You Want to Be a Band?" begins at the point of conception. You and some friends are sitting around, and somebody remembers an old electric guitar in the attic and suggests you get together to jam in the basement. This part helps you figure out what kind of band you want to be—pop, rock, hip-hop, duo, trio, quartet, one guitar or two?—and coordinate your musical ideas into a cohesive whole.

One key component of this process is communication, one of the book's running themes. If the drummer insists on playing old-school country music while the singer wants to be the Backstreet Boys, you'll stall out in frustration until somebody concocts a compromise. We help you build goals and accept your roles.

Logistics are important, too: No matter what kind of band you are, you'll need musical instruments and instructions on how to play them. You'll also need a place to rehearse that doesn't drive the neighbors insane. Slowly, as you practice and mature, the band may notice everything starting to come together. And it's time to move on to live gigs, from friends' parties to club shows.

Part 2, "Day-to-Day Business with Your Band," examines the trickier aspects of keeping a band together. Suddenly, your members may find conflicts between band business and personal lives—how can they practice every Wednesday night when their significant others have designated Wednesday as movie night? What if the keyboard player writes songs that nobody in the band thinks are any good?

Resolving these issues—and more serious ones like drug and alcohol use—is crucial to maintaining the band's forward progress. Don't let the band stop being fun. If you've come this far, getting paid for playing may soon become a reality.

Of course, when money enters the equation, everything gets a lot more complicated. Who collects it? How do you divide it up? When should you hire a lawyer? These questions are tough for every band, and the sooner you come up with operating procedures to manage them, the sooner you can focus on the music.

Part 3, "The Gig, and How to Get One," plunges into the complex, challenging world of performing live. At first, you'll have to decide at what level you'd like to play—from a friend's party to a local club. Then you'll have to do some scouting to figure out where your style of music best fits in—you won't, for example, want to play boisterous heavy metal at a quiet coffee shop.

After that, it's time to *network*. Contact club owners and bookers and try to land auditions. (If you're lucky enough to get one, play your absolute best.) But when you do get the gig, your work is just beginning. You'll have to arrange transportation to and from the show—including all your gear—and contend with things like sound checks and guest lists. Finally, once you've played around town and developed a reputation, it may be time to take your show on the road. Which means booking out-of-town gigs.

Part 4, "Getting the Word Out," deals with telling everybody you can tell about how great your band is and why they should attend your upcoming show. Begin by studying, and making contact with, the media. Local newspapers and alt-weeklies are instrumental in providing advertising and publicity for your gigs (and, perhaps later, your CDs for sale). Learn, too, how to effectively use the Internet and posters.

As your audiences grow along with your reputation, you may want to think about hiring a professional—if you're ready, well-connected *publicists* can get you into publications you never expected. Maybe *Entertainment Weekly* can write a feature. Or *Vibe*. It can't hurt to try, right?

Part 5, "Making a Record," explains both the musical and technical details of cranking up recording gear to make a *demo* or for-sale compact disc. A demo is your musical "calling card" to send to club owners, managers, booking agents, radio programmers, and record labels. A for-sale CD, of course, is a great exposure tool on many levels—also, it's a way for the band to make some extra money.

To make a record, you'll have to record at home or go to a *studio*, and it's certainly possible these days to record in your rehearsal space, but for a more professional sound, you'll have to pay by the hour. Although it's not necessary to know what every knob does on every device, the more you learn, the more prepared you'll be for the next recording session.

Part 6, "Taking Your Band to the Next Level," is the "advanced" section of the book. Up until now, you've played some gigs, had some fun, tinkered in the studio, and maybe come out with a fan base and a demo. Now you're considering music as a full-time career—or even a path to stardom and riches. It can be done. You'll need to ratchet up the level of intensity and professionalism by hiring producers, making videos, and approaching record labels.

Networking, again, is a key element of this process. Networking can mean hiring a lawyer to take your demo to a record-label A&R representative or driving your van to a music-industry festival like South by Southwest and talking to as many important people as possible. If you're good and really, really lucky, you might wind up with a hit—and a whole new set of challenges.

But you don't have to set "The Big Time" as your band's ultimate goal. Thousands of bands have made great music and perfectly respectable livings—or supplemented their day jobs—by playing weekend gigs.

You'll also find several informative boxes throughout the manuscript that you won't want to skip:

Avoiding Bad Notes

Don't do this stuff, or you might wind up in one of the common traps that dooms many a promising band.

Behind the Music

Gaffer tape is crucially important to a live performance! (And other facts and inside band dirt you probably didn't know.)

Backstage Insights

Follow these tips to make collaborating, learning to play, buying equipment, songwriting, recording, marketing, and every other aspect of the music business easier.

Words to Rock By

These definitions will help you identify each piece of gear, the elements of a press kit, technical terms, and everything else you need to know about the world of bands.

Acknowledgments

In addition to their families, Mark and Steve wish to thank the following people for valuable time and assistance: John Macy, Lisa Shively, Michael Yarmy, Michael Kudreiko, Peter Geisheker, Keren Poznansky, and Rick Gershon. Special thanks, too, to Jessica Faust, Jennifer Moore, Renee Wilmeth, and the other fine editors of this book and series.

Special Thanks to the Technical Reviewer

The Complete Idiot's Guide to Starting a Band was reviewed by an expert who double-checked the accuracy of what you'll learn here, to help us ensure that this book gives you everything you need to know about the music industry. Special thanks are extended to Todd Unruh.

Trademarks

All terms mentioned in this book that are known to be or are suspected of being trademarks or service marks have been appropriately capitalized. Alpha Books and Penguin Group (USA) Inc. cannot attest to the accuracy of this information. Use of a term in this book should not be regarded as affecting the validity of any trademark or service mark.

Part 1

So You Want to Be a Band?

You're not the first one. John Lennon, Mick Jagger, Grace Slick, Sting, Johnny Rotten, Kurt Cobain, Natalie Maines, and countless other pop stars have been in your position, too. In addition to talent, all these names had an emotional connection to making music with other people and a desire to work hard on every aspect of their art and business.

You probably won't jump from tuning your guitars in the basement tonight to the top of the charts tomorrow morning. Becoming a successful band takes much longer than that—first, all the members have to buy instruments and learn to play them; then, they have to play together. Most important, they must be willing to commit to hard work.

These tasks are more difficult and time-consuming than you'd expect. But if the band sticks with them long enough, it might just achieve its collective goals, whether they're to play every weekend at parties or sell 10 million records.

1

Building on Your Talent and Commitment

In This Chapter

◆ The exhilarating rush of being in a band

◆ The benefits of duos, trios, quartets, and more

◆ Can you make a living at this?

◆ Picking the instrument you'd like to play

◆ Getting better via practice, teachers, and shows

The lights go on, the crowd roars, somebody hits a power chord on a guitar, and suddenly you feel the rush. When you're in a band, there's nothing quite like the feeling of everybody onstage playing in perfect harmony before lively admirers. Of course, you may not achieve this feeling right away—there are instruments to buy, chords to learn, songs to memorize, party organizers to schmooze, and promotional websites to build. But eventually, if your band works hard enough, it may get a tantalizing taste of this exhilarating feeling. That's the fun part of being in a band, the part that makes perfect sense, the part that redeems all the practice, gear-schlepping, and travel.

To begin this adventure in music, which could last a few weeks or the rest of your life, start with this chapter, in which we define a band and help you decide what kind you want to be. After that it's just a matter of getting better.

What Is a Band?

The dictionary definition of *band* is a group of people getting together for a common purpose. In music, the concept of a band means much more than that.

The first official "bands" in popular music were big bands, which in the 1930s and 1940s were collectives of horn players, guitarists, percussionists, and singers who played swing jazz. (Actually, bands were around even earlier, given John Philips Sousa marching bands, military-style bands, and jazz pioneers that existed around the turn of the century.) But big bands had too many members to travel easily across the country, so rhythm-and-blues and newer jazz musicians reduced the number to roughly four or five people per band. This configuration was more flexible and affordable, and the trend continues today.

The first rock 'n' roll bands arrived in the 1950s, notably Elvis Presley and his three-man rockabilly combo, guitarist Scotty Moore, bassist Bill Black, and drummer D. J. Fontana. As the music grew, the bands expanded—The Beatles pioneered the classic pop quartet, with two guitarists, a bass player, a drummer, and four members who could sing. Rock, in addition to country, folk, blues, bluegrass, and pop, has since gone through many permutations, from a lone singer such as Joan Baez to a 27-piece harp-choir-guitar band such as The Polyphonic Spree. There are no rules on this subject; choose as many or as few members as you need to properly get the music across.

Backing Up the Star

Sometimes bands have an obvious star, who is often also the creative talent, and the rest of the musicians will step into the background. Bruce Springsteen & the E Street Band, Tom Petty & the Heartbreakers, and Lil Jon & The East Side Boyz are among the examples from pop-music history—early on, the sidemen accepted their roles as supporting players. In these situations, the star gets top billing on club marquees, while the band develops into a loyal coalition of players who take orders from the leader.

Another type of backup band involves a well-known frontperson who hires musicians to bring his or her music to life. Next time pop star Christina Aguilera comes to an arena in your town, notice the people behind her—although it may not be obvious from the audience, they're a salaried band hired to keep the music going. (Sometimes they'll play the same role in a recording studio.) But some backup bands form out of longtime friendships with the leaders, sticking with them as they climb from obscurity to stardom.

These kinds of bands are worth studying: Which musicians play solos, and when? What instruments sound good together? Can you hear the keyboardist all the time? A great way to learn broad band concepts like tempo and dynamics is to pay attention to how the professionals do it.

The players in any of these backup bands probably started exactly where you're starting now—with a few friends who think it'd be cool to be in a band. These professional musicians are proof that if you work hard and do all the right things, from booking club shows to maintaining a mailing list, you have a chance. Perhaps success in a self-contained band, in which each member has an equal role in the music and decisions, awaits you. Or perhaps you're destined to play your bass in a band led by somebody else. Both of these "working musician" configurations are equally respectable—and fun.

Self-Contained Groups

At this stage, your best opportunity to form a band is in a self-contained group of musicians who plan to pick a style, rehearse, and perform together. You'll do all the fundamental band work yourselves without hiring outside people. (Once you get bigger and need help, the hiring will begin.)

Behind the Music

Bands break up all the time, making longevity a precious commodity in pop and rock music. But here are 10 that have been together—continuously—for more than 20 years:

- The Rolling Stones
- U2
- NRBQ
- Sonic Youth
- Tom Petty and the Heartbreakers
- Bon Jovi
- Beastie Boys
- Los Lobos
- They Might Be Giants
- The Nitty Gritty Dirt Band

A self-contained group can be incredibly rewarding. (Or incredibly painful, if you fall in with the wrong combination of people.) Whether you stay together for three weeks or an entire career, band members make emotional connections with each other and can stay friends forever. If they're really lucky, they'll wind up like U2, a group of Irish schoolmates who managed to stay together as a profitable and rewarding band for two decades and counting.

Backstage Insights

Many band members start out as a group of friends who come together because they enjoy each other's company, not necessarily because they've recruited a musical ringer. It's not necessary to be a virtuoso player as long as you enjoy the music and are willing to cooperate with others.

Playing Together

Once you form a band, it won't take long to realize what you're doing isn't easy. The music may come easily to you, especially if you're starting out with basic, three-chord rock, pop, country, or blues, but concepts like *teamwork, cooperation, chemistry,* and *soul* are much more challenging to master. To do so, keep in mind that a band playing together as an entire unit is far more effective than everybody soloing at the same time.

What Kind of Band Do You Want to Be?

These days, there are more kinds of bands playing more styles of music in more configurations than anyone could possibly count. Some are party bands, playing upbeat versions of familiar rock 'n' roll songs to get people dancing. Some are wedding bands, playing a specific roster of standards predetermined by the bride and groom. Some will play original music, written and performed by the band members, in an attempt to fill clubs and sell compact discs.

It's not important, yet, to know exactly which of these configurations, if any, you'd like to be. Try to let your style evolve, rather than defining it so rigidly that there's no room for experimentation or dissent. The Rolling Stones started out as a blues band, performing Muddy Waters and Chuck Berry songs, but have evolved over the decades into perhaps the most successful rock 'n' roll band in the world.

Image and Sex Appeal

Do you have to be good-looking to be in a band? No! Check out pictures of Aerosmith singer Steven Tyler, ex-Cars leader Ric Ocasek, the Stones' Mick Jagger, and certain weird-facial-haired members of the Backstreet Boys. Not the hunkiest men in the world. But they all had a certain *je ne sais quoi,* a stage presence or charisma that made them effective and desirable as front men for bands.

Remember, too, that the image of the pop-star hero you're trying to emulate may be heavily manipulated by the time it reaches you on a CD cover, poster, or Internet page. Don't let looks intimidate you. If your band makes terrific music, it will be inherently attractive to people.

Your image will come naturally as the band progresses. Some performers have drastically changed their looks in order to present dramatic images—Marilyn Manson, for example, toiled in bands for years before becoming famous in white makeup, bright red lipstick, and creepy contact lenses. Tons of successful musicians, from David Bowie to Madonna to Britney Spears, have changed their appearance regularly to help sell their music. You can try it, too.

> **Behind the Music**
>
> When performers have a certain something that makes them magnetic on stage—even if they're not attractive in the traditional sense—they're charismatic. While performing, they may also have stage presence. These concepts mean fans won't be able to avert their eyes from the performance. Famous examples include Elvis Presley and Madonna.

Many great musical movements have arrived with corresponding fashion scenes. When The Beatles became internationally famous in the 1960s, they pioneered the extreme notion of men with long hair. Punk bands in the late 1970s created their own clothing and hairstyles, with accessories such as mohawk hairdos and safety pins. More recently, pop singers like Mariah Carey, Pink, Britney Spears, and Christina Aguilera have drawn attention to their music by wearing very little clothing. If anybody in your band has some fashion sense, consider changing the band's look to get attention.

The Dynamics of Duos (and Trios and Quartets and ...)

One of the first questions you'll need to tackle is, "How many musicians should be in the band?" Often the answer will be obvious, as you'll have three or four people who show up to practice prepared to sing or play certain instruments. But you may have to make the membership decision based on your collective musical vision—duos sound drastically different from quartets, and it's worth knowing the pros and cons of each configuration.

Duos have a rich tradition in pop, rock, and other genres, from The Everly Brothers to Simon & Garfunkel to The White Stripes—but they're limited. Many duos wind up hiring bands to flesh out the music behind them, or in the Stripes' case, hiring a bass player to complement their vocal-guitar-drums lineup. A *trio*, favored by such rock stars as guitarist Jeff Beck, the Goo Goo Dolls, and Nirvana, is a sturdy configuration that avoids "too many chefs" syndrome.

But perhaps the ultimate rock-and-pop lineup is a quartet, usually with drums, bass, guitar, vocals and, if the singer plays an instrument, perhaps a keyboard or second guitar. It may not seem like much, but when all four band members play together, they can create a powerful sound (or a horrible racket, depending on how good they are). Classic quartets include The Beatles, The Who, The Sex Pistols, The Clash, X, The Replacements, Jane's Addiction, and the Foo Fighters.

You can have as many musicians as you want, of course, as long as the lineup doesn't start to mess up internal communication. See Chapter 6 for more information on group dynamics and how to stay together in varying circumstances.

One Guitarist or Two?

Again, if only one guitarist shows up to practice, your decision is made. But some bands have a specific vision about how they should sound, and often this vision centers on *lead instruments* such as guitars and keyboards. Most bands prefer at least one lead instrument, so one musician doesn't have to do all the solo work. Great lead guitarists such as Jimi Hendrix and Stevie Ray Vaughan had such full sounds that they didn't need second guitarists. But not every player is quite so gifted.

If you have a keyboard player as a second lead instrument, one guitarist will probably suffice. Even if you don't, you may find one guitarist provides an adequately dense sound. Installing two guitarists in the same band, though, can make for unique interplay, with the players feeding off each other and trading licks, or solos.

Behind the Music

Five great albums starring two lead guitarists:

- Derek and the Dominos, *Layla* (Eric Clapton and Duane Allman)
- The Rolling Stones, *Exile on Main Street* (Keith Richards and Mick Taylor)
- Lynyrd Skynyrd, *Second Helping* (Allen Collins and Gary Rossington)
- Television, *Marquee Moon* (Tom Verlaine and Richard Lloyd)
- Sonic Youth, *Daydream Nation* (Thurston Moore and Lee Ranaldo)

Do We Really Need a Keyboardist (or Strings)?

It never hurts, especially early in a band's career, to tinker with different lineups and introduce new players. A good keyboardist who can play piano and organ offers versatility—this musician's rig may include electronic approximations of horn or string-section sounds to flesh out the band's sound. If a keyboard-playing friend gets along with the band members, why not give him or her a chance?

Eventually, as your band grows and develops a distinctive sound, the decision to add new instruments will come down to the music. If you're playing certain strains of funky jazz or 1960s soul, you'll probably need an organ. Big-band and jump-blues music begs for a horn section. And regardless of what style you play, you may come across a song that's just dying for cowbell, accordion, or a second guitar player.

Many rock and pop bands are built on lead instruments other than the traditional guitar. The 1970s progressive-rock band Yes, for example, wouldn't have been so distinctive without elaborate keyboard players such as Rick Wakeman. The pioneering German electronic band Kraftwerk used computers and synthesizers rather than guitars and basses. And hip-hop bands, of course, have favored two turntables and a microphone above traditional live instruments. If you're creative enough, you can make music out of anything.

Setting Goals

At first, when you form a band, the goal is to have fun playing together. But after you've done this for a while, and considered the idea of regular rehearsals or performing before live audiences, it may be time for the group to sit down and determine its goals.

Do members of the band fantasize about being major rock stars? Do they want to play parties on the weekends? Quit their day jobs and make a living at music? At a certain point, it may help to make a chart of where you are, where you want to be, and how to get from here to there. This process requires communication among the band members, so it may be time to start meeting (in addition to rehearsing) on a regular basis.

Making a living in a band is an extremely difficult trick, which usually requires a long trip up the ladder from parties to weddings to club *gigs*. But if you have the commitment, you'll have a chance. The band members will probably have to spend at least a few months working regular jobs (or attending school) while rehearsing nights and playing on weekends.

Words to Rock By

A **gig** is a live performance, after which (usually) the band gets paid. The more gigs you get, the more successful your band can become.

In fact, some musicians spend their entire careers as "weekend warriors," changing clothes Friday after work and heading to club gigs. Many professionals enjoy the complementary nature of these two careers. In Denver, for example, Andrew Hudson spent nights playing bass in jazz combos when he was the spokesman for then-mayor Wellington Webb. If you have a high-pressure or low-creativity job, performing music during off-hours can be a great release.

Shooting for fame isn't nearly as relaxing, although it can be incredibly rewarding. If the band is determined to be stars—which means, perhaps, touring different parts of the country, hiring a manager, and signing with a record label—the road is long, difficult, and fraught with barriers. Playing once or twice on the weekend won't be nearly enough.

Remember that making music, at least at first, is a low-paying proposition. Don't delude yourself into thinking you'll rehearse for a few weeks, land a club gig or two, and never have to work a real job again. Many musicians toil for years before they reach this point. You'd be surprised how many well-known band members continue to work day jobs.

What Instrument Can You Play?

Usually, you won't choose an instrument. It'll choose you. If you grew up enjoying piano lessons and prefer putting your fingers on keys rather than guitar frets, you'll probably stick with piano or organ. If you can't tap your foot in time to any given song, you probably won't be the drummer. If you have the need to be the center of attention, you probably won't be the bass player (unless you're Sting or Paul McCartney). And if you've got a good ear for melody, you may be destined to be a guitarist or keyboard player.

Often, band members choose their instruments out of necessity. If four high school friends converge to form a band, and three play guitar, you may have to dig up a set of drums. Or you may be the only person whose voice doesn't crack above middle C, in which case you're the singer. Even if you've never played an instrument before, it's possible to learn as you go along. The key, though, is to go home and practice as many hours as possible. Picking up your bass only once a week during rehearsal will stunt your musical growth and frustrate the other members.

Many bands come up with strange configurations because of their members' particular musical skills. The Doors, for example, recorded several influential albums in the 1960s and 1970s with no bass player—keyboardist Ray Manzarek handled the low notes. The rock trio Morphine crafted a unique sound out of two-string bass, saxophone, and drums. In other words, just because you lack a traditional rock or pop instrument, that doesn't mean you can't play rock or pop music.

In the following sections, we describe some characteristics of typical band musicians. See Chapter 4 for more specifics on how to buy, plug in, and play these instruments.

Guitar: Flexible Fingers

Guitar players, in most bands, can be *lead* or *rhythm* players—the former takes many of the solos and provides a song's melody, while the latter falls in with the bass player and drummer to flesh out the rhythm. If you're considering picking up the guitar, you should have a decent sense of melody, fingers that can adapt to many tricky string-bending permutations, and at least a slight desire to be in the spotlight. For most bands, the focal point in concert is the singer, but guitarists get almost as much attention.

Guitarists are also often the backbone to the band, the least replaceable players when things get tough. Although the singer usually gives a band its unique voice, the guitarist is the fundamental building block of its sound. Once you've located a good one, don't let him or her go.

Drums: Keeping the Beat

The drummer's job in any band—well, except for improvisational combos where the drum may be a solo instrument—is to maintain the tempo. If it goes too fast or slow, it can throw the rest of the band into disarray. So the drummer's responsibility is considerable. If you find yourself drumming on chairs and phone books, or keeping up with elaborate radio-song tempos using your hands, legs, and the steering wheel, it may be your perfect band role.

Drummers also need to stay in good shape, as they handle the most physically demanding job. The first several times you play the drums, you may feel muscle pain in your arms, legs, and back—and may develop blisters on your hands until calluses develop. (Music stores sell special drummers' gloves to prevent this affliction.) Blisters also afflict guitarists and bass players, but not with the regularity of drummers. Keep a stock of Band-Aids nearby.

Bass: Steady and Reliable

The bassist complements the drummer in the band's *rhythm section* and fills in the low-frequency range of the band. The rhythm section sets the *groove*, on top of which go guitars, keyboards, vocals, and other solo-oriented instruments. Although bass players take occasional solos—check out John Entwistle's classic lines in The Who's "My Generation"—their job is almost always to stay in the background.

Bass players should avoid delusions of grandeur. Despite anomalies such as Sting and ex-Beatle Paul McCartney, both of whom are also accomplished singers and songwriters, bass players tend not to be rock superstars. If that's your goal, consider switching to guitar or vocals. Then again, there are exceptions to every rule in music.

Keyboards: Putting Piano Lessons to Work

Keyboards, a catch-all term referring to pianos, organs, and synthesizers of all types, perform essentially the same function as guitars. They solo when it's time to solo, and lay back and play little complementary riffs while the singer handles the verses and choruses.

What distinguishes the keyboardist from the guitarist, at least on stage, is a distinct lack of mobility. Where guitarists can jump around and kick their legs in the air while playing, keyboardists are normally trapped behind their instruments. So it's much harder for a piano player, say, to become a band's charismatic star than it is for a guitarist. Again, there are exceptions: Pianists such as Fats Waller, Little Richard, Jerry Lee Lewis, Billy Joel, Elton John, and Ben Folds have become huge superstars by leading bands.

Other: When Trombones Fit In

We're being facetious here. Trombones don't belong in rock and pop bands. Or as The Mighty Mighty BossTones and other ska bands have shown us, maybe they do. If The Beach Boys could add a spooky, arcane, electronic instrument called the theremin to happy surf-rock music, maybe your band can have a trombonist. More typically, the trombone is simply one element of a band's larger horn section.

When adding instruments beyond the bedrock vocals, guitar, drums, bass, and keyboards, try not to let them get in the way of your basic sound and framework. It's fun to experiment, but frills can be distracting and convoluting. At least at first, expand your sonic palette in small doses—maybe the drummer can pound a cowbell to the beat. Maybe the keyboardist can play the accordion. Think about what the song needs, and make adjustments accordingly.

Behind the Music

Well-known songs that rely on "untraditional" instruments:
- ◆ The Beatles' "Within You Without You" (sitar)
- ◆ Blue Öyster Cult's "Don't Fear the Reaper" (cowbell)
- ◆ The Rolling Stones' "Under My Thumb" (marimba)
- ◆ The Beach Boys' "Good Vibrations" (theremin)
- ◆ The Troggs' "Wild Thing" (ocarina)

Getting Better

Four basic activities will help you improve your musicianship: group rehearsal, individual practice, lessons, and playing live. And they should complement each other. After rehearsing a new song or riff with the band, go home and practice it over and over until you can play it by memory. Plunge into practicing difficult passages.

Playing live will help the band get immediate feedback, figure out what to work on, and fix weak passages quickly. But you may not yet be in a position to play regular live gigs.

Just as athletes usually can't go from good to great without an experienced coach, musicians normally can't become accomplished without a decent teacher.

Finding a Teacher

Finding a traditional music teacher is pretty simple—they're all over the phone book; faculty at your high school or college can probably make solid recommendations; and some schools offer lessons as part of their music programs. Finding a rock, blues, jazz, pop, or hip-hop teacher may be a little more difficult. The classified ads can help, especially in alt-weeklies (see Chapter 14), but the best search method may be through word of mouth.

Piano players might take an excursion to a club or hotel lobby where the longtime local boogie-woogie master holds court. After the set, approach the musician and ask if he or she gives lessons—the receptive response may surprise you. Ask around at school; a jazz-orchestra teacher may know local blues-night veterans willing to give lessons. And check bulletin boards at record stores, bookstores, and coffeeshops, as well as local websites.

How do you know if a teacher is any good? Sit through a lesson or two. If you're interested in rocking out to Limp Bizkit and Led Zeppelin, and the teacher wants you to endure scales for two hours a week, it may not be the right situation. (Still, don't scoff at music-theory instruction; it may not pay off immediately, but in the long run you'll be surprised at how much it improves your playing.)

Screen teachers the same way you'd screen a new car. Find out who else they've taught and what kind of music they like. Ask about experience. Cost may play a role in your decision. Try to get a sense of pieces you'll learn as you progress—although you'll want to be exposed to different musical styles, playing what you like is important.

Practice Without Driving the Neighbors Nuts

Especially if you play potentially obtrusive instruments like the drums, you'll want to check first with nearby friends, roommates, parents, and neighbors before setting up a practice area. See Chapter 5, where we discuss rehearsal space in detail, for more information on this tricky topic.

The Least You Need to Know

- Whether you're backing up a charismatic frontperson or joining a self-contained group, a band will be a lot of fun and a lot of responsibility.

- Quartets are the basic, bedrock configuration of most rock, pop, country, and blues bands—but duos, trios, and more can be effective as well.

- Do you want to make a living through music? Or just play at weekend parties? As you progress, set goals.

- Guitarists, singers, and keyboardists generally handle the solo stuff and get the most attention. Bass players and drummers provide the rhythm.

- How will you get better? Practice and rehearse, of course, but also seek out a good one-on-one teacher.

Chapter 2

Expanding the Band

In This Chapter

- ◆ Fleshing out your band's lineup
- ◆ Putting diversity to work for you
- ◆ Becoming a solo artist
- ◆ Finding new members
- ◆ Making sure that everyone gets along
- ◆ Learning to handle rejection

Congratulations! You've made it past the stage that splinters many a fledgling band—finding a musical partner, setting rough goals, and figuring out what kind of band you are. You may have even started regular rehearsals. But where do you go from here?

If you're a traditional electric rock band, it may be time to find a rhythm section. Or you might want to add some new musical elements, like a second guitar player or a keyboardist, for texture and depth. Either way, the trick now is to mesh disparate musical visions into one cohesive whole and try to locate band "add-ons" who'll contribute their own particular styles and idiosyncrasies. As you start to define a "set list" and think about performing somewhat regularly in public, you may need the perspectives of talented, imaginative new members. Read on to determine what you need and how to find it.

Is Your Band a "Mutt"?

Jane's Addiction had a goth weirdo as a singer, a metalhead teenager on guitar, an African-influenced drummer, and a pure punk rocker for a bass player. Combined, they created a shrill, oddly urgent bastardization of funk, punk, and metal that became one of the key building blocks of 1990s alternative rock. Today, bands from Limp Bizkit to Audioslave clearly draw from Jane's Addiction's example, but in the mid-1980s their strange individual parts seemed bizarrely incongruous. Your challenge, then, is to merge people with diverse backgrounds and tastes into a cohesive, successful whole.

What If You Have an Opera Singer and a Funk Drummer?

Very rarely do band members' record collections contain the same artists—the world's biggest Blink-182 fan can easily find himself in a band with the world's biggest Mariah Carey fan. And you'll just have to deal with it.

> **Words to Rock By**
>
> Covers, or cover songs, are tunes artists perform that are widely associated with other artists. To name one example, Pearl Jam has for years, off and on, covered Neil Young's "Rockin' in the Free World" in its live set.

The important thing is to avoid being too dogmatic. If your favorite band is the Donnas, and all you want to do is play Donnas *covers*, you may have to compromise to accommodate a Celine Dion–loving singer and Red Hot Chili Peppers–loving bass player. Only after each band member embraces diversity and starts to value other members for their unique musical personalities will the band develop a group identity and make cohesive music. Any type of music, played by band members listening to each other and working toward the same goals, can be cohesive—even on records as strange as Jane's Addiction's *Nothing's Shocking*.

Technically, jamming disparate musical visions together can be a difficult trick. For example, if your guitarist loves to imitate folk singer Ani DiFranco while your bass player cranks Metallica up to 11 on his spare time, you'll have to do something about the combination of soft acoustic guitar and gigantic bass amplifier. One of these two players—preferably both—will have to make a change. Be magnanimous about it. Be the band member who volunteers to turn down his or her amp so as not to drown out the acoustic guitarist. Be the classically trained opera singer who translates complex sheet-music passages to the self-taught drummer.

A Word on Musical (and Other) Communication

In this book, you'll frequently encounter marriage as a metaphor for being in a band. As you grow and develop, you'll spend long hours in close contact, and will have to learn to communicate and compromise in order to stay together. Learning to play your instrument really, really well is important, of course, but so is getting along.

The bottom line of communication is staying open to other people's ideas. Allowing personal resentment to fester is the fastest way to kill a band, so do your best to avoid it. (We deal with group-dynamics issues in more depth throughout Chapter 6.)

One way to communicate effectively, in terms of playing music as a group, is to write everything down before you start. If everybody can read music fluently, great—that will make rehearsals easier. More likely, though, at least one of your fellow musicians won't have music-reading skills. So you'll have to transcribe the lyrics and print the chords in such a way that everybody can understand them. Make the charts simple—"A for four beats, then E for four beats, then back to D for one beat" may be the most efficient way of communicating musically, in a language everybody can easily understand. A slightly more complex type of chart is the *head arrangement*.

Words to Rock By

A **head arrangement** is the opposite of writing out a piece of music on paper. It means that a band verbally agrees on chord changes, basic orders, and solos. Although some jam bands base their entire careers on this type of arrangement, most quickly learn that preparation makes a song coherent.

Or Maybe You're a Solo Artist?

As artists from John Mayer to Jewel have discovered, being a full-fledged member of a band may be too constrictive or complicated. You may have such a distinctive artistic vision that it's impossible to find a bass player or guitarist to go along with your complex ideas. Or personality-wise, you may be so set in your ways that you just can't compromise to get along with other musicians. The sooner you figure this out, the less frustrated you'll be.

One way to proceed as a solo artist is by hiring a *backup band*. As leader, you'll oversee a group of professional musicians paid to perform according to your instructions.

Very rarely in frontperson/backup band situations do players come up with their own musical ideas and eclipse the boss. Many musicians, from Godfather of Soul James Brown to country hitmaker Travis Tritt, find such control liberating.

The other configuration is *solo artist*. That's just you, and probably your instrument, with nobody else to cover up your mistakes on stage. Obviously, in this situation, you're in complete control. You can play whatever solos you want, whenever you want, without throwing off a drummer's timing or stepping on a guitarist's showcase. A solo artist may find it easier to land certain kinds of quiet wedding gigs— particularly during the ceremony—or appear at coffeehouses.

Solo artists' expenses tend to be considerably lower than band expenses. You probably won't need the amplifiers to get your sound across. And you won't need cumbersome transportation options to carry yourself and your instrument to the gig. Then again, solo artists tend to get paid less than bands.

Whether you front a hired band or not, you'll have to be pretty talented as a musician to justify a solo career. (Some well-known artists, such as The Beatles' Ringo Starr and the Backstreet Boys' Nick Carter, were never successful on the level of the bands they left. Of course, Beyoncé Knowles of Destiny's Child went on to huge success as a solo artist.) Even if you're good at your instrument, you'll need to work on new show-business skills such as charisma and stage presence to succeed with any kind of longevity.

Where to Find Members

Unless you have the good fortune of having siblings who play bass, drums, and guitar, or unless you're married to your musical soul mate, you'll have to go out and find band members. This process may be as easy as hooking up with the person who sits next to you at music class or the next-door neighbor who admires your Velvet Underground LP collection. More often, though, it's a long, drawn-out process. Many bands, including Yes and The Red Hot Chili Peppers, can't seem to solidify a consistent lineup even after they become successful. So be prepared for some hard work and frequent changes of personnel.

Classified Ads

Unless you can draw from personal talent wells, such as friends' broken-up bands or school music classes, the search for new band members often begins with the classified ads. This is how Susanna Hoffs, singer for 1980s hitmakers The Bangles, met guitarist Vicki Peterson.

Hoffs came across a "bandmates wanted" ad in the *Los Angeles Recycler* in 1981 and contacted the author, who liked The Beatles, The Byrds, and a couple of early 1980s punk-rock bands. When Hoffs called, the woman who placed the ad wasn't home. But she clicked with the woman's roommate—Peterson.

"I guess I waited about three weeks, and I saved that copy of the paper and I called back and said, 'You know what? We should hook up.' So we went into the garage, we played together that night and that was it. We all knew," Hoffs told Steve in a 1997 *Chicago Tribune* interview. "It's pretty remarkable. But I always say, I met my husband on a blind date."

Other well-known acts who found each other via the classified ads include …

◆ Elton John and songwriter Bernie Taupin

◆ KISS

◆ The Pixies

◆ The Exies

Keep in mind not every musician is as lucky as Hoffs and Peterson, who went on to record hits like "Hero Takes a Fall" and "Walk Like an Egyptian." In the late 1990s, Chicago singer Jonny Polonsky placed a "bandmates wanted" ad in the *Chicago Reader* and was dismayed to find out who called back.

"It's really been a cross-section of humanity, with the psychotic depravity [that] people commit to tape," he said in the same *Chicago Tribune* article. "You'd think people were answering an ad for the midway in the carnival. It's unbelievable how many freaks you get."

"I don't know where these clowns come from. This one guy called on the machine and said, 'I'd like to send a tape, but I don't want to bore you with my playing. I'd rather just have you over and I'll play for you live and we'll just talk,'" Polonsky continued. "Ideally, I'd like to just find a great band and fire their singer."

If you do go the classified-ad route, always request that people send you a demo tape—that way you can prescreen candidates and only meet with the musicians that you are interested in. And always be professional and polite. In a local music scene, you never know when you'll encounter someone later.

Backstage Insights

An effective "musicians wanted" ad should spell out your needs and include a brief description of music played. Here's a recent one from *Westword*, the Denver alternative-weekly tabloid:

BASS & DRUMS: Two experienced singer/songwriter/guitarists forming band to play locally. Beatles, Stones, Dylan, etc., and lots of originals. Bassist must sing backup. Call Dan at [phone number].

And here's one in the opposite direction:

PRO DRUMMER seeks vocal, guitar, bass, keys, DJ/sampler 4 a beyond the norm band, diversity a +. (Sigur Ros-Elliot-Massive Deep Dish) John [phone].

Bulletin Boards at Coffeeshops

Even cheaper than classified ads are *community bulletin boards*. These are all over the place, especially in college towns—check kiosks at local outdoor malls, boards in student centers, entrance areas of record stores, libraries, bookstores, community radio stations and, yes, coffeeshops.

Take a chance and scrawl an eye-catching ad on colorful paper. Include those little tabs at the bottom people can tear off so they don't have to copy down your phone number.

Be sure to scan the ads that already exist. If you're a metal band covering Limp Bizkit, Metallica, and other macho headbangers, you may not want to post at the campus Classical Music History Association. Then again, maybe you will—you never know where you'll find the person who perfectly fits your music.

Words to Rock By

Networking is the art of making contact with people who can help your career. At first, this may mean members of other local bands who can give you insight on which musicians are good, experienced, and available. Later, you might network—or, less formally, schmooze—with club owners, radio-station programmers, or even record-label representatives.

Group Music Lessons

Taking music lessons can be a great benefit, both to you and the band. If another member is a little more advanced than you, and it's difficult to keep up with him or her, you can advance a couple steps via private training.

Music lessons also give you *networking* opportunities. Your teacher, who is more experienced, is better connected locally, and probably has performed in a few bands, may know other students who'd fit your needs. The teacher may also suggest other contacts, or even local bulletin-board opportunities, for you to try out. In a pinch, this person may even be willing to step into your band temporarily until you find the right person.

Group music lessons, with more people, obviously present more opportunities.

Another common way bandmates find each other is in high school or college band classes. You may be playing second violin and strike up a conversation with the tuba player about how boring the class is. "We should rock" is a common invitation to start a band. So why not?

The Web

Although Chapter 16 deals with the web as a promotional device once you have a relatively established band, the technical tips in that chapter also work for seeking band members online. Post eye-catching "bandmate wanted" ads on your homepage and draw attention to the page via search engines, link exchanges with other webmasters, and even on physical banners you hang at local gigs.

You can also post to musician-friendly message boards, from Usenet newsgroups (news.google.com) to specialty classified sites such as Harmony Central (harmony-central.com/Services/#cla) and the Internet Classifieds (theinternetclassifieds.com/cgi-bin/index.cgi). Although these services may not be specifically local—use Google to find online regional publications—you'll likely find discussion threads that deal with your geographic area.

Be creative and aggressive when using the web for this sort of thing. Perhaps locally written web logs, or personal homepage diaries, contain gossip about bands looking for members in your town. Maybe your high school has an online bulletin board where you can post a bandmates-wanted message. Maybe an established band's site, like metallica.com, has bulletin-board threads dealing with Metallica-loving musicians in certain parts of the country. Cast your net widely in cyberspace.

Auditions

Once you've identified a prospective bandmate, the next step is to get together and play. An audition, another word for a job interview in the entertainment world, will give you a feeling for how well this musician can play. Perhaps more importantly, it will help you get to know the player personally—remember that the most talented musician in the world may not get along with the rest of the band. Conversely, the most easygoing person in the world may be far from the greatest musician. Consider both angles when hiring.

In rock history, auditions have been both famously elaborate and famously minimalist. In early 2002, Limp Bizkit embarked on a highly publicized quest for a new guitarist, auditioning literally thousands of regular Joes at guitar stores all over the country. Some applicants waited in freezing outdoor temperatures for hours. More than a year later, though, the popular rap-metal band simply hired a ringer singer Fred Durst knew from an established band, Snot.

At the other extreme, The Who didn't even know that they needed a replacement musician until a kid named Keith Moon approached the band after a show and declared himself better than their existing drummer. He started hammering away with the band and they asked him to show up at the next rehearsal. He kept showing up, and even after The Who had become superstars, nobody ever said, "You're in the band."

Try to stay focused on your needs as a group. If a guitarist shows up and blows you away with fiery heavy-metal leads, and you're a quiet folk-rock combo, don't get "new car fever." Tell the person you'll come to see his concerts someday, but he just isn't right for your band. You're looking for a musician, ultimately, who will stick with you for perhaps months or years—maybe even longer, if you follow The Rolling Stones—so make the decision intelligently.

How to Know When They're Good

Talent will almost certainly be apparent. A serious band candidate will be able to play with you, rather than against you—not only in tune, but in time. He or she will know the difference between a verse and a chorus. This person will understand the subtleties of dynamics, or when to play soft and when to play loud. The ultimate bandmate will know to lay back when the singer sings and not rip off a loud, impressive solo in the middle of somebody else's verse.

Backstage Insights _____

Questions for the ultimate bandmate:

- ◆ Can you play the same songs we play?
- ◆ What records are in your collection?
- ◆ Can we borrow them sometime?
- ◆ Have you been kicked out of other bands?
- ◆ Do you own your own equipment?
- ◆ Are you willing to share your equipment?
- ◆ Do you own transportation for use to and from a gig?
- ◆ Are you old enough to play in bars?

Will They Fit In?

Just as job interviews rarely indicate definitively whether a prospective employee will fit into the corporate culture, a musical audition won't screen for nebulous issues like compatibility. Play with your potential bandmate several times if necessary, but if you're really serious about this person, hang out with him or her in other settings.

Go out together for a cup of coffee. Have dinner, see a movie, attend a baseball game, or naturally, hear other bands. Do things as a group. Through such rigorous "screening," you'll probably find out whether this person will fit in with the rest of the band.

Behind the Music

When they've just started, many bands will hire an easygoing friend who doesn't even know how to play an instrument—and teach him or her along the way. Perhaps the most famous example was Stu Sutcliffe, a hipster friend of The Beatles' John Lennon who knew such little bass that he stood with his back to the audience. The Pixies' Joey Santiago learned lead guitar, The Sex Pistols' Sid Vicious learned bass, and The Breeders' Kelley Deal learned rhythm guitar—instruments they'd never played—while their bands became famous.

The Art of Polite Rejection

Rejection can be traumatic for both the rejecter and the rejected. If you're unlucky enough to be in the latter category, get used to it. The music business will reject you frequently, whether it's kicking you out of a band, keeping you out of a club, keeping you off the radio, or keeping a record label from signing you. Don't take it personally. It isn't a conspiracy. It's just the way people do business. Learn from it and move on.

Your first musical rejection may come in the form of a failed audition. This can be extremely stressful, especially if the band expressed so much interest that they took you for a cup of coffee or a movie (as we suggested earlier). In such cases, the rejection probably has nothing to do with you personally, or even the way you play. Another band member's mother may have insisted her niece become the bass player. Or maybe somebody else owned a car and you didn't.

Once rejected, try to ask questions if they're appropriate. What did and didn't the band like? Would it be possible to re-audition in the future once you've learned certain songs? Then again, if somebody in the band just didn't like you personally, or if you have history with a band member's significant other, it'll be almost impossible to glean constructive criticism. So move on.

Rejecting an applicant may be just as stressful and depressing for the band members themselves. They may have really liked a certain musician but ultimately couldn't hire him or her for some of the reasons we've described.

Rejecters should be honest but gentle. Obviously, "You're crap, so pack up your gear and go home" is never an acceptable thing to say. Not only will it needlessly depress your applicant, it could give your band the reputation of abusing prospective members and being difficult to work with. This can make a difference later on, when you're trying to earn auditions with club owners or record labels. In the music business, even just the local club scene, gossip is prevalent and everybody's trying to damage your reputation somehow. Don't give anybody fuel by being a jerk for no good reason.

Effective things to say when rejecting an applicant:

- "We really like your playing, but you seem better suited for a different genre of music."

- "You were one of our top two candidates, but the other guy had just a little more experience."

- "We thought you fit in really well, but were worried about your lack of music-reading ability."

- "We went with somebody else the band knew a little better."

- "Sorry we can't use you, but here's the name and number of another musician looking for good people."

The Least You Need to Know

- You might wind up with bandmates who have totally different musical influences and opinions. That's a good thing! Diversity will help you build a sound in the future.

- If the band members have varying musical skills and backgrounds, consider transcribing the songs onto paper in the simplest possible way—just chords and lyrics.

- To add new musicians, search for them using classified ads, local bulletin boards, and the web.

- Don't just audition a prospective member—take that person out for coffee or to a movie.

What Kind of Music Do You Want to Play?

In This Chapter

◆ Selecting a genre … or creating your own

◆ The fluid nature of "rock"

◆ Where three or four chords can take you

◆ Building on the basics

◆ Picking a really good name

Choosing a musical style is one of the first major decisions you'll make as a band. Sometimes it's simple: Everybody in the band listens to the same rock radio station, likes the same rock songs, and therefore agrees to play the same Aerosmith and Maroon 5 covers. Usually it's more complicated: The drummer grew up worshipping James Brown, the guitarist is a Tool kind of guy, and the bassist likes Irish folk ballads. (This latter combination may actually be more original and interesting than the Aerosmith scenario.) Regardless of what style you settle on, you'll find plenty of easy-to-play songs to start the band's repertoire. No genre of popular music is too difficult for a beginning band to master—even jazz is often based on basic pop standards. Here, we run down prominent styles, show you how to play some songs, and help you choose a name that fits the sound.

Throughout the chapter, we also include "essential album" picks in several different genres. Many bands learn material by carefully listening to a famous song, and then reproducing it during individual practice or group rehearsal.

Basic Genres

In the early days of pop music, genres were easy to define. Rock 'n' roll meant Elvis Presley and, later, The Beatles. Folk meant Joan Baez and Pete Seeger. Blues meant Muddy Waters and old Robert Johnson records. Jazz was John Coltrane, country was Loretta Lynn … you get the picture.

These definitions have expanded, almost to the point of meaninglessness, over the decades. "Rock" today refers to punk band Sleater-Kinney as well as pop diva Britney Spears. Thus, marketers, writers, radio programmers, and the musicians themselves have found it necessary to break down the genre into dozens of hair-splitting subcategories: hard rock, classic rock, punk rock, hardcore punk, pop-punk, emo, rap-metal, funk-metal, punk-metal, and so forth. Your options, when deciding on a genre, are all or none of the above. And feel free to invent your own.

Rock, Punk, Metal, and Alternative

Whether you believe Elvis Presley, Little Richard, Chuck Berry, or somebody else invented the style in the 1950s, rock 'n' roll music began as an exciting merger of white country-western music and black rhythm-and-blues. It has more or less stayed close to that original definition, although the "rock" category has expanded to all sorts of non-Elvis-like sounds.

Generally, the minimum number of players in a rock band is three. The core rock-band configuration is usually guitar, bass, drums, vocals. Rock music is mostly played in the standard 4/4 time. For each of these rules, however, you can probably name 100 exceptions.

As rock matures and ages, it splinters. During the mid-1970s, for example, New York City's The Ramones, and then England's The Clash and The Sex Pistols, decided rock was boring and needed to be simultaneously simplified and sped up. Thus, they invented the faster, shorter *punk rock* genre; over the years, younger bands like Nirvana, Green Day, Rancid, and Sum 41 picked up the style and added their distinctive personalities.

Backstage Insights

Five essential punk-rock albums:
- The Sex Pistols, *Never Mind the Bollocks Here's the Sex Pistols*
- The Clash, *London Calling*
- Nirvana, *Nevermind*
- The Ramones, *Rocket to Russia*
- The Stooges, *Raw Power*

Alternative rock began in the early 1990s, when Seattle *grunge* bands Nirvana, Pearl Jam, and Soundgarden took punk rock's inspiration and turned it into something heavier. As grunge began to catch on at MTV and traditional rock radio stations, others copied the style—Bush and Stone Temple Pilots made grunge more palatable to larger numbers of listeners. As more and more bands jumped into the format, radio stations and record labels marketed it as *alternative rock*, or an alternative to the mainstream. (That this kind of rock *was* the mainstream didn't matter.)

Metal is loud, deep, and often obsessed with gothic fantasy images of death and destruction. Its inventors were Black Sabbath and Led Zeppelin in the late 1960s and early 1970s; later, Motorhead, Iron Maiden, Metallica, Anthrax, Megadeth, Pantera, and Korn would add their idiosyncrasies. As various bands expanded the genre, metal became hyphenated—Slayer will always be *thrash-metal*, whereas you could call Limp Bizkit *rap-metal*. In the 1980s, pop bands with big hair juiced up metal's catchy melodies and invented what's now called *hair metal*: Bon Jovi, Poison, Mötley Crüe, and so on.

You can play all of this rock stuff with rudimentary musical skills. Beatles bassist Paul McCartney, famously, never learned to read music. Joey Santiago, guitarist for Boston's influential Pixies, picked up his instrument the day that he joined the band and learned as he went along. Although we'll stop short of saying it's better *not* to know how to play your instrument, we believe passion and soul are far more important than technical musical ability.

Folk

Like rock, *folk* is a catch-all category that can cover everything from Nigerian drummers to American protest singers. So named because of its "music for the people" spirit, folk began as a network of sea chanties and field hollers passed down from generation to generation. Its major renaissance came in the 1960s, when political-minded "folkies"—Baez, Bob Dylan, Tom Rush, Phil Ochs—filled New York City coffeehouses with acoustic guitars.

That's not to say folk groups necessarily have to be political. Since the 1960s, the definition of folk has come to mean "a soft-spoken singer or singers with original songs and acoustic guitars"— James Taylor, Joni Mitchell, Shawn Colvin, and Dar Williams fit this broad category.

Backstage Insights

Five essential folk albums:

- Bob Dylan, *The Freewheelin' Bob Dylan*
- Joan Baez, *Diamonds and Rust*
- Various artists, *The Anthology of American Folk Music*
- Simon and Garfunkel, *Bookends*
- Iris DeMent, *Infamous Angel*

Groups can play folk music—The Weavers and The Kingston Trio are some of the most influential artists in the genre—but more common configurations are solo artists or duos.

The style is similar to rock, in terms of tempo and chords, although folk is usually a little slower and a lot quieter. The songs also tend to be personal, told from the narrator's first-person perspective or telling the classic story of John Henry the steel-driving man or the shady Philadelphia lawyer. As with rock and country, if you know three basic guitar chords and how to keep time, you can play folk.

Country and Bluegrass

Country began, informally, as old-timey tunes in the Appalachian Mountains and other rural areas before the turn of the twentieth century. Like folk, country's origins are in self-taught, sing-around-the-fire songs passed down through word of mouth among friends and family members.

Beginning in the late 1920s, when the recording industry started to mature, singers such as Jimmie Rodgers, The Carter Family, Roy Acuff, and Hank Williams Sr. became stars in the genre. They sang in high, lonesome tones about living tough lives and finding relief in God, traveling, and drinking (although not necessarily in that order).

Over the years, country would shift in many different directions, from big-band-jazz-inspired *western swing* in the 1930s to the heavily produced, pre–rock 'n' roll "Nashville Sound" in the 1940s. One offshoot came from Kentucky mandolinist Bill Monroe, who with his Blue Grass Boys invented an influential, soulful sound known as *bluegrass*. One of Elvis Presley's early rock hits was a hopped-up version of Monroe's "Blue Moon of Kentucky."

In the 1970s, The Byrds, The Nitty Gritty Dirt Band, Gram Parsons, and Poco merged two genres, creating *country-rock*, which proved influential in the early 1990s. Garth Brooks, Clint Black, Alan Jackson, and others streamlined this sound into massive record sales and huge superstardom. With Faith Hill and Shania Twain turning country into pop, the sound continues to evolve and—for better and worse—turn away from its hillbilly roots.

Backstage Insights _____

Five essential country albums:

◆ Hank Williams Sr., *The Original Singles Collection ... Plus*

◆ Marty Robbins, *Gunfighter Ballads and Trail Songs*

◆ Loretta Lynn, *Coal Miner's Daughter*

◆ Johnny Cash, *At San Quentin*

◆ Steve Earle, *Guitar Town*

To play country or bluegrass, do you have to be from Kentucky? Of course not. But you need to know those three basic chords we keep talking about, and preferably have a good, soulful singer—many country stars are individuals, backed by an anonymous band.

Today's country, like rock, can pretty much sound like anything—Nashville's Steve Earle plays it like early 1970s Rolling Stones, Chicago's Waco Brothers turn it into punk, the late, great Johnny Cash sang the occasional Nine Inch Nails song, and Shania Twain is more like a pop diva than a country crooner. Bluegrass, however, is almost always played in the traditional manner, with rickety vocals and a band of mandolinists, fiddlers, and soft, acoustic instrumentation.

Blues

A purely American song form, *blues* began in the early twentieth century as an informal series of slave shouts and field hollers. The blues' roots are in Africa, where the music traveled to other countries via the slave trade; the music's brutally honest expressions of suffering and joy eventually influenced all levels of popular song.

Early blues were generally played on acoustic guitars, harmonicas, and washboards, by then-unheralded giants such as Charley Patton and Robert Johnson. The myths made the music richer: Johnson was one of several Mississippi Delta singers to have ostensibly sold his soul to the devil at the crossroads. They played at juke joints and house parties; folklorists sporadically tracked them down for recordings.

By the 1940s, many southern bluesmen joined the mass African American exodus from the South to industrial cities a little farther north. Muddy Waters wound up in Chicago, where he pioneered blues on electric instruments; John Lee Hooker took his "stomp" to Detroit; B. B. King landed in Memphis. Their recordings were vital precursors to rock 'n' roll.

Backstage Insights

Five essential blues albums:

- B. B. King, *Live at the Regal*
- Robert Johnson, *The Complete Recordings*
- Howlin' Wolf, *Evil*
- Muddy Waters, *His Best*
- Bessie Smith, *Greatest Hits*

Today's blues performers are usually traditionalists; some do the sitting-on-a-stool, singing-with-a-guitar thing, while others ape Muddy Waters and learn to play guitar in an electric band. They almost always use the *12-bar blues* as a musical foundation—this refers to a repetitive structure using three particular chords.

A little music theory: To learn chords in the 12-bar blues figure out the I, IV, and V notes of any given scale. For example, if you're playing in the key of C, go up the scale to the first, fourth, and fifth notes—which would be C, F, and G. Thus, the C, F, and G chords are the three you'll play (generally speaking) in the C blues.

Once you know this pattern, you can play almost any blues standard—from "Stormy Monday" to "Sweet Home Chicago"—and lots of country, folk, and rock, too.

Jazz

They say Buddy Bowlen invented *jazz* in New Orleans in the 1910s, although no recordings of him exist. Pianist Jelly Roll Morton, also from New Orleans, staked his claim to the "inventor of jazz" title a few years later, turning pop standards into rich boogie-woogie originals.

Jazz is by nature improvisational, so the musicians solo regularly and often make up the song as they go along. As jazz has grown and changed dramatically, players such as saxophonists Lester Young, Charlie Parker, and John Coltrane; trumpeters Louis Armstrong and Miles Davis; guitarist Charlie Christian; bassist Charles Mingus; and pianist Thelonious Monk have become legendary innovators.

Originally, jazz was usually played in the New Orleans *Dixieland* style. Armstrong came along and gave it personality. Later, it morphed into *big-band swing* orchestrated by black bandleaders such as Fletcher Henderson and Count Basie, but, by World War II, it was turning into pop music played by white talents Benny Goodman and Glenn Miller and their big bands.

By the 1940s, Parker and Davis eschewed the rulebook and created *bebop*, a more free-form, soloist-centered style that built on the framework of blues and pop standards. After that, important figures such as Coltrane, Mingus, Monk, and Ornette Coleman laid the foundation for *modern jazz*, which has almost no rules at all, just instinct and soul. Another strain is *smooth jazz*, like that played by Chuck Mangione and Kenny G., which is usually a melodic, radio-friendly version of traditional jazz standards with lots of soothing solos.

Backstage Insights _____

Five essential jazz albums:
- ◆ Miles Davis, *Kind of Blue*
- ◆ Louis Armstrong, *The Complete Hot Five and Hot Seven Recordings*
- ◆ John Coltrane, *Blue Trane*
- ◆ Ornette Coleman, *Music of My Mind*
- ◆ Various artists, *The Smithsonian Collection of Classic Jazz*

Jazz is a little more difficult to play, and certainly to master, than three-chord rock, blues, or country. Jazz combos—trios, quartets, or more, all the way up to multi-musician big bands—require at least one talented soloist. And the rhythm sections must know how to do more than simply keep a "one, two, three, four" beat; like classical music, jazz is often performed in complicated time signatures.

That's not to say you can't play jazz. Many standards, from Parker's "A Night in Tunisia" to Davis's "So What" are written in basic blues and pop arrangements. But your goal, as a jazz group, should be to eventually excel as a collection of soloists. Often, jazz groups form out of jazz-club jam nights or school orchestras.

Words to Rock By

Note that while many people use **hip-hop** and **rap** interchangeably, hip-hop is a broad term reflecting the entire culture of fashion, break dancing, graffiti, and rapping, while rap specifically refers to the music.

Hip-Hop and Techno

Hip-hop began in the late 1970s, as New York City DJs took existing funk and disco songs, sliced up their beats, and chanted over the resulting grooves. The first major hip-hop song was The Sugarhill Gang's "Rapper's Delight," in 1979, and artists such as Kurtis Blow, Grandmaster Flash and the Furious Five, Run-D.M.C., LL Cool J, Public Enemy, Queen Latifah, N.W.A., Ice Cube, Dr. Dre, Outkast, and Eminem followed.

Backstage Insights

Five essential hip-hop albums:

- Public Enemy, *It Takes a Nation of Millions to Hold Us Back*
- Run-D.M.C., *Raising Hell*
- N.W.A., *Straight Outta Compton*
- Outkast, *Stankonia*
- Eminem, *The Marshall Mathers LP*

Hip-hop took punk-rock's "do it yourself" philosophy to an extreme. Although the rappers had to have a gift of gab and a certain amount of poetic skills, none played a musical instrument or followed any traditional song structure.

The "musicians" of rap are DJs, which isn't to say the disc jockeys you'd hear on radio stations. These sonic gurus pioneered the "two turntables and a microphone" approach, scratching vinyl records and turning samples, or snippets of classic funk and disco tracks, into completely new songs.

To start a hip-hop group, you'll need at least one lyricist, a DJ with a sense of rhythm and a strong record collection, and perhaps a dancer or two. As with rock, hip-hop stage moves are distinctive and stereotypical: Every emcee (lead rapper) at some point tells a crowd to "put your hands in the air and wave them like you just don't care!"

Note that while rap groups began by breaking down the traditional band concept, many performers these days tour with live bands such as the Roots.

Like every other pop genre, hip-hop has splintered into a million pieces. *Gangsta rap* grew out of Los Angeles band N.W.A.'s early 1990s imagery of guns and fighting back against police brutality. *Jazz rap* comes and goes, with groups like Digable

Planets and Gangstarr showing how seamlessly classic jazz and modern rap fit together. *Trip-hop* is a spacier, more dance-club-oriented spin-off, exemplified on Tricky and Portishead CDs.

Although *techno* music doesn't sound much like hip-hop, the instrumentation is often the same. Growing out of warehouse dance parties in London, Detroit, and Chicago in the early 1980s, techno creates repetitive, loud, dance-able noise from turntables, drum machines, and these days, computers.

> **Behind the Music**
>
> The DJ is responsible for electronically stringing funk and dance songs together at a nightclub. The DJ's equipment consists of two turntables and a microphone—which you can buy as a package for as little as $299 through catalogs like Musician's Friend (musiciansfriend.com).

Briefly nicknamed *electronica* in the late 1990s, techno is what you'd usually hear at an all-night *rave party*. Its best-known artists include Moby, Orbital, and Paul Oakenfold.

Pop

Pop, short for *popular music*, is technically "whatever people are buying." It has come to represent Top 40 music from Olivia Newton-John in the 1970s to Britney Spears and the Backstreet Boys in the 1990s. Today, aspiring singers flock to reality-TV shows like *American Idol*. Rarely do pop singers form bands; they stay home and work on their voices and try to "make it" via talent shows and music-industry Svengalis.

Power-pop bands were allies of punk-rockers in the 1970s, and tried to reduce rock songs to their essence—short songs, short solos, unflashy singers, and punchy, powerful lyrics. Songs like Nick Lowe's "I Love the Sound of Breaking Glass" and Dave Edmunds's "Girl Talk" sound simple but they're deceptively hard to play well and require much rehearsal.

What Songs Are Right for You?

To start out, you'll want to play basic songs in the genre you've picked. If you're in a funk band and aspire to play any gathering where people dance, you'll have to know Kool & the Gang's "Celebration." If you're in a blues band, you'll have to know "Sweet Home Chicago." Every genre has its signature song, and every band in that genre must be able to play it.

Having said that, it's worth thinking about long-term goals as you figure out what songs to work into your "we can play that" list. If you aspire to perform original material and make CDs for a record label someday, you won't want to get pigeon-holed as "that band that plays Kool & the Gang." Of course, if you aspire to make money on the wedding-and-party circuit, "Celebration" will work just fine.

Covers or Originals?

Initially, unless you're like Jim Morrison and have notebooks filled with brilliant, unheard poems, you'll want to play familiar covers. Everybody in the band probably knows the lyrics already, they're easy to learn, and fans, when you have them, will react enthusiastically. Plus, the more covers you play, the more you'll learn about universal chord changes, lyrical twists, and song structures.

For now, you may want to avoid originals. Once you've mastered a dozen cover songs, it may be time for somebody in the band to introduce original material. Until then, your focus should be on working together as a group and learning each other's musical nuances.

Originals add several new elements into the song-learning process—particularly ego, as the new writer may not yet be prepared for the band's critical feedback. But that's not to say you should never introduce new material. You should; when the time is right, it may take the band to a new level.

Three Steps to "Louie, Louie" and Hundreds More

Whether you're a guitarist or keyboardist, learn three chords: A, D, and E-minor. That progression, the foundation of the Kingsmen's incomprehensible 1960s rock classic "Louie, Louie," will take you almost everywhere. They're three standard strumming chords that are often the basis of rock, country, blues, and folk songs. The Ramones' "Beat on the Brat" and Nirvana's "Smells Like Teen Spirit" are variations on this "three chords and a cloud of dust" formula. (This is a slight variation of the 12-bar blues, which we discussed in the blues section, earlier in this chapter.)

Now, put everybody in the same key, have the drummer set a tempo everybody is comfortable playing, and you're on your way to songs. From here, everybody can learn and rehearse their individual parts at home. Later, you can play them together, over and over and over, until you know the song in your sleep. That's when bands start to get fun.

> **Backstage Insights**
>
> Invest in a variable-speed recorder (cassette or microcassette, available at many electronics stores) and slow down the song you want to learn. The solos, especially, will be easy to copy. Repeat them until you know all the notes, and then increase the speed as you learn the tune.

Choosing a Name

In Mark's view, the best band names are always short, simple, and easily memorable: Oasis, Blur, Kraftwerk. Often they're preceded by "the": The Beatles, like Buddy Holly's The Crickets only with a "beat"; The Rolling Stones, named after Muddy Waters's classic blues song; and so on. Steve, however, is partial to Austin's … And You Will Know Us by the Trail of Dead. In any case, the most important thing is to pick one that's fairly representative of the music you play.

Another serious consideration, which we'll deal with in Chapter 16, is whether you can register your band name as a domain name on the Internet. Check registrars like networksolutions.com to see if your preferred name is taken. Although you can easily get an alternative website address—fabulousdogs.org rather than fabulousdogs.com, say—at this stage it may be just as easy to change the band's name.

Brainstorming

Don't get obsessed with cleverness. Again, simplicity rules. Pick out characters' names from famous books. Ask your Aunt Byrxegus if she'd mind if you borrowed her name. One band named itself after *The New York Times*' science writer, Gina Kolata (and wound up with bonus publicity when another writer interviewed the real Kolata about her namesake band).

To speed up the process, there are tons of Random Band Generators on the Internet. But perhaps the best way to generate a name is to relax, sit on comfortable chairs (*outside* your rehearsal space), and start throwing ideas around. Remember, in brainstorming, there's no such thing as a bad idea. Come up with a list of 100, and then narrow it down.

History: From Meat Puppets to Flaming Lips

Famous band-name origins:

- Toad the Wet Sprocket took its name from a Monty Python sketch.

- "Chumbawamba" is what one of the Ewoks, in *Return of the Jedi*, exclaimed while falling over.

- Duran Duran is the villain from *Barberella*, doubled.

- The Sex Pistols grew out of the London punk-fashion store "Sex," then added Pistols to sound dangerous.

◆ Despite rumors to the contrary, Pearl Jam is named after singer Eddie Vedder's grandmother, Pearl, who apparently made jam.

◆ Pink Floyd is an amalgam of singer Syd Barrett's favorite blues musicians, Pink Anderson and Floyd Council.

◆ … And You Will Know Us by the Trail of Dead is reportedly a prayer to Mayan corn gods.

How the Dead Kennedys Got Their Name

Before Boulder, Colorado, record collector Eric Boucher became the notorious punk-rock singer Jello Biafra, he befriended Mark (yes, the co-writer of this book) in the late 1970s.

While swapping records with Boucher one day, Mark said, "I have this all-time great name for a band—the Dead Kennedys—but nobody could ever use it." (This was before Christian Death and the Butthole Surfers.) "Several years later, when Eric morphed into Jello," Mark recalls, "he was able to prove me wrong."

For years, after his prime with the Dead Kennedys, Biafra did a spoken-word performance segment titled "Names for Bands." His best suggestion: "Mondale."

The Least You Need to Know

◆ Among your musical choices are rock, punk, alternative, folk, country, blues, jazz, hip-hop, techno, and all or none of the above.

◆ Start by covering other artists' well-known material in your genre. After you've learned perhaps a dozen cover songs, think about writing your own material.

◆ From "Johnny B. Goode" to "Louie, Louie," rock, folk, blues, and country are built on three basic chords. Once you know what they are, you can play almost anything.

◆ The 12-bar blues formula is a bedrock in most popular music styles; learning the I-IV-V progression will help you in countless ways.

◆ How do you pick a good name? Brainstorm. And take lessons from famous examples, such as the Dead Kennedys, Toad the Wet Sprocket, and, of course, The Beatles.

Chapter 4

Plugging In

In This Chapter

- ◆ Finding good deals for instruments
- ◆ Sticking to your role in the band
- ◆ Singers and their microphones
- ◆ Guitarists, bass players, and their axes
- ◆ Drummers and their kits
- ◆ Keyboardists and their rigs

Whether you're a trio like the Goo Goo Dolls or a 27-piece orchestra like The Polyphonic Spree, you'll make music not as individuals but as a collective. Which means you'll have to discuss with other band members what instruments you want to play and spend some money on the corresponding equipment. Although great bands have formed by playing their siblings' hand-me-down instruments, gear will probably be your first major expense. And depending on which instrument you choose, you'll accept certain roles and responsibilities. From here on, your drummer may need a bigger car to lug instruments between home, rehearsals, and gigs. Your guitarist will be a regular at the local music store to replace broken strings and occasionally buy effects pedals.

Plugging in your gear and starting to play is one of the most exciting milestones in a band's history. Have fun with it.

How Much Do Instruments Cost?

A better question might be "How much do you want to spend?" In most price ranges, almost any brand, style, or condition of musical instrument is available. The guitar you buy for $25 in a pawnshop won't sound as rich as the one you order for $3,500 from a catalog, but both will play the same songs. Subtle sonic nuances probably won't matter as much when you're just learning to play an instrument.

The pawnshop doesn't have to be your only option, even if there's not much money in the budget. "Student" instruments, or guitars, drums, and keyboards designed for beginners, are reasonably priced. And used instruments, found online or through local classified ads, are often bargains.

Types and Prices

No matter which instrument you choose, you'll encounter a wide range of styles, brand names, conditions, and prices. To get a sense of what's available, try websites like Musicians' Friend (musiciansfriend.com) in addition to your local music store. Perusing our catalog collection, we find these ranges:

- **Drums.** A five-piece Pulse Percussion set, with snare, bass, hi-hat, cymbal, and tom-tom (we'll explain these terms later), goes for $299. But you can also buy high-end DW and Ludwig models for thousands of dollars.

- **Classic electric-guitar** brands such as Gibson, Fender, Gretsch, and Rickenbacker are available in many different price ranges—a new Fender Squier Stratocaster goes for $149.

- **Electric bass guitars** tend to be slightly more expensive than regular guitars. Most guitar companies sell both styles, and you can find a Fender Squier bass or a similar-sounding Ibanez for about $200.

- Price and style range for **keyboards** is probably the most diverse, from an $88 Yamaha with 60 electronic "voices" to baby grands worth hundreds of thousands. You'll probably want something mid-range, like a $1,000 Yamaha with weighted keys and good piano and organ sounds.

New or Used?

Buying a musical instrument is a little like buying a car. If you're careful and shop around, you can usually get a good deal. However, you always risk ending up with a lemon.

Begin with the classified ads, in the local alt-weekly or daily newspaper, all of which have substantial sections titled "musical instruments." There's no shame in buying a used instrument. Just make sure that you test it out before buying, and consider bringing a superior player along to make sure there aren't any dead spots.

Also, talk to friends or relatives who have old instruments left over from their days in bands. They may be pleased somebody's putting their old guitar or snare drum to use. As you become more serious with the instrument, and in the band, you can upgrade to a higher-quality product. It's always possible, though, that you'll never want to part with the 1960s Telecaster you rescued from your uncle's dusty attic.

> **Backstage Insights**
>
> The classic company Fender has a line of Relic guitars designed to look like instruments from the old days. Just as Levi's makes jeans with designer holes in the knees, Relics come with nicks, dents, and fake cigarette-burn marks. But they're well built, selling for roughly $2,600 apiece.

Where to Shop

Almost every city has at least one music store, so start hanging around and befriend the clerks. They're generally musicians, and while their agenda is to sell high-priced instruments, they're usually honest about what's worth the money.

One of the biggest music-store chains is Guitar Center, which has competitive prices, knowledgeable clerks, and a range of brands and styles. You can also move beyond your surroundings and shop online, where many music stores, established and new, have set up shop. Search sites such as Musical Instruments @ Net Instruments (netinstruments.com) make the price-tracking process extremely easy.

Pawnshops can be excellent sources of old instruments, but buyer beware. It's easy to lose the negotiation with a practiced haggler, and the pawnshop owner probably won't be quite as nurturing toward young band members as local music-store clerks.

Finally, check for deals on the Internet auction site eBay (ebay.com). We searched for "guitar" while researching this book and came up with 15,530 listings, including a Carlo Robelli bass (with case) for $102; a Paul Reed Smith custom electric, $2,699; a Dean Avalanche One electric, $149; and effects pedals, cords, and tuners of every style and price.

Getting a Good Deal

As with any kind of merchandise, shop around. Try to avoid "new guitar fever," imagining yourself in a classic Jimmy Page pose as soon as you encounter a Gibson Les Paul. The more you're aware of instrument prices in general, the less likely you are to succumb to unreasonable markups.

The retail price for musical instruments tends to be considerably higher than the basic wholesale price. This means there's often plenty of barter room. Good salespeople, especially if you're a regular customer, might be willing to give you a deal.

Other Equipment: Cords, Amps, and Tuners

Budget for the accessories. If you buy an electric guitar, you won't be able to hear anything without an amp. And neither one of those things will work particularly well without the proper cords to connect them. In addition, most guitarists will probably want to buy electronic tuners and perhaps some effects pedals. (See "The Guitarist," later in this chapter, for more on these accessories.)

Amplifiers, or amps, give electric instruments sound—and can make them as loud as you want. You'll need them for most rehearsal and gig situations, and they can be expensive, so shop carefully. And be ready to spend the rest of your band-member career loading them in and out of vans and venues.

Amps come in a wide range of sizes and prices. Guitarists' amps are perhaps the most elaborate—one of the most famous brands is Marshall, which sells amps anywhere from $1,100 to $2,500. You can also opt for a mini amp, also called a practice amp or studio amp, for considerably less money—as low as $100 for some models.

For best results, every player should use an amp specifically designed for his or her instrument's needs. A bass player should buy a bass amp, for example. But often singers and guitarists can economize by plugging their microphones and guitars into the same amps. If you plan to do this, make sure the amp you buy has enough inputs. Music-store clerks can show you what gear works best for this approach.

Backstage Insights

If you position your electric instrument or microphone too close to an amp, you may get a burst of noisy feedback. Musicians mostly try to avoid this jarring nuisance, as it can really screw up a song. But often, as in the famous style of Jimi Hendrix, musicians incorporate the feedback noises into their music. Position your instrument and amp in different configurations, and mess with the volume knob, to determine just how much or little feedback you prefer.

Finally, the drummer needs sticks and a throne, a special stool that stands up to years of loading and performance abuse. And you may want to pay a few bucks for an old music stand so everybody at rehearsal can see the song lyrics. None of this extra stuff is costly, but it can add up if you buy it all at once.

Finding Your Niche in the Band

As we've already noted, your role in the band, to a great extent, will be determined by the instrument you play. The drummer and bass player, traditionally, are in charge of laying the rhythmic foundation, on top of which other instruments provide melody, harmony, and flourishes. The drummer and bass player tend to be steady, reliable, and nonshowy—characteristics that may translate to the players' personalities.

(There are exceptions, of course: Keith Moon of The Who was one of the flashiest drummers and drummer-personalities in rock history. And thanks to rockers such as Cream's Ginger Baker in the late 1960s, drummers are almost required to play long solos during concerts. Bass players, sometimes, too.)

Guitarists and keyboardists are more likely responsible for the melodies. A lead guitarist flies above the rhythm, playing solos rather than perpetuating the beat. A rhythm guitarist works in tandem with the bass player and drummer, fleshing out their beats with a fuller sound. Keyboardists tend to plug into the mix where necessary. The Doors didn't have a bass player, so organist Ray Manzarek handled the low frequencies with his left hand; most keyboardists, however, trade solos with the lead guitarist.

The singer, of course, is responsible for the words, and rarely solos unless he or she is known for Whitney Houston–style vocal histrionics. In those cases, moaning, groaning, and yodeling is standard procedure. In general, the singer's role is to hold the song together by providing the story and the lyrical continuity. The rest of the band members should follow his or her lead as the song progresses.

The Singer

As far as equipment goes, the singer has the most minimal role in the band. (Unless, of course, the singer plays an instrument as well—guitar and keyboards are common.) In most amplified bands, a singer will simply need a reliable microphone, preferably one that can stand up to abuse.

Microphones: How to Sing Into Them and How They Work

The microphone's job is simply to amplify the singer over the din (in most rock and pop bands) of guitar amplifiers, bass amplifiers, and thudding drums.

As with musical instruments (and cars), microphones are available in a wide range of brands and prices. The standard "workhorse" microphone is Shure's SM57, which can supposedly pound nails into lumber. This style usually sells for about $79. You can go one step higher with the Shure SM58, a stage microphone that has a slightly better sound, for roughly $99. The AKG D590 goes for $70 and is often packaged with a pair of headphones for home-studio use.

Microphones are also used to amplify instruments, such as drums (see Chapter 20) or non-plug-in violins and cellos on stage. Ask at your local music store about which model fits better for instruments and vocals.

Generally, you'll want to use the same microphone in rehearsal as on stage, so you're used to the sound. The last thing you need, while overcoming stage fright during a gig, is to hear yourself differently through the PA system.

Backstage Insights

Many singers these days use wireless microphones, which operate just like regular microphones only without the cumbersome cords. They're a little more expensive than cord-connected mikes because they come with high-tech receiving devices. You can buy the mike and receiver in one package.

As with any instrument, remember to budget for the accessories. A microphone stand is a necessity, both for storing the microphone so you don't have to leave expensive equipment on the ground, and for having something on stage to dance with. (Aerosmith's Steven Tyler and Pearl Jam's Eddie Vedder are among the many rockers who romance mike stands in elaborate, creative ways while performing.) Mike stands run anywhere from $20 to $50.

One other note about microphones: They can give you an electrical shock on stage. Be careful not to step into any puddles before grabbing one—and wear rubber-soled shoes just in case.

Words to Rock By

Shredding is a guitarist's slang term for playing a really excellent, fast, rocking solo during a song. It's usually used in the context of hard rock and heavy metal.

The Guitarist

The guitarist is expected to be perhaps the most versatile member of the band. Sometimes, this musician will strum the strings rhythmically, to augment the bass and drums. Other times, he or she steps to the edge of the stage, leans back, and delivers a high-pitched solo in the *shredding* tradition of Led Zeppelin's Jimmy Page or Metallica's Kirk Hammett.

Should You Play Acoustic or Electric?

While guitarists sometimes play acoustic and electric instruments in the same band—or even the same song—there's usually a line of demarcation between the two styles. Because acoustic guitars are much, much softer than electric guitars, acoustic players generally perform in folk, country, bluegrass, or soft rock, while electric players deal in pop, punk, metal, and hard rock.

But acoustic guitars often fit harder sounds as well. Many hard-rock and metal bands use acoustic instruments to flesh out their sounds with greater depth and texture. And many electric bands, from Stone Temple Pilots to Staind, include "acoustic" bits in their shows, when they play well-known songs on softer instruments. MTV's *Unplugged* series of the 1990s turned this trend into a franchise, with artists such as 10,000 Maniacs, LL Cool J, Nirvana, and Eric Clapton reinventing themselves in a softer way. Often, their *Unplugged* albums sold extremely well.

Electric guitars are generally less expensive than acoustic guitars of the same condition. That's because the sound of electric guitars is amplified electronically, whereas the sound of acoustic guitars resonates from the wood itself. Although electric guitars have their own character and can be lovingly built, acoustics are more like prized furniture.

Almost any guitarist who plays an acoustic can play an electric, and vice versa. If you're in an all-acoustic band, it won't be a huge stretch for the guitarist to pick up an electric on occasion and play a solo. Similarly, if a hard-rocking, fully amplified band needs a strummed acoustic passage, any of the guitarists can probably handle it without trouble. If your guitarist has the funds, it can't hurt to maintain both an electric and an acoustic guitar for future arrangements.

Rickenbacker or Gibson?: Brands and How They Sound

A guitar is a guitar, basically, but certain brands have distinctive tonal qualities that set them apart—and give them a certain mystique. Some of the best-known guitar-making companies are Fender, Gibson, Rickenbacker, Gretsch, Martin, Paul Reed Smith, and Ibanez, most of which put out electric and acoustic instruments.

Invented by Leo Fender in the early 1950s, the Fender Telecaster and Fender Stratocaster quickly became famous for their sleek, curved, basic rock 'n' roll look—among the adopters were Buddy Holly, Jimi Hendrix, and the Rolling Stones' Keith Richards. The Telecaster, for example, has a more aggressive "biting" sound than other types of electric guitars.

The 12-string Rickenbacker, known for its distinctive chiming sound, was a signature instrument for the Byrds' Roger McGuinn. The Beatles' George Harrison and rocker Neil Young became well known for playing a larger-bodied Gretsch. These models, among others, have become mythological in pop culture.

The Les Paul, one of Gibson's most popular guitars, was designed by its namesake, a pop-rock legend and musical instrument designer who began playing guitar in the 1930s. Originally marketed in 1952, Les Paul guitars have a distinctively "fat" tone and are famous for their sustain.

Backstage Insights

Several glossy guitar magazines critique brands, interview star musicians about their styles, and print hit-song transcriptions. They include *Guitar World*, *Guitar One*, *Guitar Player*, and *Acoustic Guitar*.

Gretsch guitars have huge, curvy bodies and a heavy, raw sound that works more effectively in rockabilly and punk music than jazz or classical.

As for acoustics, the most renowned company is Martin, which has been building guitars since 1833. Many country, folk, and rock artists, from Hank Williams to Dave Matthews, have sworn by their Martins' super-smooth wood finishes and impeccable vibrations.

Backstage Insights

Have you ever watched professional guitarists' feet while they perform on stage? You may notice them stomping onto effects pedals. There are many different kinds of these boxes on the market to make your guitar (or other instrument) growl, cry, and scream. They have names like the Crybaby from Hell and the Vox Wah.

Whammy Bars and Other Luxuries

Electric guitars are famous, in part, for their effects. Funk bands in the 1970s, for example, turned the wah-wah pedal, which presents a distinctive, rhythmic *wah-wah* sound, into a pop and rock music fixture. The fuzztone effect—pioneered by 1950s rockabilly instrumentalist Link Wray but used most famously in the Rolling Stones' "(I Can't Get No) Satisfaction"—clouds a guitar tone with dense feedback noise. And the whammy bar, which is built onto a guitar body rather than coming separately in an effects kit, allows guitarists to make a curvy, echoey, vibrato noise.

Basic Riffs

Before you're able to jam with other musicians, you'll have to develop a repertoire of your own—that means learning riffs, or distinctive short melodies that sound really good when played over and over.

Begin with the classics—Chuck Berry's archetypal rock 'n' roll line in "Johnny B. Goode," "Roll Over Beethoven," and dozens of other 1950s hits; the bluesy picking of Muddy Waters' "Honey Bee"; the fuzzy three chords of the Kingsmen's "Louie, Louie"; the pretty, soaring opening of Jimi Hendrix's "Little Wing"; the stomping power chords of the Stooges' "Search & Destroy," the Sex Pistols' "God Save the Queen," Nirvana's "Smells Like Teen Spirit," and Metallica's "Enter Sandman." Buy these records, slow them down, and learn to play them. Eventually, when you're accomplished at other people's inventions, develop your own.

The Bass Player

Stereotypically, the bass player is the stoic member of the group, who provides the band's bottom, or lower frequency levels. You may not hear the bass overtly, the way you can pick out a guitar or keyboard in any given song, but if the bass player is doing his job you'll feel it. (Some bass players take solos, but this is recommended only if they're very, very good.) Bass provides crucial punch and rhythm.

Electric or Upright?

In all-acoustic groups, the bass player will often use a large upright bass that belongs to the violin family. He or she will pluck the thick strings to achieve a soulful, rhythmic effect, or occasionally bow it like a cello. Note that some newer upright basses are electric, combining the full sound of an acoustic with the flexibility of a smaller model.

Although they can be amplified just like electric basses or acoustic guitars, acoustic basses won't work quite so well in loud bands. If you're trying to compete with heavy-metal guitarists, you're likely to get lost in the mix. So most rock bass players tend to go electric.

Four or Six Strings—or More?

A standard electric bass has four strings, although some basses have five, six, or even eight. Because bassists generally don't play chords, and instead of soloing they tend to pluck notes, beginners won't need more than four strings.

Behind the Music
Ex-Beatles bassist Paul McCartney and the legendary Jimi Hendrix are among the few left-handed guitarists who have had to restring their instruments upside down in order to play in reverse. This isn't as necessary today, as many guitar companies design guitars specifically for left-handed players. Remember, though, you'll have to learn to play songs from sheet music a totally different way.

Most of the same companies that make guitars also make basses. And they're often just as mythological, but in a less flashy way. The Rickenbacker Bass is known for its punch. The Hofner Violin Bass is more mellow and flexible and is the instrument of choice for ex-Beatle Paul McCartney.

While standard guitar strings break all the time, bass strings tend to last forever.

The Drummer

The drummer's job is similar to that of the bass player—maintaining the rhythm—but with several key differences. Most of the band will look to the drummer to maintain the tempo, or speed, of the song. If the drummer goes out of tempo, it will throw the entire band off. Also, while bass players tend to stay in the background, drummers usually have more license to be flashy—they use cymbals, snares. and other high-frequency noises to enter guitar-and-vocals territory.

Types of Drums

A drum is an ancient instrument that comes in a wide variety of forms, from sticks banging on rocks or gourds to African hand drums to a standard rock drummer's kit to sophisticated electronic percussion. Rhythm is a universal language, and drums draw children at early ages who are thrilled to bang on objects with sticks even if they have no formal musical training.

A standard drum kit has the following core:

- A bass drum, played by foot, with a pedal attachment.
- A snare, with a higher-pitched sound, generally played on the beat.
- Cymbals, which come in a variety of sizes and sounds.
- A hi-hat, or two cymbals on a stand that click together through the use of a pedal attachment.
- A tom-tom, fuller than a snare and more flexible than a bass, for fills and emphasis.
- Sticks, a throne, and percussion of your choice (we'll get to that later).

The easiest way to buy a drum kit is to purchase everything as a unit. That way you won't have to worry about mounting tom-toms to the bass drum.

But it may be cheaper to mix and match, just as you would with home-stereo components or computer equipment. To build a custom kit, start with the snare, which is the predominant element of your sound and needs to be properly responsive.

When buying the hi-hat, bass, and accompanying foot pedals, test them to make sure that they're comfortable. The last thing you want is to throw a bunch of money at drum components and wind up playing in discomfort. And be sure you have a reliable place to practice—drums are the loudest rock instruments.

> **CAUTION**
>
> ### Avoiding Bad Notes
>
> Before embarking on a career as a rock drummer, keep in mind it's one of the most difficult instruments to play physically. You have to keep in shape to perform, and even then, drummers such as Anthrax's Charlie Benante and the E Street Band's Max Weinberg wind up with painful variations of carpal-tunnel syndrome. If it hurts to play, arrange the drums differently or work on developing your muscles.

Drums vs. Percussion

Percussion is a broad term for rhythmic instruments—including drums—sometimes played with sticks or mallets. Aside from drums, one of the most common percussion instruments in rock and pop bands is the tambourine, used to rich effect in Motown hits and other classic rock and pop songs.

Again, drums are the best-known form of percussion. But many bands use percussionists to supplement their drummers, or the singer will shake a tambourine if he or she doesn't play another instrument. Percussionists can use many different instruments to vary the sound and feeling in a song: egg shaker, cabasa (a Latin instrument that makes an urgent zipping noise), maracas (bulbs attached to sticks with gravel inside), triangle, wood block, cowbell, even trash-can lids. Percussion instruments are generally affordable, so try different ones out to flesh out various songs.

The Keyboardist, Et Al.

Often, due to years of childhood piano lessons, the keyboardist's music-theory knowledge is the most extensive in any band. So keyboardists are often musical directors by default, arranging the songs and teaching band members their parts.

At least at first, most bands' keyboardists will get by with standard pianos or organs. Eventually, they may opt for more complex synthesizers, or electronic instruments containing many different sounds and effects. Some keyboardists, however, are traditionalists who eschew synthesizers in favor of old-school instruments such as the Hammond B-3 organ, the Fender Rhodes electric piano, and the Farfisa organ.

Modern electronic keyboards come equipped with your choice of dozens of different sounds—grand pianos, organs, accordions, steel drums, handclaps, breaking glass. Many professional bands, lacking the money for horn or string sections, simply program their keyboards to approximate these sounds. Some higher-end models also contain built-in drum machines and computer-recording equipment, so keyboardists can literally be their own band.

But you may want to resist the urge to give too many musical roles to the synthesizer player. Some electronic sounds, especially on cheaper keyboard models, may come across tinny and corny. These sounds were big in the 1980s—check out Harold Faltermeyer's hit "Axel F." theme to the movie *Beverly Hills Cop* for evidence—but feel dated today. Nonetheless, keyboards have advanced with technology, so for midrange prices you can get noncorny organ and piano sounds.

And yes, as an alternative, you can hire an entire horn or string section if you have the money.

The Least You Need to Know

- Once you've picked an instrument to play, the next step is to decide on amplification and buy the equipment.

- Guitars, amps, basses, drums, and keyboards are available in a wide range of prices. Try shopping at pawnshops, online, and through the newspaper classifieds for good beginners' deals.

- Your choice of instrument, to an extent, will determine your role in the band.

- Classic guitar brands include Fender, Rickenbacker, Gretsch, and Gibson. Each style has a different sound dynamic.

- Electric basses are usually equipped with four strings, although you can choose an acoustic upright bass or experiment with more strings on your electric.

- Drummers can customize by buying individual instruments, but it's easier to buy the whole kit at once.

Part 2

Day-to-Day Business with Your Band

After you've (more or less) finalized your band lineup and learned to communicate constructively as a group, the next step is to expand the music. You'll initially do that in rehearsal, where the band hones its sound, perfects its craft, and figures out how to do new things.

Soon, though, you may start thinking about how to make money. It may take a while—early gigs at parties, clubs, and other small venues may pay very little or not at all. But after your band has established a reputation and started to draw crowds, salaries may start to arrive semi-regularly.

That's when things start getting complicated: How much should you make? Who gets what? Do you have to sign a contract? Also, once you play in public before larger and larger crowds, potential challenges such as the presence of drugs and alcohol can start to creep in. Remember to stay focused on the band—making music is your top priority—and you'll grow quickly.

THE MOST IMPORTANT THING IN KEEPING A BAND TOGETHER IS OPEN DIALOGUE. WELL, *THAT* AND A KICK-BUTT DRUMMER.

Chapter 5

Rehearsal

In This Chapter

◆ How to find the perfect rehearsal space

◆ The basics of playing songs

◆ Choosing a leader—and accepting your role if you aren't the leader

◆ Constructive criticism—and figuring out if you're any good

◆ When and how to tape your rehearsal

Until now, you and your bandmates have probably jammed together purely for fun. Whenever you happened to be free at the same time, you gravitated to the instruments, fired up an amplifier or two, settled into roughly the same key, and let loose. But if you're considering a regular rehearsal, it means you're ready to graduate from noodling around to serious business. Rehearsal is where you grow and develop as a band. You learn songs, become better musicians and—perhaps most important—develop into a cohesive unit. To improve, every band must rehearse regularly. That means settling on a reliable time and place, hammering out each member's role, and learning to communicate as a group.

Can I Bring a Date?

The short answer: no! Nothing against dating, of course. But if the band is ready to take music seriously, that means focusing on the music and not on distractions. Do you bring your date to your day job? We hope not. Being in a band is more fun than working at an office or industrial plant, but it's work nonetheless.

Where and When to Do It

Where? Wherever you can. It's often difficult to find a rehearsal room, especially if your music leans toward loud guitars and thudding drums. Parents and neighbors may balk at the noise, so you have to be creative—and willing to give something in return. Volunteer the band for garage cleanup duty in exchange for two weeks worth of practices. And check with any neighbors in advance for opportune times.

When? It depends on the band members' schedules. At a minimum, we suggest one two-hour session a week—the better you want to be, the more you should rehearse. Nighttime rehearsals are often the most convenient for everybody, but they're not required. Try the morning, before school or work. Or two or three lunch hours per week.

> **Backstage Insights**
>
> Build in at least one 15-minute break for each rehearsal. No matter how exciting your groove, the drum throne and piano bench start to feel terribly hard after a certain point. Refreshed brains and muscles are conducive to good ideas.

The single hardest thing about planning rehearsals is setting up the schedule. Invariably, the singer's best day is the bassist's worst day. But once you set up the schedule, stick to it. (If a change becomes necessary, make it together, then stick to that.) If it's every Wednesday at 8 P.M., don't show up at 7:30 or 8:20. Be on time. Nothing's worse than keeping an eager band waiting.

Find the Perfect Basement

The perfect basement—or garage, bedroom, or backyard—is one the owners will let you use for free. Beyond that, it should have plenty of space for each band member, and enough electrical outlets to accommodate many amps.

Often it's not so much a matter of finding the perfect rehearsal room as creating one. If you're in an apartment building, and your rehearsal time happens to be smack in the middle of *Friends* or the Stanley Cup playoffs, be sensitive to neighbors' needs. Maybe you can muffle the drums by putting towels over them, or use soft mallets instead of sticks. Maybe everybody can rehearse with headphones. Or instead of using your gigantic Marshall Stack amplifier, plug your guitars into a tiny practice amp. Sometimes the solution is as simple as moving to another room.

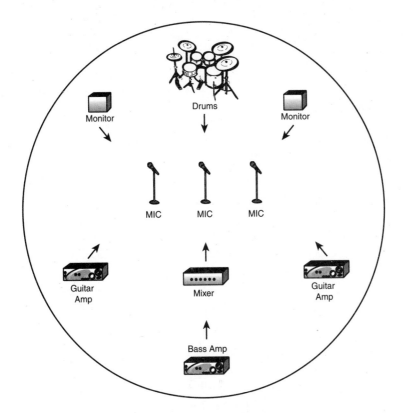

Your band can set up in any configuration, but here's a basic one that works for most rehearsals.

Communication, as always, is crucial. Here's a conciliatory thing you can tell the neighbors: "Every Wednesday night from 7 to 9 it may be a little noisy in here. If it's too noisy, just let us know and we'll adjust." Better yet, work with them to find an opportune time. Nobody wants to squander useful rehearsal time and energy on cat-fights with unsympathetic neighbors.

Whatever rehearsal space you use, make sure it's properly ventilated. If there's a propane heater, don't hang blankets or egg crates or other flammable soundproofing unless you're sure the heater functions properly. Have a fire extinguisher on hand, and know how to use it. And remember all the stuff your parents told you about garage safety: Don't start the car with the door closed and so forth.

Renting Rehearsal Space

Early in your band's career, the cost of rehearsal space—from $10 an hour in a cheap warehouse to $150 an hour for a luxurious room with a PA system—will probably be prohibitive. But if you have that kind of money, and all your free-basement leads have fizzled, check the local paper. Often, classified ads will list rental spaces. And if you live in a big city, try the musician's union (afm.org), which has experience linking bands with rehearsal spots.

Short of that, again, be creative. Maybe the local high school music teacher will let you use the facilities during an off period of the school day. Try the youth center or even the local church.

Graduate from Jamming to Songs

Improvisation is fun, and you might be the kind of band that wants to agree on a musical key and solo, solo, solo. (Some big-time bands, including the String Cheese Incident and Phish, have made entire careers of this.) But at a certain point somebody—maybe you—will inevitably say, "How about if we learn some songs?" In some bands, the collective answer might be: "Nah!" In others, the musicians may be just as bored as you are and crave structure.

The hard part is agreeing on what kind of structure. To start playing basic rock, blues, folk, and pop songs, start with the lyrics to the songs—and perhaps the chord changes. (These days, almost every popular song is fully transcribed on the Internet; use the Google search engine or broad-ranging websites such as lyrics.com.)

As we pointed out in Chapter 3, when using preprinted lyrics and chord transcriptions, it's not necessary to have music-reading ability. (Although sometimes it helps.) If everybody in the band knows three or four particular chords, you'll have an endless repertoire, from rock classics like The Kingsmen's "Louie, Louie" and Nirvana's "Smells Like Teen Spirit" to country and blues standards like Leadbelly's "Goodnight Irene" and Robert Johnson's "Sweet Home, Chicago."

Again, band communication is crucial. If one guy insists on Limp Bizkit's "Break Stuff" and another can't live without playing "Kum Ba Ya" on stage at least once in his lifetime, you'll have to compromise. Indulge each person with a favorite until, after many rehearsals, the band becomes good at certain songs and not so good at others. (This will become obvious.) At that point, reshuffle.

> **Behind the Music**
>
> Can't figure out Jack White's guitar solo on The White Stripes' "Seven Nation Army"? Bring a CD player to rehearsal and listen to the relevant bit over and over. Or better yet, invest in an old-fashioned record player and buy The White Stripes' LP. Then slow the record down and pick out the notes. Some computer programs and variable-speed recorders will help you do this, too.

Playing In Tune

"Why doesn't it sound right?" is the most frustrating question a rehearsing band can ask. Especially if the question comes up after every song, for hours at a time. Usually the answer is simple: "Because somebody is way out of tune." Tuning takes just a few minutes—less time with experience—but can prevent hours of irritation.

An electronic tuner costs as little as $10 (or as much as $250) and is a worthwhile investment. In the old days, guitarists used tuning forks and plucked individual strings until their ears told them they were on target. Today, a tuner smaller than a cell phone will lead you to the right pitch using LED lights. Tuners are simple to figure out, and you can even turn off the amp and tune in silence, using your eyes rather than your ears. Buy them at any local music store, or on music-gear websites such as guitarcenter.com.

Before you start rehearsal, take time to tune up. And if you play piano or drums, be patient and avoid the distracting urge to fiddle around while the guitarists tune up.

It sounds so simple: Decide on a musical key and have everybody play in that key. But … what if the guitarist prefers E and the pianist can only play in C and F? What if everybody enjoys B-flat, but you insist on playing Roy Orbison's "Oh, Pretty Woman," which, according to your *fake book*, is written in A?

> **Words to Rock By**
>
> A **fake book** is a thick collection of popular songs, from jazz to standards to folk to rock, printed in rough sheet-music form. They almost always contain lyrics and basic chord changes, although they rarely transcribe famous solos. (To learn the saxophone solo in Charlie Parker's version of "A Night In Tunisia," you'll have to listen to the record—and be an incredible player.) They're available at most music stores and online.

The basic rule is to let the singer pick the key. Otherwise, he or she will have to strain and the song will sound terrible. Guitarists and pianists can always learn new chords, but inexperienced singers comfortable in C will have a hard time switching to D-flat on short notice.

If the band insists on playing a more complicated song, tricky chords and all, you may want to table it until the members have had a chance for individual home practice. Learning a new song at group rehearsal is valuable, but learning how to play a new chord tends to be a one-person activity—and will likely frustrate the rest of the group. Start with songs you all can play, and grow from there. *Guitar tabs* can help all the musicians, not just guitarists, figure out what chords to play when.

Words to Rock By

A **guitar tab,** short for *guitar tablature,* is a style of writing down music for guitar and bass. It's usually found on websites (Guitar Tab Universe, at guitartabs.cc, is particularly thorough), and the text characters tell you exactly where to put your fingers on the strings and frets. The charts also show how to use effects like string-bending or vibrato. Tabs are amazingly helpful in learning how to play well-known songs.

Beginnings and Endings

A song is like a story, with a beginning, middle, and end. Bands, unlike individual writers, have to agree on how to approach each of these segments. In most bands, the drummer begins a song—by clicking sticks together in the agreed-upon 1, 2, 3, 4 tempo. Often, however, the guitarist will end the song by lifting up the guitar neck to get everybody's attention, and then dropping it down for "cut!"

Then again, in some bands, the singer or accepted bandleader will be the point person for these details. Either way, you'll have to accept the decision—unilaterally ending a particular song yourself, even if you think it has dragged on long enough, is likely to create tension in the band.

These details, of course, must be frequently rehearsed for smooth execution.

Eventually, after slogging through these decisions and rehearsal repetitions, you'll start to become

Avoiding Bad Notes

Metronomes and click-tracks, or electronic drum patterns built into a synthesizer or drum machine, are handy for individual practice. With groups, they can be restrictive and difficult. Consider using these techniques if you're really having trouble staying on time, but otherwise, relying on your drummer's instincts is excellent practice.

more comfortable with each other. Experienced bands begin to communicate with a sort of telepathy, using eye contact and other unspoken cues to coordinate instinctively. If you're in the mood for a band field trip, try to catch a veteran band in concert—watching Pearl Jam or The Rolling Stones communicate nonverbally is a rich learning experience. You can pick up the same knowledge—although it won't be nearly as fun—by watching concert DVDs.

Mixing Guitars with Keyboards

Although every musician uses the same palette of notes, keys, and chords, different musical instruments speak different languages. Inexperienced keyboardists hate to use too many black keys, while inexperienced guitarists are uncomfortable stretching their fingers from one difficult chord to the next. And it's often hard for a guitarist to recognize what a keyboardist is playing, and vice versa.

Communication, as always, overcomes these concerns. It may take a minute in practice for a pianist to *transpose* a song he knows in C to a song that better fits the singer and guitarist in B. (Transposing means converting a set of chords from one key to another; many electronic pianos will do this with the push of a button. Otherwise, the musician will simply have to write down the new set of chords.)

It can't hurt for musicians to learn other instruments. A drummer who knows a little guitar will better understand certain musical cues—if the rhythm accelerates after a key change, for example, the drummer will more quickly adapt to what's going on. Similarly, there's nothing more frustrating for a pianist than a guitarist who says, "Just watch my fingers and do what I do." Basic guitar lessons can help. But that's not a necessity; communication is.

The regular group rehearsal shouldn't be your band's only rehearsal. Each musician should plan to spend several hours at home learning new parts and smoothing out kinks. And the bassist and drummer may want to schedule separate "rhythm-section rehearsals" to lock down the groove. What will they do? Play the songs. It'll only make things better when the guitar player arrives for regular rehearsal. Similarly, "vocal-only rehearsals" are effective for bands that emphasize group harmonies.

Basics of Rhythm

Rhythm, or *tempo*, is as easy as counting and feeling the beat of the music. Your drummer will certainly want to learn about time signatures—rock-and-country-time 4/4 or waltz-time 3/4, for example, which fundamentally define a song's rhythm. But the rest of the band will have to align itself to the drummer's speed and avoid dragging or rushing.

If everybody counts to four at the same speed, your band has itself a rhythm. If this seems impossible, you may want to invest in a metronome, a small automatic musical counting device, but as mentioned earlier, this can lead to restrictions and frustrations. A better plan might be to let the drummer play the groove alone for a bit while the rest of the band counts silently.

Most songs, by acts ranging from Frank Sinatra to Dashboard Confessional, are built on these basic elements:

♦ The *verse*, as with a verse in a poem, is where you lay out your lyrics and essentially tell the song's story.

♦ The *bridge* is exactly what the name implies—the link between the verse and the chorus.

♦ The *chorus* is a more repetitive summary of the verses, or if you will, the "sing-along portion" of the song. It often contains the *hook*.

These elements won't appear in every song—sometimes you'll encounter a classical, jazz, hip-hop, or just plain experimental piece that ignores such structure altogether. (Nirvana, to name one popular rock band, actively mocked this structure—one of the band's early 1990s tunes was called "Verse Chorus Verse." The song was surprisingly traditional.)

Words to Rock By

The **hook** is whatever makes a song stand out and appeal to people. It may be a melody, like a bluegrass band singing "you are my sunshine, my only sunshine." Or it may be a catchy guitar riff, like AC/DC going *deedle deedle deedle dee* at the end of every verse in "Back in Black." Hit songs, especially those on the radio, almost always have prominent, repetitive hooks.

By playing other people's songs, you'll get a feel for traditional verse-chorus-verse structures—and maybe get some ideas on how to structure your own material later on.

Arrangements

Arrangements are basically what you do with the verses, choruses, and bridges. They're the blueprint of your song, and once the band decides how to put one together, everybody must stick to the plan. Unless you're playing experimental, purposely dissonant jazz, the pianist can't decide to take an impromptu break while the guitarist is in the middle of a solo, or it will throw everyone off.

When to Add Horns

Avoid making a song overly busy if it's not necessary. Often, however, you'll detect something missing. Trust your ears to be your guide. If you're covering an old Benny Goodman swing song for a wedding reception, and the piano player's synthesizer-horn sound comes across too tinny, consider inviting a saxophone-playing friend to accompany you.

Just remember, early in a band's history, it's hard to rehearse with extraneous players. Stick with more manageable configurations—two guitars, bass, and drums; or maybe bass guitar, keyboard, and drums. As you gain experience, expanding the sound will become an obvious next step.

Recognizing the Leader

Rehearsals may be going pretty well—you've found a place to set up, you can play a few songs all the way through without mistakes, and the jams are sounding tighter and tighter. So why not do it like this forever? Because at some point, to progress creatively or even financially, you'll have to become more sophisticated.

The first step in this direction is choosing a leader. (See Chapter 6 for more detail about the leader and other band personalities.) Certainly it's possible to function, as a group, without a leader. But then who settles the arguments? Who picks, or writes, the songs? Who decides which gigs to play?

Choosing is perhaps too strong a word. Somebody in the band will probably emerge without discussion as the leader. You'll recognize that person when he or she starts making assertions, like, "I think we should play this song" or "What if we started trying to play in public?" or "Here, I've written a few of my own lyrics for us to try." There is nothing inherently wrong with this; if one person wants to assume the responsibility and extra workload that comes with being the leader, why not give that person a shot?

If you're a competitive person, or if you just can't stand following orders, a certain amount of resentment toward the leader is natural. But give the new leader a chance. Maybe the decisions will be pretty good, and maybe vision is just what the band needs. If the would-be leader becomes too controlling or manipulative, you can deal with that later through communication and compromise. Or, yes, firing.

The Myth of the Democratic Band

Some bands are purely democratic, which means everything that happens goes up for a vote. Feel free to try this approach. *Everything*—where to park the van outside the gig, who collects the money from the event organizer, who writes the thank you note to the neighbors for not complaining about the loud rehearsals—goes up for a vote. As you can imagine, this process can be quite cumbersome.

There's a certain amount of democracy to every band. Every member should be involved in important financial decisions (like whether to open a band bank account or hire a manager), for instance. But it's easiest for one person to set a direction, and too much input can confuse or cloud the issues. Endless debate kills any band quickly.

More often than not, the leadership role just sticks to somebody like a magnet. If you find the rest of the band coming to you with questions, whether they're musical or business matters, you might be the leader. If you wind up doing little things nobody else does, like buying supplies for rehearsal, or proposing a rhythm-section rehearsal, you might be the leader. If that's the case, accept the role. You can make decisions, but don't be mean. Benevolent dictators are the most effective dictators.

Knowing Your Role

You're in a band, a unit, a group, a marriage, so don't let little things eat at your ego. If it's your job to play a little guitar bit between two verses of a song, do that. Don't act like you're the talent who's slumming until something better comes along.

Have we mentioned communication yet? The best way to figure out your role, if it's confusing, is to ask. As the keyboardist, maybe you aren't sure whether to augment the bassist by playing along with your left hand. Ask the bassist or the leader. Bring issues out in the open—during calm moments, rather than stressful ones—and discuss them until you're satisfied. This is a key component of successful marriages.

In a rehearsal situation, defer to the leader. But if anybody feels he or she needs to rehearse a part again, speak up. Just pay attention to the structure of the rehearsal. Deal with a particular song while you're working on it. If you've long since moved on to the fourth song, it'll only frustrate everybody if you return to the second.

"Hey, I've got to learn this one a little better—can we take it up again next week?" is an appropriate thing to suggest. That way, you don't have to muddle through several frustrating versions of a song. Of course, if you're playing that song at a gig the following night, it behooves you to practice until you get it right.

Backstage Insights _____

The easiest way to obtain constructive criticism is to play in public—or, at least, in front of people not in the band. Avoid surrounding yourself with "yes people," such as significant others or even parents, who won't deliver the pointed comments you desperately need. If you get "you suck," or "that was pretty good," press for specifics. If none is forthcoming, consider finding other critics.

Are We Any Good?

If you play in front of people, and they like it, then yes, you are good. On a more personal level, as rehearsals continue, and you feel yourself uplifted by certain chord changes or solos, chances are the band's on the right track. At some point, once you've learned the songs and don't have to worry so much about frantic memorization, try to really listen. Is it something you'd turn up if it came on the radio?

Still, no matter how intently you listen, it's difficult to step outside the music and get an objective perspective. Consider inviting a member of another band, especially one you like, to rehearsal. Or a friend with a reputation for good taste. Press this person for specifics, especially if the comments are purely positive. And accept negative comments gracefully and try to learn from them; you'll know whether the critic is simply being jealous or abusive. It can't hurt to play to several listeners with diverse musical backgrounds.

Roll Tape! (When and How)

It's essential, if the band wants to improve, to tape a rehearsal and require each member to sit down and listen. Self-critique sessions are invaluable, but only if everybody remains constructive. Don't make these criticism sessions personal.

At this stage, whatever tape recorder you can afford will work fine. A cassette recorder with a built-in microphone will run $25 or so at Radio Shack, and despite the murky sound, it should give you enough raw material for group criticism. Expensive home studio gear, of course, is much more precise and effective—but not yet necessary. (More on buying recording equipment in Chapters 18 and 19.)

Certainly each band member can borrow the playback tape and listen with more scrutiny during personal time. But beware of tampering with fragile group dynamics. If one musician takes the tape home and returns to say the bass playing isn't in time, and the defensive bass player says, "prove it," you're in danger of upheaval. Individual listening can help correct unrecognized problems, but it should supplement the group critique sessions, not replace them.

The Least You Need to Know

◆ Be especially kind to parents, neighbors, and others who might potentially offer free rehearsal space.

◆ Inexpensive electronic guitar tuners are immeasurably helpful.

◆ Communication, during rehearsal, is hugely important—decide together who will start and end each song, what key to play in, when to solo, and so on.

◆ Democratic bands are well and good, but bands with strong leaders are much more efficient. When somebody—maybe you!—emerges as leader, decide on your role and stick with it.

◆ Impartial, constructive criticism will help you improve. But it can't replace your own personal listening.

◆ To record rehearsals, a cheap tape recorder and microphone will work just fine. Be sure to listen to playback, on a somewhat regular basis, as a group.

Chapter 6

Staying Together

In This Chapter

- Typical personality types that make bands work
- How to synchronize members' busy schedules, establish common goals, and speak up constructively
- A group dynamics primer—what to say, what not to say, and how to keep the discussion moving forward
- Communication, communication, communication
- When to hire and fire members, and how to avoid hurt feelings

Every successful band member leaves behind a long resumé of unsuccessful bands. Before Pearl Jam had anything close to a hit record, members played in Green River, Mother Love Bone, Mookie Blaylock, and several other short-lived collectives. And that's just one of millions of examples. At some point, you'll probably play in a band that breaks up, too. But if you've made it to this chapter, you've survived expanding the band, choosing a musical style, learning songs, and rehearsing—and are, therefore, pretty serious. So it's time to start thinking about how the band will stay together in the long run. Which means hanging on to the musicians who are as serious and driven as yourself and weeding out the musicians who are in it exclusively for the post-show parties.

Band Personality Types

A band is like a marriage. (So in theory, more than 50 percent of them end in divorce, but that's a subject for a different book.) All the musicians will spend so much time together—rehearsing, performing, dreaming, scheming, handling the business—that they'll feel they're in a long-term relationship. And just like husbands and wives, boyfriends and girlfriends, band members must figure out how to deal with each other in constant close quarters.

The usual relationship rules apply: Try not to get too picky; don't take things too personally; subvert your ego to reach a collective goal; and, perhaps most important at this stage, figure out your role in the band. Then stick to that role as best you can, whether it's a personal, getting-along-together kind of role or a musical, play-a-certain-chord-at-a-certain-time kind of role.

A key component of marriage is commitment. The day you join a band and the day it breaks up are often memorable—a lot like a wedding or a divorce. You may feel elated that first day, and emotionally spent on the last. As with marriage, it's important to learn to commit and to know, if necessary, when to move on when the sad time comes.

Following we list several general personality types in bands. Of course, you can't reduce complex musicians to simple stereotypes, and these rough categories can't possibly cover every band character. It's not necessary to obsess over recognizing the "comedian" or "friend," although it's usually important to pick a leader. If the band functions smoothly, and the music is progressing, chances are you've got a strong, complementary mix of personalities already.

The Leader: Earning Respect

We briefly discussed the concept of a leader—and concluded it's good to have one—in Chapter 5. It's possible you're the leader and must start making decisions and generally setting direction for the band. If you're not the leader, learn to subvert your ego and acquiesce to the leader's decisions. At the least, give him or her a chance.

A strong leader helps direct the group in a specific musical or business direction. If this person has true leadership skills, he or she will consult the group for its input and make decisions, easy or hard, that make everybody feel valued and important. A weak leader may create resentment and disharmony—and if such behavior continues, you may have to start the difficult process of choosing a new leader.

The leader will most likely be the hardest-working member of the band. Among the leader's duties are negotiating with neighbors over where and when to hold rehearsals, researching songs and lyrics and presenting them to the band, casting the tie-breaking vote for rehearsal time if members' schedules conflict, halting rehearsal to ensure that everybody's input is heard, and arriving early to a gig to determine where and when to set up the equipment.

Who gets to be leader? Again, the band's "alpha personality" will usually just emerge naturally. If you have to sit around and figure out who the leader is, you're probably in a democratic band, which, as we've suggested, can mean big trouble. A good leader will naturally earn respect. And the rest of the members are usually glad to accept leadership: "Just tell me when to be there" is a common refrain.

The leader doesn't necessarily have to be the best or most experienced musician in the band—although sometimes that helps. To be effective, he or she has to work hard, take initiative, make decisions, and be aware of others' feelings.

The leader will have to do certain things individually: signing any kind of contract, collecting the money the night of the show (because the entire band can't show up in the club office), and conducting media interviews (because reporters often have trouble focusing on multiple voices).

Some situations, though, demand a group vote:

- Whether you'll play a gig at a certain time and place (and for a certain amount of money)

- Certain financial decisions that affect everybody, such as opening a band bank account

- Whether to make a large group purchase, such as a PA system

- Choosing a band name

- How to disperse money from gigs, recordings, and so on

- Set-list disputes

- Choosing common goals (keep reading)

Behind the Music

James Brown, the legendary Godfather of Soul, is notorious as a bandleader for maintaining control and order over his musicians. Some called him "militaristic," as he required each member to wear a three-piece suit, fined late employees, and scolded musicians who arrived with crooked ties. He paid the price for these dictatorial tendencies in the late 1960s, when several hot young members, including the great bassist Bootsy Collins, left to become famous in other bands.

The Talent: Making Your Bandmates Better

In the early Rolling Stones, if singer Mick Jagger was the leader, guitarist Brian Jones was the talent. (Sadly, Jones drowned in his swimming pool in 1969.) He was the heart and soul of the band, the guy who introduced country and Indian influences, suggesting a sitar bit in a certain song when nobody else would have possibly thought of such a thing.

The talent has just that—innate musical or show-business sense. This musician pushes the creative envelope and often winds up as the primary songwriter. During rehearsal, the talent will often make germane musical suggestions and encourage other members at precisely the right times. He or she might suggest a six-string bass instead of the usual four-string on a particular song—and might be right.

The Arranger: Directing the Music

Traditionally, an arranger is the behind-the-scenes person who sees to it that many disparate musicians play in harmony. Famous arrangers include Paul Shaffer, bandleader for the *Late Show with David Letterman*, and Nelson Riddle, who conducted the orchestras for Frank Sinatra's classic Capitol recordings in the 1950s and 1960s.

In your band, the arranger most likely has a little more formal musical training than everybody else. This person understands the basics of music theory, knows a few extra chords and can help, say, quickly transpose a song in the key of C to an easier-to-sing key of E. Without an arranger type, bands can sit around for hours trying to help an untrained guitarist figure out a flatted-seventh note.

The Friend: Keeping the Peace

Although the leader has the authority (we presume) to tell others what to do, often the friend has the credibility. This easygoing personality type may be the only person who can kindly explain to the bassist that he consistently wears black clothes covered in dandruff to the gig. Or politely tell the singer he's flat.

The friend helps everybody get along. In a way, this person is the liaison between band members. If the drummer isn't speaking to the singer, the friend will take both characters out and communicate messages until finally coaxing them back onto speaking terms. Factions and camps are inevitable in every group, and the peacekeeping friend is invaluable to bring them together.

The Comedian: Lightening the Mood

Bands have a nasty habit of taking themselves too seriously. The exception is the comedian, who's always quick with the one-liner and prepared to make even the angriest musician laugh. This character is almost always "on," and knows the difference between laughing at and laughing with other people. Drummer Keith Moon famously played this role to excess in The Who—and took it a bit too far, as he died of complications from drug and alcohol abuse in 1979.

Behind the Music

Excellent jokes for aspiring band-comedian types:

◆ What's the difference between a drum machine and a drummer? You only have to punch the information into the drum machine once.

◆ How do you make a double bass sound in tune? Chop it up and make it into a xylophone.

◆ How can you tell when a singer is at your door? He can't find the key, and doesn't know when to come in.

◆ What do you throw a drowning guitarist? His amplifier.

◆ Why was the piano invented? So the musician would have a place to put his beer.

Synchronizing Your Schedules

Nothing kills a new band faster than scheduling conflicts. We have no easy solution to this problem. The best you can do is be flexible and prioritize. If the band is more important to you than swim class, and three of the other four members can practice only during your swim class, consider canceling pool time. Before discussing times with everybody else, block off large chunks that are good for you and be willing to give something up. Invest in a date book.

And as mentioned in Chapter 5, do what you promise to do. If rehearsal is at 8 P.M. every Tuesday, don't show up at 8:20. Occasional explained absences are understandable, but consistent erratic behavior is a good way to wreck a band—or, at least, get yourself kicked out.

Activities you'll probably have to schedule on a regular basis include the following:

◆ Rehearsal (and more specialized rehearsals such as vocals and rhythm)

◆ Band meetings

◆ Gigs (plus loading in and out)

Establishing Common Goals

Now is the time to dream. Do you want to perform at stadiums someday? Sign with a major record label? Open for Linkin Park? *Be* Linkin Park? Or just play around town, stay together for a while, and then look back on the good old days?

All of these goals are reasonable. But if people in the band disagree on them—especially without communicating their desires—it can make even the smallest decision difficult.

Now might be the time for a band meeting, where everybody can discuss ideas and determine who agrees with whom. Once you've written everything down, take a vote, or allow the leader to make the final decision. Your goals will change as the band progresses, but for now it's helpful to know whether you're in it for the fun or the fame.

How to Speak Up Constructively

Eventually, as your band learns how to communicate and holds several successful meetings and rehearsals, you'll develop a framework for constructive criticism. Again, don't make it personal. If you want the bassist to know he's not playing in time during the second chorus, separate that issue from the issue of fighting with him over your girlfriend.

Try to break down every issue into a separate, bite-size discussion and stay focused on that. And stay focused.

Also, it's the little things that often break down group dynamics. Resist the urge to fold your arms, or worse, roll your eyes, when somebody else is talking. When addressing another musician, avoid "you" statements—"you're doing that wrong," "you're stupid," and so forth. Best to stick with "I" statements—"I feel perhaps this isn't sounding right." It's okay to be blunt on rare occasions, but keep in mind basic concepts of respect, kindness, and communication.

Words to Rock By

The technical definition of **group dynamics** is "the personal interrelationships among members of a small group." Learning to deal with these interrelationships is one step toward making your band successful—or at least making rehearsals easier.

Basics of Group Dynamics

Group dynamics is a fancy psychology term for "several people getting along together." Researchers and business analysts have tons of theories for how to do this, but as usual, the basics apply. For example, don't let difficult issues linger; deal with them quickly and openly, at band meetings. Keep personal issues separate from musical or business issues. Communicate, communicate, communicate.

General Psychology

Psychologists have studied group dynamics for decades, and one prominent theory comes from researcher B. W. Tuckman in the mid-1960s. (Doomed rock bands of that era, such as Buffalo Springfield and The Beatles, probably could have used his help.)

Tuckman identified the following five stages of group dynamics:

- ◆ **Forming,** or trying to avoid conflicts and keep things simple while beginning the task at hand

- ◆ **Storming,** or dealing with competition and conflict as members get deeper into the task

- ◆ **Norming,** or starting to get along with each other and function smoothly as a unit

- ◆ **Performing,** or beginning to achieve your goal as a group

- ◆ **Adjourning,** or breaking up the group altogether

The trickiest progression here is from storming to norming, and Tuckman recommends listening as a key transitional device. In other words, try to give up your personal baggage and ego issues. Figure out who the other band members are and why their needs are important. If everybody learns to do this consistently, jumping to the performing stage will be simple—and perhaps you can avoid the adjourning stage.

The most exciting Tuckman stage, for your purposes, is performing. Often, after the band hashes out its personal issues, that's when the best music starts to emerge. You'll be able to play your parts without resentment or frustration, satisfied that you'll get to solo as much as you want and you may reflexively find yourself humming along to the chorus. This is often the most rewarding point in a band's career, and the experience may stick with you forever.

Learning from Team Sports and School Bands

Every sports team has one or two big stars and several other guys who do their jobs extremely well. Consider the Chicago Bulls of the 1990s—they won six basketball championships, largely due to the amazing talents of Michael Jordan. But several other players performed key roles: John Paxson hit a key three-point shot to win the 1993 championship series, and Ron Harper provided crucial defensive punch for the last three titles.

Bands function the same way. Bruce Springsteen may be a gigantic rock star and major talent, but his organist, Danny Federici, provides just the right sonic touches on several different songs, and drummer Max Weinberg keeps the beat big and steady and always avoids the urge to upstage his mates. Booker T and the MG's, The Band, and Crazy Horse performed similar roles for, respectively, Otis Redding, Bob Dylan, and Neil Young. In other words, the front person doesn't have to shoot the big shot on every play. It's the final product—the group product—that's important.

Behind the Music

Al Kooper, who played keyboards on Bob Dylan's 1960s classic "Like a Rolling Stone" and has been in many prominent rock bands, including Blood, Sweat & Tears, has his own group-dynamics theory.

He compares bands to a stack of books on a table, with each book representing one musician. If you pull certain books out as far as they'll go, the stack will be wobbly— but it will often remain standing. This is a dangerous way to run a band, with various characters stretched as far onto the fringe as they can go. Kooper recommends stacking the books evenly, so everybody's easy to get along with.

Hiring and Firing Members

It's often necessary to "change parts" as a band progresses. Sometimes this decision will be obvious: If nobody in the band can read a note of music, and you're having trouble transposing keys or staying in tune, you may want to recruit a ringer. Conversely, somebody in the band may have unsalvageable music skills or may just not fit the group's personality. At this point, for the good of the band, you'll have to make a move—and the decision is often difficult.

Mark Rubin, bassist for the punk-bluegrass trio Bad Livers, advises bands to choose members based on how well they get along with other people. You may discover the greatest musician in rock history living in your town, but if that person has serious problems getting along with other people, it may make more sense to hire the mediocre musician who everybody likes. Group dynamics can be that fragile.

Behind the Music

Rock and pop bands have often changed members on the route to fame. The best-known example is The Beatles, who fired Pete Best and hired Ringo Starr in the early 1960s. Country's Dixie Chicks, who began as a down-home bluegrass band, fired two original members, hired singer Natalie Maines, and sold millions of records. And Destiny's Child went through several different configurations before settling on its hugely successful R&B-trio format with singer Beyoncé Knowles as the star.

When Should You Add Somebody New?

"When somebody leaves" is the obvious answer. Or when the music requires it. Once the band has rehearsed and maybe even performed a few times, you may want to broaden your palette. Keyboards can add color, texture, and density. More simply, if you're playing a wedding, you may want to hire a saxophonist or other horn player for big-band-dance-style numbers or similar special requests.

There are excellent nonmusical reasons to add players as well. If the band is filled with flamboyant, difficult personalities, it may behoove you to find a down-to-earth, laid-back type to keep everybody grounded. When Mark drummed in the W.C. Fields Memorial Electric Blues Band, in the mid-1960s, the musicians added a player because he had a car. "The bonus was he also played the organ," he recalls. "I don't want to say poorly … but he did play very poorly."

When Should You Cut Dead Wood?

Unless you're really lucky—the worst or most difficult player has prior commitments, say, and decides independently to leave—firing a bandmate is an emotional process. But if every other member agrees a particular personality doesn't mesh or a person's musical skills are inadequate, it's time to take this extremely difficult step.

The key is to remain businesslike and try not to be rude or mean. (Now is not the time to tell somebody, "Your drums sound like garbage cans!") It does you no good, really, to insist this musician throw away his instruments and consider another occupation. Instead, say the playing isn't exactly right for this band's style of music. This process isn't about hurting anybody, it's about maintaining the band's forward momentum.

The Least You Need to Know

- Getting together is easy, staying together is hard—and doing so for a long period of time defies the odds.
- "Democratic bands"—in which every decision is made by vote—are almost impossible to maintain.
- Almost every band needs a leader, who will probably just emerge and start making decisions before you know it. Give this person a chance, and accept your role.

- Other important band personality types include the talent, the arranger, the friend, and the comedian.

- Hold group meetings at certain times every week, speak up constructively, and determine common goals.

- There are reasons to hire and fire members. When firing, don't get personal.

Chapter 7

Sex, Drugs, and Rock 'n' Roll

In This Chapter

- Why artists, writers, and musicians, including poet Rimbaud and rocker Hendrix, are susceptible to excess
- How to prevent excessive behavior from affecting the band
- Staying away from drugs, especially the hard ones
- Myths and realities of one-night stands
- Maintaining a long-term relationship while you're on the road

From French poet Arthur Rimbaud to American writer Jim Carroll to rockers Jimi Hendrix, Jim Morrison, Janis Joplin, and Kurt Cobain, the history of art is filled with tragic talents seeking inspiration via mind-altering substances. As a musician, you may encounter similar temptations, from all the alcohol you can drink at a bar gig to drug dealers trying to get you hooked on heroin. Partying all night can be enticing, but if you want to maintain your long-term health, and keep the band together and performing to the best of its abilities, it's crucial to avoid excessive behavior.

On the other hand, sex is the reason many people join bands in the first place—a successful band can make a musician seem immediately cool and attractive. We'll leave it to you to determine your moral standards, but suffice to say you should always practice safe sex and be knowledgeable about AIDS and other sexually transmitted diseases. Moderation just might be the most effective policy.

How to Know When They Affect the Band

Although drugs and sex are stereotypically linked in the context of rock 'n' roll, we're really talking about two different things—with many levels of intensity.

Drug use can mean anything from one glass of wine before the gig to a desperate addiction to crack cocaine or heroin. The wine, of course, won't affect the band (unless your 13-year-old drummer decides to try it for the first time)—some performers contend that it loosens them up and staves off stage fright. The addiction is far more serious, and if you suspect you or anybody in the band is developing a problem, seek help immediately. The Musicians' Assistance Program (www.map2000.org) is one of many available resources.

And there is a lot of gray area in between. Is it an addiction if your bass player smokes the occasional joint? What if the drummer sometimes binges with three pre-show Long Island iced teas? These are judgments the band will have to make together, by communicating openly about group behavioral standards. The important thing is to not let these extracurricular activities affect the music; if heavy machinery is unsafe to operate while intoxicated, a guitar solo is difficult to play under the same circumstances.

 **Backstage Insights** _____

No matter how old you are, and how far behind you believe you've ditched the designated driver concept, it's relevant again if you perform at beer-serving events. It's easy to forget everything else and jam all night, but remember, you have to drive a vehicle packed full of equipment and band members after the show. Designate at least one driver for this duty, and switch drivers with every gig.

When you're abusing substances, simple things like staying in time and remembering the next song can be far more difficult than they should be. While some artists will argue drugs loosen you up and set you free, if you're in a recording studio playing to a click-track, that definition of "freedom" may be suspect. Take care of your health.

You'll have to decide as a group which level of use is uncomfortable and distracting. In the long run, being an addict or junkie will make it impossible to keep a band, let alone a life, together.

Aerosmith singer Steven Tyler and guitarist Joe Perry used to be known as the Toxic Twins. They kicked their habits, however, and Tyler frequently gives public addiction-related advice.

Among his suggestions in recent years:

- ◆ "You can't do a lot of business when you're in McLean Hospital, weighing 136 pounds." (*Berklee News*, 2002)

- ◆ "I shot coke in my arm and OD'd, so I shot it again. I lost my first wife, so I did it again. It's called using in spite of adverse consequences. It's called the big [expletive] DUH!" (*The Guardian*, 1999)

Sex is another area that ultimately comes down to each band member's standards and morals. Practically speaking, it probably won't hurt the group if the singer "sleeps around." But allowing this band member's "friend" to hang around afterwards, and later take part in rehearsals and business decisions, will only create extreme tension in the band. For evidence, we'll refer you to several key scenes in the movie *This Is Spinal Tap* and the history of The Beatles.

Alcohol

Although alcohol use is legal among adults over the age of 21, it's the most commonly abused substance. And it presents a unique problem for rock musicians, who constantly spend their professional and leisure time in nightclubs, bars, and other venues that sell liquor.

Some people say alcohol's benefits as a social lubricant can be helpful for performance purposes. But alcohol use can be a danger. Peer pressure, among both screaming, beer-guzzling fans and other band members, can circumvent whatever device you employ to know when to stop. Early on, it's important to establish how much you can handle and still remain in control.

If you're going to consume—and this assumes you're of legal drinking age—don't go overboard. It's easier than you'd think to arrive at the club hours before the gig and just start drinking until the show begins. But no musician ever had a serious health problem by indulging in a beer or two onstage (although the dehydrating effects of any alcohol can be harsh on a singer's vocal cords).

"It took me years to figure out that after that second or third drink, I wasn't going to feel any better—and was probably going to feel worse," says one veteran band member. "It's hard to tell someone who's 21 that his solo isn't going to be any good if he drinks 18 beers. If you must imbibe, do it in moderation—and understand that topping it off with one extra isn't good. That's my public service announcement."

> ### Behind the Music
>
> Many nightclubs deny entrance, as a general policy, to patrons under the age of 21. Occasionally bar managers will grant exceptions to underage musicians scheduled to perform at the club. But not always. Be sure to check first with the club long before you accept the gig. And if the club owner grants an underage band performer an exception, under no circumstances should that band member indulge in a drink.

Drug Culture and Rock

As we mentioned in the introduction, artists for centuries have experimented with mind-expanding drugs—and, more often than not, dealt with the tragic consequences. Nineteenth-century poets Arthur Rimbaud and Paul Verlaine spent decades addicted to drugs and alcohol, screwing up their family lives, shooting at each other, and in Rimbaud's case, dying relatively young. The great jazz saxophonist Charlie Parker had a notorious heroin addiction, which, some will tell you, may have improved his music, but more generally made him unreliable, annoying, and difficult to work with.

Rock musicians have had a depressingly cozy relationship with excessive drug use. Rock mythology is based on excess of all forms—The Who destroyed their equipment onstage, Elvis Presley locked himself up in an elaborate mansion, and Cream played 25-minute drum solos in concert. It's only logical that these acts of excess would lead to further exploration. Some artists, including Jimi Hendrix, insisted hallucinogens improved their creative process. Many classic rock works are clearly drug-inspired.

Drug references are common in rock songs, too: Singer Roger Daltrey stuttered the syllables of the Who's "My Generation" to imitate the amphetamine-high stuttered speech of the pill-popping British "Mods" who followed the band. Artists from rappers Cypress Hill to country singer Willie Nelson have advocated marijuana use in their songs. Rapper Eminem has a running lyrical theme of mushrooms and "purple pills." Again, the individuals in your band will have to determine their comfort level with this sort of thing.

Eventually, of course, a lifestyle of drug abuse catches up to you. Presley, Hendrix, the Doors' Jim Morrison, Janis Joplin, Nirvana's Kurt Cobain, Alice in Chains' Layne Staley, and countless other talented rockers have died from drug-related causes. When Cobain committed suicide in 1994, after an adult life of heroin addiction, his mother told reporters: "Now he's gone and joined the stupid club. I told him not to join that stupid club." She was referring to rock stars who died young of drug-related causes. It was sound advice. You can't play good music if you're dead.

Behind the Music

Many rock stars have overcome a life of drug use and embarked upon successful "second careers," including the following musicians:

- ◆ Eric Clapton
- ◆ Aerosmith's Steven Tyler and Joe Perry
- ◆ Joe Cocker
- ◆ Steve Earle
- ◆ Jim Carroll (author and "People Who Died" singer)
- ◆ Bonnie Raitt
- ◆ David Crosby
- ◆ Everclear's Art Alexakis
- ◆ Dr. John
- ◆ The Red Hot Chili Peppers' Anthony Kiedis

Drugs as Inspiration

"Look, *Exile on Main Street* wouldn't have happened without Keith Richards' heroin addiction. *Young Americans* wouldn't have happened without David Bowie's cocaine addiction. Alcohol played a big part with Vincent van Gogh," John Taylor, bassist for the drug-indulgent 1980s pop band Duran Duran, told *Blender* magazine in 2003. "You need that edge. The trick is to find the edge without killing yourself."

That's certainly one way to look at it. Without some level of drug use, The Beatles' "Lucy in the Sky with Diamonds," The Velvet Underground's "Heroin," The Rolling Stones' "Sister Morphine," Jimi Hendrix's "Spanish Castle Magic" and many others— not to mention the entire reggae genre— wouldn't have existed.

But listen closely to these songs. Some endorse marijuana use or occasional acid trips as mind-expanding behavior. But few of them are blanket endorsements of hard drugs. "Heroin," by rocker Lou Reed, paints a frightening musical picture of a place with "dead bodies piled up in mounds."

All we're saying is, know the risks.

Avoiding Bad Notes

Few fans want to see a drunk band. Some stars, from Mojo Nixon to Jimmy Buffett to the late Dean Martin, have used alcohol as part of their onstage shtick, but they still sing the right lyrics in the right key onstage. This implies that they weren't as drunk as they wanted you to believe.

What You Might Encounter

Because rock has such an association with drug use, the entire concert experience often attracts dealers and other questionable characters. This won't happen at your early dance and party gigs, but as soon as you achieve a certain popularity, you may find that you have access to drugs of all kinds.

Some famous rockers have studiously avoided the party scene. The late shock-rocker Frank Zappa, although he was known for his outrageous behavior onstage, condemned drugs throughout his career. (He said it messed up his music, among other things.) Artists from Ted Nugent to Good Charlotte to Neil Young (his landmark *Tonight's the Night* is a scary exploration of drugs' dark side) have either avoided drugs entirely or learned their dangers firsthand.

Avoiding Temptation

The best way to not develop a drug addiction, of course, is not to start taking drugs in the first place. We don't want to give a Nancy Reagan–style "Just Say No" lecture in this chapter, but remember that the drugs that make you feel so good may one day make you feel really bad.

Should you find yourself with a problem, we suggest any of the following organizations, all of which have contact information on their websites:

- ◆ Musicians' Assistance Program (www.map2000.org)
- ◆ Community Anti-Drug Coalitions of America (cadca.org)
- ◆ Alcoholics Anonymous (alcoholics-anonymous.org)
- ◆ Narcotics Anonymous (www.na.org)

Finally, in case you're tempted to romanticize the lives of tragic artists such as Hendrix, Joplin, Morrison, Cobain, country-rock star Gram Parsons, and scores of others, check out books like Gary Herman's *Rock 'n' Roll Babylon* or ex-groupie Pamela des Barres's *Rock Bottom: Dark Moments in Music Babylon*. After reading about Sex Pistols bassist Sid Vicious allegedly stabbing his girlfriend, Nancy Spungen, to death, and then dying of a heroin overdose before he could be tried, it's difficult to view this lifestyle as glamorous.

Sex

If you've joined a band to meet members of the opposite sex—or the same sex, if that's your preference—it won't be the first time in rock history. "The only reason

I ever got on stage was to meet girls," says pianist Billy Joel, who married (and later divorced) supermodel Christie Brinkley. Joel's sentiment is hardly uncommon, but the meeting process isn't as easy as you'd think from the band's perspective.

You'll definitely meet attractive, friendly potential dates at gigs—but they'll often be in the audience with their significant others while you're onstage. Or they'll be partying while you're preoccupied with loading your equipment before and after the concert. Being in a band can be a lonely existence, in fact, especially if you're successful enough to go on tour, when you'll find yourself on the road for long hours between gigs. For days at a time, the only people you're likely to encounter will be bandmates, bartenders, waitpeople, club owners, and the occasional truck-stop cashier.

Still, if you attain a certain level of regional and national stardom, your level of personal charisma automatically rises. More than ever before in your life, you may find attractive strangers approaching you simply because you're a popular musician. Some would call this a potential danger. Others would call it a fringe benefit.

"Groupies"

Groupies are celebrated figures in rock lore—Chicago resident Cynthia "Plaster Caster" Albritton, who made statues of her male-rock-star subjects' most prominent features—based on real experience—remains a mythical figure. Cameron Crowe's movie *Almost Famous* turned a young journalist's loss of virginity to a rock groupie into a sweet rite of passage. In the 1960s and early 1970s, groupies were just another part of the rock generation's social norms.

Groupies, as they'd be the first to tell you, can be more than hangers-on who show up to have sex with rock stars. In the words of *The New York Times*'s Ann Powers, rock groupies "transformed 'hanging out' into a form of creative expression." Pamela Des Barres used her tell-all autobiography *I'm with the Band* to become a music journalist of sorts. And ex-groupie Margaret Moser is a longtime staff music writer for *The Austin Chronicle*.

Words to Rock By

A **groupie** is a super-fan who follows around a particular rock group in order to make a personal backstage connection with the star. Although groupies are commonly associated with sexual conduct, many are obsessive figures who just want to hang out with their heroes and heroines.

For a while in the 1960s, groupies inspired artists, too. Frank Zappa put a likeness of super-fan "Miss Christine" on the cover of his *Hot Rats* album. Groupies in general were reputed to have influenced Jimi Hendrix's entire *Electric Ladyland* album. KISS, no stranger to groupies, has a song titled "Cynthia Plaster Caster."

Famous groupies include …

- ◆ The aforementioned Cynthia "Plaster Caster" Albritton, whose works went on display at New York City's Thread Waxing Space in 2000.

- ◆ Bebe Buell, a 1970s *Playboy* model who bedded (and "inspired") rockers Todd Rundgren, Steven Tyler, Jimmy Page, Iggy Pop, Mick Jagger, and Elvis Costello, among others. Her daughter with Aerosmith's Tyler, Liv, grew up to become a well-known movie actress.

- ◆ Barbara the Butter Queen, who apparently did interesting things with butter to stars such as teen idol David Cassidy.

- ◆ Sable Starr, who hung around with early 1970s punk acts Iggy Pop, the New York Dolls, and others.

- ◆ Margaret Moser, ringleader of the three-woman "Texas Blondes," who dallied with many touring new-wave and underground bands in the early 1980s.

- ◆ "Sweet" Connie Hamzy, who gets name-dropped in Grand Funk Railroad's hit "We're An American Band."

The goofy, harmless spirit of groupies waned in the age of heavy metal, as Led Zeppelin and others became infamous for abusing their young followers in hotel rooms. (In a way, Stephen T. Davis's *Hammer of the Gods: The Led Zeppelin Saga* is the ultimate chronicle of groupie culture.) KISS, Poison, Mötley Crüe, and almost all the hair-metal bands of the 1980s turned Zeppelin's mythology into a lifestyle.

For a while in the early 1990s, as AIDS became a reality and grunge bands Nirvana, Mudhoney, and Pearl Jam eschewed groupies as rock clichés, the culture receded somewhat. Groupies still hung around in metal clubs and on Guns N' Roses tours, but they were rarely celebrated as backstage rock heroines.

That changed again after grunge died out. Younger rock stars, from Korn to Kid Rock, started to openly celebrate their trysts with groupies and relationships with porn stars. Although old-school groupies still exist, Barbara the Butter Queen has largely been replaced by performers from all levels of the adult industry.

> **Behind the Music**
>
> Although its language can be crude and the stories explicit, Groupie Central (www.voy.com/16357/) is an "insider's guide" to the backstage rock-star scene. You'll find tips—we can't vouch for their accuracy—on big-name rock stars' approachability. You'll also find ongoing discussions of personal grooming habits and physical characteristics. It's probably useless as a How to Meet Rock Stars guide, but the exchanges are funny and risqué.

It's your decision whether to partake in the groupie scene if it materializes backstage. Just be sure to practice safe sex and try not to let groupie-related romantic issues interfere with band relationships.

One-Night Stands

Groupies or no groupies, the issue of one-night stands may come up after performances. Just make sure it doesn't affect the band—if you're in charge of loading out your drum kit, and you skip the job to party with a new friend, you'll anger your fellow musicians. Similarly, if you start showing off during a song, when it's time for somebody else to solo, your personal relationships are getting in the way.

Another trap to avoid is bringing a newfound friend into the band's inner circle as a sort of honorary member. In the classic rock spoof *This Is Spinal Tap*, David St. Hubbins brings his girlfriend onboard as a costume designer, much to the irritation of the rest of the band members. As with everything else in *Spinal Tap*, these scenes were fictional exaggerations of real problems that afflict many bands.

Long-Term Relationships

So you have a nice relationship with somebody at home. And you want to maintain that relationship, but you're traveling all the time with the band. What do you do? You can't really bring that person on the road because, one, he or she will probably get bored as toast; and, two, your bandmates may become frustrated that you're spending too much time with your significant other and not enough time with them. This is a common band dilemma.

One way to solve the problem, of course, is to decide the relationship isn't as important as the band and break it off. But when wives, husbands, and children are involved, obviously, you'll need to find a better option.

There is no easy solution to this age-old problem. With cell phones and e-mail–equipped laptops, you can stay in better communication than ever before with your boyfriend or girlfriend back home. (Send flowers!) And it's acceptable to occasionally bring a friend on the road, as long as everybody in the band gets to do it now and then and the person doesn't become a distraction.

If your long-term relationship isn't totally secure, life on the road will exacerbate the tension. At this stage, many musicians start creating drama in their lives by cheating on their sweeties back home. Without getting into the moral implications of this practice, we'll simply say such drama makes your life very, very complicated. And if you're the type who likes to talk about it, your hijinks will eventually annoy the rest of the band.

CAUTION

Avoiding Bad Notes _____

Spending too much time with the band and not enough with the significant other, you say? Well, why not hire this person as a part of the lighting crew, a bus driver, or even an assistant manager? Buzz! That way danger lies. Blurring the lines between personal and band/business relationships can make for complications. No matter how lonely you are, leave home at home and work at work.

In this scenario, why bother keeping both the long-term relationship and the string of one-night stands? Choose one or the other. Then again, this is no relationship-counseling book. As far as we're concerned, if the other band members aren't angry with you, go ahead.

The Least You Need to Know

♦ Artists for centuries have indulged in mind-expanding drug use—some with tragic results. Proceed with caution; what's initially enticing may wind up deadly.

♦ Alcohol, the most abused drug, is prevalent and easily accessible at clubs, parties, weddings, and other places your band will play. Figure out your limits and stick to them.

♦ Whatever you do, put the music first. Never indulge to the point where anything will negatively affect the band.

♦ Although many bands, from The Rolling Stones to Nirvana, have used drugs as inspiration, this is a very dangerous road—be careful walking it.

♦ Groupies are a funny part of rock 'n' roll lore. They aren't as romantic these days as in the 1960s—or the movie _Almost Famous_.

Chapter 8

Money

In This Chapter

- Why "paying your dues" means you won't make any money—at first
- How to recognize and appoint the band's "money person"
- Who gets to be the manager?
- What's a booking agent, and why should you hire one?
- How to find the right lawyer—and what the right lawyer can do for your band

People join bands for lots of reasons—to hook up with attractive fans, to create works of art, to share with other people the songs and strange howling noises that just have to come out. But at some point, every musician starts to fantasize about another goal: achieving all these things *while earning a living*. That brings us to the intersection between art and commerce. At some point, you may realize creating music isn't a totally philanthropic enterprise. That's when you'll want to make enough money to give up your day job. To do so, you won't necessarily need an MBA—just basic money-management skills and some simple knowledge about terms, rates, and negotiating. If money just isn't your thing, consider hiring a trustworthy manager (or asking a friend or relative to do the job). Eventually you may want to hire specialists—booking agents and lawyers—too.

Money: Why You Won't Make Any (at Least for Now)

If it were up to us, your band wouldn't have to play its first few shows for free. And we'd see to it you received guaranteed $600,000 advances on multi-city concert tours, with all expenses paid. But the reality is your early gigs will be in the "leisure-time activity" category rather than the "paid professional" category.

As with almost every other business, bands have to pay dues. In the small picture, the initial gigs can be tiny affairs, such as friends' parties, high-school dances, and maybe tiny coffeehouses or nightclubs. But in the big picture, they're valuable first steps toward exposure and, yes, money. If you're diligent and keep the band together for a long time, these small steps can lead to bigger ones.

> **CAUTION**
>
> **Avoiding Bad Notes** _____
>
> Early in your band's career, you may land a pay-to-play opportunity. A night-club may offer a gig, but, in exchange, you'll have to guarantee that a certain amount of money comes through the front door. Which means it's your job to draw customers—say, with custom-made drink-discount coupons distributed to your band's e-mail list.
>
> Pay-to-play situations are rarely in the band's interests, because you could wind up owing money by night's end. Occasionally, though, the exposure is worth it.

The main reason you won't make any money at first is because your band is still an unproven entity. A nightclub booker won't take a chance unless you've shown you can draw crowds of beer drinkers. A wedding planner won't take a chance until you've generated a few recommendations from other wedding planners. Nonetheless, maybe your mother's company is planning a barbecue and can pay $100 for live entertainment. And after the show, maybe the company's CEO will be willing to write a recommendation, or talk to another CEO about yet another party. Again, small steps lead to big ones if you stick with it.

Getting Paid to Play

For an entry-level band—that's you—a $100 gig at a company barbecue isn't a bad deal. Neither is a $150 gig at a small club. These scenarios obviously won't make you rich, as you'll have to deduct expenses and divvy up the money among the band members. (This helps explain why some musicians spend their entire careers as solo artists.)

After a gig or two, though, you may have a little bit of leverage to negotiate for a higher salary. What salary should this be? Have a number in mind when you deal with potential clients. Figure out how much it'll cost to play your gig—regular expenses include gas, guitar strings, drumsticks, gaffer tape, and possibly, renting sound and lighting systems. In a perfect world, your gig salary will cover these costs and leave the band with spending money.

Nonetheless, until you're a big star, it's generally better to make a little less money and get the gig. Stubborn negotiating has its place, but don't shut yourself out of an opportunity, especially if you know the club booker or wedding planner doesn't have much of a budget to play with.

Do you need a contract? Ultimately, yes, to protect yourself. If the club doesn't do contracts as a matter of policy, consider writing one up yourself: "Crash Cat Boogie Cat will play on this date and receive $100 at the end of the performance." Some clubs will refuse to deal with contracts, which is a shame, but if you're interested in playing the gig, you may have no other choice but to submit. Wedding and bar mitzvah planners are likely to pass you a contract, while less formal party planners and many clubs almost never do.

Scrutinize every contract you receive. Under optimal circumstances, as we explain further in Chapter 11, an attorney should read over any contract that spells out more than the basic time, place, and salary.

> **Backstage Insights**
>
> When you do get money for a gig, you'll receive payment in cash, personal check, or, perhaps later on in your career when the fees are higher, a cashier's check. Usually you'll get paid after the show's over.

Parties, Dances, and Clubs

To secure your first party, dance, or club gig, you'll need to begin *networking*. Talk to everybody you know who might need live entertainment.

For dances, approach the local high school student council or a nearby university's campus activities board and ask about upcoming events. Ask if those entities can pass information about your band to the proper committee.

To secure party gigs, spread the word more broadly. Print up several fliers, with little perforated tabs at the bottom, announcing your band for hire. Put them up at record stores, campus radio stations, city kiosks, and whatever public bulletin boards you can find. Clever advertising expressions never hurt: The musical description "polyethnic Cajun slamgrass" took Boulder's Leftover Salmon a long way.

Club gigs are the result of auditioning. We'll deal more with this process in Chapter 11, but suffice to say, you need connections and a reputation to land an audition. Be prepared for less-than-optimum circumstances. Your first gigs may involve playing for free on a Sunday night.

Appoint the Band's "Money Guy"

It's not absolutely necessary to appoint a band member to handle the finances. But it sure helps. As with many other roles in the band—the leader, for example—who will be the money person may well become obvious. He or she is scrupulously honest, can balance a checkbook, and earns the trust of the entire band. Although an MBA degree isn't a prerequisite, business savvy and negotiating skills are a bonus.

The band's "money guy" (or gal) takes on time-consuming and important responsibilities. Serving as a sort of band treasurer, the money person collects all the money from gigs, writes checks for group expenses, and takes care of band bills. Ultimately this person maintains a checkbook, whether it's out of a personal account or a central band account, and makes certain that the band never bounces a check. Keeping a budget—the gig paid $100 on a certain night, $5 went for gas, $10 went for equipment, and the rest was profit—is always handy. Ideally, the fund grows according to the paid gigs you play.

Everybody should keep an eye on the money person—it's your money, too!—but ultimately the money person should be trustworthy enough that you don't have to watch him or her. And remember the band treasurer is taking on tons of extra work and responsibility, so don't give him or her too much grief. Also, the band treasurer should never have to front personal money to pay for expenses; this road leads to frustration and resentment and could ultimately break up the band.

It goes almost without saying that no band member gets to dip into the collective fund for individual purposes. No matter how hard up you are, it isn't "your money."

Establishing Financial Goals

Financial goals, for a band, can be as simple as opening a bank account or as complex as investing in the stock market with the band's collective funds. Early on, if you're playing parties, your immediate goals will be to cover expenses and have a little beer money left over. If you're playing weddings or bar mitzvahs, the salaries may be a little more lucrative, so perhaps you'll supplement your existing yearly income with a regular cash stream. Or maybe you'll want to quit your day job and play in the band full-time—and, someday, make millions with a record contract. Either way, as we noted previously, it's important for the band to discuss these goals periodically.

Should You Hire a Manager?

A *manager*—at least, a good one—takes care of almost every band detail save the music-making itself. He or she can be your most valuable ally, a well-connected businessperson who will give answers to questions like "how come we didn't get the merchandise settlement yet?" and "when's the gig?" This person should be experienced, helping you wade through the music industry on several levels, and give you straight-up advice that will advance your career. Such a person is hard to find, especially at first. For now, you may have to settle on a trustworthy, somewhat business-savvy friend, relative, or even band member. Eventually, when you start to make money, the band can upgrade.

> ### Behind the Music
>
> The standard deal for rock managers is 15 percent of the band's gross (though it can vary from 10 to 50 percent). So if you make $100 for a show, $15 of it goes to the manager—which means a paid manager may not make sense yet for the band. If you start grossing $100,000 per show, definitely, hire a manager. And maybe two or three.

Do It Yourself

An entry-level band—which is to say, musicians who've played a few gigs at most and have been together a few months or less—probably can't afford a paid manager. Until 15 percent of your salary per gig is worth something, a professional won't be interested. It's possible you'll get lucky, or just be really, really good, and a manager will catch your show and want to work with you right away. These things happen in the music business. But don't count on it.

Still, somebody has to deal with the band's boring business stuff. Staying in touch with party planners, negotiating gig salaries, and collecting money can be a pain, but in addition to saving the band money on a paid manager, the do-it-yourself manager will learn how to do the job. When it's time to hire a manager, that person will know what to look for.

A drawback to the do-it-yourself approach to band management is it may take away from your music-making time. Try not to let this happen. Art and commerce intersect in many ways, but your guitarist-manager shouldn't be so busy working the spreadsheet that he or she can't make it to practice.

Can a Friend or Relative Manage Your Band?

Say you've done it yourself for a while and it's not working. You need more time to practice and rehearse, and economics isn't your favorite subject at school. But there's still not enough money in the band kitty to hire a pro. Try hiring a friend or relative to take over.

Maybe the drummer's father has some extra time on the weekends and used to be in a band himself. Maybe the bassist's aunt, who runs a small business, loves your music so much she just has to contribute.

Make sure whomever you hire shares your vision. Get him or her involved in the "goals" meetings, if not the music rehearsals themselves. Oh, one more thing: If you're a punk-rock band and scream your rage against the world, your uncle/manager probably shouldn't book you on Caribbean cruise ships.

Managing 101: Negotiation, Leverage, Terms

What does a manager *really* do? When it's time to book a gig, somebody has to sit down with the intimidating concert promoter or wedding planner and attempt to get a reasonable amount of money for the band. These *negotiations* aren't usually complex, at first, but they do require finesse, conversational skill, and perhaps courage. If the band wants $150, and the club owner offers $50, it's difficult to say, in a nice way, "No way, you're screwing us, we need more." But such is the lot of the band manager.

> **Backstage Insights**
>
> Ask for a little more money than you really want. Then, when the club owner knocks down the price in the negotiation, you'll still be in good shape. Keep in mind, however, that a smart promoter is probably thinking the same way in reverse.

Early in the band's career, you probably won't have much *leverage*, which means enough clout to significantly influence the negotiations. Joe's Local Band, which hasn't played many gigs and has demonstrated little ability to draw a crowd or media coverage, won't have the leverage to ask for much more than the promoter offers. R.E.M., on the other hand, can expect to get almost anything it requests. It can never hurt to ask for more money, but if you desperately want the gig, at least at first, you'll have to compromise.

Terms are the basic details of any gig you play. (Or any record deal you sign, but that's a subject for Chapter 22.) How much money will you make? How much time will you be onstage? How many breaks do you get to take? Do you have to play any specific songs? Can you videotape the band? Do you have to bring in your own sound system? All these questions are part of the negotiation, and while not everybody is out to bamboozle you, some people are.

A good manager, in addition to having the time and energy to simply do the work, has a built-in "B.S. detector." This person won't be seduced when the club owner drops the salary below a reasonable level but accounts for it with "one free beer per musician." A good manager will also have the instinct to know when to stop—you never want to alienate your boss or burn an important bridge—even if the deal isn't perfect. These skills come with time and experience.

Who You'll Negotiate with: Club Owners, Promoters, and So On

On a smaller scale, your negotiating partners will probably be honest, regular folks who just want to create a good event. For dances, it could be the representatives on a college activities board or high school student council. For parties or weddings, it could be your next-door neighbor, or someone from a local banquet hall. For extremely large events, such as a large theater, arena, or stadium show, you'll deal with a big-time concert promoter. But that'll come much, much later in your band's career, if at all.

Club owners—or, in many cases, bookers or promoters—are not generally "regular folks." They're usually honest and straightforward, but keep in mind these people make their livings dealing with all-night beer drinkers, bouncers, and rowdy crowds. They tend to be a little tough.

They also tend to be aggressive, high-energy, and busy. On any given night, a club owner has 8,000,000 things to do—making sure the bar is stocked, keeping the fire marshal happy, denying entrance to underage patrons, and so forth. To deal with them effectively, meet them at their pace. As with any business negotiation, it helps to connect on their level. Is a particular club owner a classic-car collector? Maybe you have some knowledge of these topics and can work your uncle's 1954 Austin Healy into the conversation. To a point, "schmoozing" is an acceptable and honorable way to develop a business relationship. There's an art to it.

Promoters

While a promoter may own a venue and serve as a booker in some cases, this character generally books bigger shows—national attractions in the ornate downtown theater or the basketball arena. Generally, working for a promoter is a step or two up from playing in clubs.

Promoters also make important decisions about *opening acts.* When a national star comes to town, the promoter may want to warm up the crowd with a hot local artist. Often this decision is a matter of simple math: If the local band consistently draws 200 people to its shows, and the promoter needs to sell 200 tickets to fill up the venue, that local band may be perfect.

Behind the Music

Headlining performers frequently get a bonus percentage of ticket sales for a sold-out show.

Examples of national promoters include *Clear Channel Entertainment*, which owns many major venues in the United States, *House of Blues Concerts*, and *Concerts West/ AEG Live*.

Early in your band's career, you probably won't appear on the stadium concert promoter's radar screen. To get there, build your fan base by playing clubs and parties, and send regular updates to influential local promoters about how well you're selling tickets and perhaps CDs. Some promoters, who are often music lovers, may enjoy taking chances.

When and How to Find a Big-Time Manager

Big-time managers aren't always angels. Many have signed agreements they—and, more specifically, their artists—have lived to regret. When he was still a nobody, rocker Bruce Springsteen fell in with Mike Appel, who negotiated most of his record and publishing deals. Within a few years, the singer spent laborious months in the prime of his career suing Appel to escape what he considered an unfair deal. This kind of story is common in the music business.

Again, before attempting to hire somebody who will take 15 percent of all your gig and recording profits, we suggest managing your own band for a while. The more you do, the more you'll learn, and the more you'll know when the band is in a position to hire a professional manager.

When should you hire a pro? When 15 percent of what you make is worth something. When crowds are obviously enthusiastic about your music. When you reach a level of success so that your well-intentioned friend or relative can no longer handle the day-to-day business details.

How? The most effective way to find a decent manager's name is by asking other musicians whom you trust, whether they're contemporaries on the local concert circuit or "name acts" you've encountered on the road. These bands will have war stories, and they'll be happy to suggest names to pursue (or avoid). Another resource is a simple compact disc: Check out the latest release from a band roughly on your level, and see which name it lists under "management." (This information may also be available on the band's website.)

Another resource is the music-industry confab, like the annual South by Southwest (sxsw.com) in Austin, Texas, or the *College Music Journal*'s New Music Marathon (cmj.com) in New York City. Whether or not your band performs at these festivals, it may be worth the entrance fee to send a representative. By talking to people and attending industry panels, you'll make contacts and get ideas about all sorts of things. Maybe even a tip on finding a good manager.

Should You Hire a Booking Agent?

A *booking agent* sets up gigs for your band to play. This person will have experience and connections that a do-it-yourself musician or manager can't possibly match. You may, for example, want to play in Chicago but can't get an "in" simply by sending your demo to clubs and following up. A good booking agent will know all the connections and have experience dealing with them—and may score you a gig by making a few phone calls.

The more you can do on your own, without a booking agent, the better off you'll be. That way, when you finally do hire a booking agent, who finally lands that elusive Chicago show, you'll have enough connections to set up smaller gigs along your travel route in St. Louis, Omaha, and Kansas City.

Are you ready to hire one? Use the same math you used for hiring a manager. Most booking agents take 10 percent of your profits. If you're making $100 per gig, and a booking agent takes $10, and you have $30 in expenses, that leaves $60 to split among four band members—just $15 each. So no, under that scenario, you aren't ready yet.

As with a manager, it's best to find someone who "gets" your music. A booking agent whose clients are Pink and Lenny Kravitz may not understand your band's predisposition toward country-punk songs inspired by Lefty Frizzell and Son Volt. This agent probably won't know the right clubs in which to book your music. So make sure you get references and do some research before signing any contract.

How can you find one? The same way you'd find a good manager. Ask friends in bands. Ask the slightly larger band for whom you've just opened a local show. Play at regional festivals, from newspaper-sponsored band showcases to "Taste of" events to the aforementioned industry conference South by Southwest. Managers and booking agents tend to gather at these things to catch more than one band at once. But as we've suggested throughout this chapter, it's also smart to network, schmooze, and work the crowd for connections.

You can, of course, send your demo tape and press kit to big-time booking agents throughout the country. And you may get lucky, or bowl somebody over with your talent. But unsolicited packages are a tough way to go and lead to a ton of rejections. Best to have a connection first.

Should You Hire a Lawyer?

Ultimately, if you plan to stay in the music business in the long run and hope to draw larger and larger crowds, you'll need a lawyer. Unlike a manager or booking agent, this specialist won't be involved in the band's day-to-day operations. But any time you have to sign a legal document, from a club contract to a record-label deal, you'll definitely want advice from a lawyer. But use these experts sparingly, because they can charge hundreds of dollars an hour.

First and foremost, lawyers can protect you from legal problems down the road. If the nightclub you play has a fire, somebody gets injured, and the club owner tries to sue the band, you won't want to scramble for counsel at the last minute. (The fire scenario hardly ever happens, but you never know.) If a label scout shows up at your gig and wants to sign you right away—again, a rarity, but a welcome one—you'll need a lawyer to peruse the paperwork. Also, lawyers can provide an introduction to record labels and help you "shop" for a deal.

Backstage Insights

California Lawyers for the Arts (www.calawyersforthearts.org) helps artists, writers, musicians, and other creative people connect with legal representation. Consultations are in the $20 to $30 range, and the attorneys handle issues from copyrights to contracts. The group is based in the Bay Area but handles clients all over the country.

Although the "do-it-yourself" approach works reasonably well, at first, for managers and booking agents, the members of your band can't possible generate adequate legal expertise on short notice. You'll need to hire an expert.

Finding the right lawyer can be a difficult process. Early on, bands will be able to ask their real-estate-attorney cousin to look over a club owner's basic contract. But eventually you might need an attorney who specializes in the entertainment industry—specifically music. To find a solid local music attorney, contact your local music-advocacy group.

The Least You Need to Know

- Don't expect to get rich from music. If it happens, it will probably be much later.

- You don't necessarily need a contract, especially if you're starting out at a friend's party or a school dance. But as you start dealing with nightclubs, a contract can protect you from liability and ensure payment.

- Should you hire a professional manager? At first, do it yourself, or ask a friend or relative to help. Eventually, though, you'll want somebody with experience in negotiation, signing contracts, leverage, and terms.

- Should you hire a booking agent? Again, not at first. But this professional's connections will eventually prove invaluable.

- Should you hire a lawyer? Yes, when you can afford one. Try to find a music-industry specialist. You'll pay by the hour, so use a lawyer sparingly.

Part  3

The Gig, and How to Get One

Whether you're playing "The Hokey Pokey" on the wedding circuit or tearing up original songs before club crowds, the gig is an important developmental step in the life of any band. Some may be dingy and depressing—and you won't even get paid! Others may be rewarding and fun. But either way, the point of almost any band is to play in public, so try not to let annoyances get in the way of the ultimate reward.

What's not to like about playing onstage with your best friends, with adoring fans screaming in front of you? As the crowds start to grow in your hometown, the next step is to expand the band's base to other cities. That's when it's time to go on the road—which leads to a whole new level of complications, from renting (or buying) a van to negotiating with unknown club bookers. Part 3 deals with gigs of all shapes, sizes, locations, irritations, and rewards.

Chapter 9

Breaking In

In This Chapter

- ◆ Graduating from the garage or basement to the stage
- ◆ Networking to find gigs
- ◆ Making the most out of college campuses
- ◆ Hitching yourself onto the lucrative wedding circuit
- ◆ Finding out if you're ready for the club scene
- ◆ Hooking up with club owners and bookers

By now you've had the "how do we make money?" discussion, and it's time to turn theory into practice. This chapter shows your band how to pack up its gear, drag it out of the rehearsal space, and haul it to a stage where people will (maybe) pay you real money. But whether or not you play for cash, performing gigs in front of audiences is a crucial way to get hands-on experience and learn how to become a good or even great band.

So how do you land this performance opportunity? Many bands hook up their first gigs through friends or family—maybe your brother needs a band for his wedding, or maybe your aunt needs a band for her corporate picnic. Any time you recognize an opportunity to perform in front of people, grab it and put on the best show you can. You just might get some objective feedback (not just the accolades you're accustomed to from parents and friends). And you may learn whether the stuff that sounds so perfect in practice translates equally well to less-comfortable surroundings. Once you've broken in—which is to say, hooked up with real audiences—it'll get easier and easier to stay in.

What Level of Gig Do You Want?

Initially, the answer to this question is "any gig you can get." If you're determined to play exclusively original material, you may not attract a lot of people looking for wedding and party cover bands. Conversely, if you're strictly a cover band, you probably won't line up the artier gigs at local coffeehouses. Be realistic. Don't overreach and contact the promoter who books Aerosmith into the local basketball arena. But don't underestimate your potential and simply invite two or three friends to hear you play in your drummer's backyard.

Until you generate a reputation, which could take months or even years, you'll probably have to play some of your town's smallest venues—like tiny campus clubs, coffeehouses, and friends' parties. You may be tempted to leapfrog these joints and go straight for the bigger-time clubs, but lightning rarely strikes like that. Unless you're Kelly Clarkson or Ruben Studdard, the first two winners of the smash television reality contest *American Idol*, you'll have to perform in public many, many times before landing on a stage in front of 10,000 or even 1,000 fans.

Amateur vs. Professional

As with sports, or any other field, the basic distinction between amateur and professional involves money. If you're getting paid, you're a professional. If not, you're an amateur.

Nonetheless, even if you're playing a gig for free, it's important to act like a professional. Show up on time, do your best to entertain the crowd (even if it's small), be courteous to the organizers and fans, don't throw tantrums if the sound system isn't perfect, and so on. With any luck, you'll find that most of your early gigs will pay at least enough to cover gas expenses. If you get something beyond that from your early gigs, you're heading smoothly in the professional direction.

Deciding How Good You Are

Until now, your band has been relatively isolated, rehearsing in private spaces and allowing only friends, relatives, and the musicians themselves to hear the songs. So your only critiques have come from people who are predisposed to be optimistic and encouraging. (Not to say that's a bad thing! Early support from friends and family is crucial to your collective self-esteem. But at some point you'll need to move to the next level of feedback.)

To determine how good you really are, you'll need constructive criticism. Start this process by taping your rehearsals. Playback, as we mentioned in Chapter 5, is an excellent way for the musicians to decide what parts they need to work on. But it's also instructive to pass your tape along to more discerning people—music teachers, friends in other bands, people you know who work for clubs or radio stations, or maybe, if you're adept at ripping songs into MP3s, random strangers on the Internet. (Be careful, though, not to send your best stuff to people who might steal or co-opt it. Once a song is online, it's everywhere. Be sure to *copyright* all your material before sharing it with anybody.)

Words to Rock By

A **copyright** protects your original song—or any creative work, for that matter—from unauthorized reproduction. In other words, nobody else can copy or profit from your copyrighted song without your permission.

To officially copyright a song, go to the U.S. Copyright Office webpage—www. copyright.gov/register/performing.html for unrecorded songs, or www.copyright.gov/ register/sound.html if you've actually put it on tape or compact disc—and follow the instructions. It costs $30 per work.

Before you play in public, you'll want to nail down the basics of continuity and flow (essentially, the art of not sounding choppy); keys and tempos (playing together in the same harmony and rhythm); and, most of all, listening to the other band members. "That's one of the pet peeves I have when I go out to see young groups: 'If you're not listening to each other, you can't play together,'" Mark says. To learn how to play together, pay attention to each other and get feedback.

Accepting Your Identity—and Defining "Successful"

Once you've accepted your identity, whether it's a wedding band or a club headliner, you'll have more focus and a better sense of what songs to pick and what bits to re-rehearse. But that doesn't necessarily mean your band has to keep that identity for the rest of its career. After rehearsing for two months and accepting one bar-mitzvah gig, for example, you may wind up with other bar-mitzvah connections. But you won't have to be a bar-mitzvah (or bat-mitzvah) band forever (unless you want to). At any point, whether it's a month or five years from now, you can try to write original songs.

But being realistic will help your band's collective psyche. If you've played several weddings in a row and you've gotten good feedback (and a paycheck!) every time, try not to be frustrated that you aren't on the fast track to becoming the next Good Charlotte. (That may happen later.) Do what you're good at, bide your time, and work on expanding in your own direction.

> **Backstage Insights** _____
>
> Success doesn't always have to do with how much money you're making or the number of times per month you play in public. To repeat a cliché—because it's true—success comes from within.
>
> Also, set your own standards of success. If your band is satisfied that it has performed a good show, don't let others convince you otherwise—even if the club owners are refusing to pay you and the crowd is throwing rotten tomatoes toward the stage. (We direct you here to a crucial scene in 1980's _The Blues Brothers,_ in which the band performs at a country-and-western bar where rednecks hurl beer bottles at the band through chicken wire.)

Party Band (Sororities, Fraternities, and Schools)

The party band, to put it simply, knows how to rock the house. It specializes in danceable, up-tempo, familiar material—from the Kingsmen's "Louie, Louie" to the Village People's "YMCA" to Billy Ray Cyrus's "Achy, Breaky Heart" (complete with line-dancing instructions). The party band will rarely succumb to the temptation of rolling out experimental, original material. (That's for another time and venue.) It will be prepared to honor fan requests as long as they're upbeat and encourage people to dance.

If you become successful as a party band, you'll be hired at schools, private events, fraternities, sororities, pep rallies, and plain old house parties. The key to landing gigs is in exposing your band name wherever possible—from campus bulletin boards to local newspaper classified ads. Word of mouth is incredibly important on this level. We've already suggested this, but it bears repeating: Check with student councils, at local high schools and colleges, for open slots and announce your availability. You won't get gigs if people don't know you want them.

Backstage Insights

Ten party songs guaranteed not to fail (if you play them enthusiastically and well):
- "Celebration," by Kool and the Gang
- "Shout," by the Isley Brothers
- "Fight for Your Right," by the Beastie Boys
- "Super Freak"/"U Can't Touch This," by Rick James/MC Hammer
- "Louie, Louie," by the Kingsmen
- "Johnny B. Goode," by Chuck Berry
- "What I Like About You," by the Romantics
- "Blitzkrieg Bop," by the Ramones
- "YMCA," by the Village People
- "We Are Family," by Sister Sledge

(Thanks to partydirectory.com for song suggestions.)

And by all means, have fun with party gigs. Whether they're your financial base or just a "slumming" exercise until you find the resources and experience to write great original material, perform them with enthusiasm. If you're bored, the crowd will know it. Get into the party vibe and throw yourself into the songs—wear costumes, string cheap strands of holiday lights across your amplifiers, and make jokes if you think it will enhance the experience. It can't hurt to attend shows by other party bands. Singer-songwriter Jimmy Buffett puts on a classic party show, complete with skits, masks, dancers, and calypso rhythms. Rapper Snoop Dogg may be lewd, but his onstage manifesto is to make everybody in the crowd jump and shout. "Jam bands" such as Phish, String Cheese Incident, and Leftover Salmon are adept at making huge masses of people wiggle uncontrollably. You may not want to emulate these exact types of music, but study the performers' moves and styles.

Playing the Wedding (and Bar-Mitzvah) Circuit

Playing weddings is a little like playing parties, only you'll probably have to please a much wider audience demographic. Whereas a party is usually a bunch of people who work for the same company or attend the same school, wedding crowds range from 88-year-old, Glenn Miller–loving great-uncles to flower girls obsessed with Elmo.

Your challenge is to prepare a set list broad enough to satisfy everybody. You'll need to know the standards, of course, so buy plenty of Nat King Cole, Frank Sinatra, Tony Bennett, The Beatles, James Brown, and Ray Charles CDs. You'll also need to know several audience-participation standards, from the Chicken Dance to the

Macarena, plus ethnic traditions like the Hora (Jewish) and Tarantella (Italian). And keep an eye on the contemporary pop charts; if a band like the Backstreet Boys has had a No. 1 hit for the last six months, don't get caught unprepared when the bride's sister begs you repeatedly to play "I Want It That Way."

The more songs you learn for a wedding situation, the better. A wedding isn't like a party, where it generally doesn't matter what you play as long as it's upbeat. Attendees will be particular about their favorites. It's acceptable to politely refuse a request if it's obscure, but under no circumstances should you not be prepared to churn out the Village People's "YMCA" or Benny Goodman's Louis Prima–penned "Sing, Sing, Sing" (and yes, you can play that one without horns).

Behind the Music

Many famous pop bands, including Los Lobos, the Gipsy Kings, and NRBQ, started out on the wedding circuit. "If you were Mexican-American and got married in Los Angeles between 1973 and 1980, we probably played your wedding," Los Lobos drummer-songwriter Louie Perez told reporters a few years ago. Some bands accept the gigs even after they become famous: Alternative-rock hitmakers Jimmy Eat World performed at blink-182 front man Tom Delonge's wedding in 2001.

You'll also have to be more organized than usual to play weddings. At these events, it's not like you can just load in your gear, start at the designated time, play your songs, and leave. A harried bride, groom, family member, or planner will undoubtedly want to meet with you well in advance of the big day and may have very specific song requests and schedule demands. The first three or four songs at the ceremony, for example, are usually special dances for the couple and certain family members and friends. And you'll have to pause at particular times to allow for toasts. Beyond that, you'll have to pace the set list in such a way that the older attendees dance first to the slower, more traditional songs. As it gets later, generally, the younger crowd will stick around and demand faster, more contemporary hits. Either way, pay close attention to the crowd and have the flexibility to alter your set list as circumstances dictate.

A few other tips about playing weddings:

◆ Dress up, at least in matching suits and ties, unless you're given specific instructions to wear certain informal outfits (like Hawaiian shirts for a luau theme).

◆ Consider hiring a second singer who specializes in particular songs—many wedding bands, for example, will bring in a female R&B belter to handle Etta James's "At Last" and Aretha Franklin's "Respect."

♦ Be prepared for control-freakishness. The bride, groom, or members of their families will almost certainly require you to play (or not play) certain songs. Be polite and do as you're told, even if it means smiling through gritted teeth during "The Hokey Pokey."

♦ Use extreme care when dealing with hecklers. They may well be rich relatives who are paying your salaries.

♦ Work out the meal details in advance. More often than not, the organizers will accommodate the band's eating and drinking needs. But if not, you could wind up in an embarrassing and potentially unprofessional situation if your drummer jumps next to grandma in the food line.

♦ Don't ask too many questions of the organizers. They've prepared much more intensely for this day than you. Take their instructions, and then do your job.

A *bar mitzvah* is a rite-of-passage ceremony for 13-year-old boys in the Jewish faith. (A *bat mitzvah* is the equivalent for girls.) Often, local bands are asked to provide the background music—just as they are at other ceremonies. Like weddings, these gigs can be lucrative and fun, and formal enough that you shouldn't show up in sandals and T-shirts. (Again, check with the planners beforehand regarding the dress code.) Generally these events aren't quite as micromanaged as weddings, so you have a little more freedom to improvise the set list. (And at least for bar mitzvahs, your dominant audience is likely to be undiscerning 13-year-old boys.) But be ready for anything.

Nightclubbing

There's nothing wrong with playing weddings, bar mitzvahs, and parties for your band's entire career. But if you aspire to write original material and perhaps get a record deal or some radio airplay, the next step is almost certainly clubs.

We delve into the club circuit more thoroughly in Chapter 11, but suffice to say clubs are places where people go specifically to hear music. Often, they charge admission. Often, they make their money off liquor and food sales. Not always, though. Some clubs don't or can't serve alcohol and are therefore accommodating to a much wider range of ages. To prepare for the club circuit, you'll need to do two things: Get better as a band, which means tightening up your cover versions and writing a few solid original songs; and network with other local musicians and club owners. The entrance exam for club gigs is often an audition, and when that opportunity comes around, be ready. Almost every famous band you can name started out playing one club or another.

Identifying Possible Venues

If no wedding, party, bar mitzvah, or club will have you—yet—consider organizing your own gig. Where do they hold rave parties in your town? Maybe you can rent out the same warehouse, set up your gear, and advertise the show via fliers and hand-bills. (See Chapter 15 for more advice on "guerrilla promotions.")

You can set up and play almost anywhere, pending local crowd-control laws and fire-marshal approval. Does your band rehearse in a basement or backyard that would fit a few dozen spectators? Start a party, and book your own band as the headlining act.

And don't forget to invite all your friends and relatives. They may well be the sup-portive core of all your early concerts, and they're likely to stick with the band as it gets bigger and bigger. Don't take these "early groupies" for granted—they may be the difference between a crowd of 5 strangers and an energetic crowd of 50 or 75 fans. Later (see Chapter 13) you can sign them up on the mailing list and (see Chapter 16) contact them via e-mail.

Backstage Insights _____

If your band has at least one really good singer, consider auditioning to sing "The Star Spangled Banner" or "O! Canada" at a sporting event. The New York Yankees probably won't need your services to open the World Series, but there may be a minor-league, college, or high school team willing to give you a chance (or an audi-tion). Although you won't be able to show off what the band does for real, these showcases are excellent promotional and publicity opportunities.

Making Contact

The rules for making contact, whether you're approaching the media (see Chap-ter 14), a club owner (see Chapter 11), or even a record label (see Chapter 22), are almost always the same. First, send a letter containing your press kit and, if you have one, a CD, demo tape, or video. Wait a week or so, then follow up by phone—and be polite to a fault, even if the voice on the other line doesn't remember your name or tries to blow you off. If you follow these procedures enough times with enough recip-ients, you'll probably get somewhere.

Start this process by contacting gig organizers.

Be Persistent Without Being a Pest

This won't be the last time you hear this advice in this book. In general, to land a job, gig, record deal, or date, you'll have to find the line between laying off the recipient completely and pestering him or her to the point of annoyance. There's an art to finding this balance. Networking, again, is crucial. To get gigs, you'll want to make contact with school or municipal committees and family members who know someone on school or municipal committees. Check the phone book, too, for local wedding planners. Often, they have rotating lists of bands they recommend to clients—getting on them is a certain path to regular work, solid money, and plenty of local exposure.

You'll almost certainly have a better chance of making contact with a wedding, bar mitzvah, or party planner than with a prominent club booker, radio station, or record company. Although wedding planners may be predisposed to hire a relative or go with a friend's referral, they differ from club bookers in that they're not swamped with 50 similar packages from local bands.

Will You Get Paid?

One primary benefit of playing weddings and bar mitzvahs is you'll almost certainly get paid—reliably and often generously. As with any other gig, set the terms in advance to avoid potential disputes later. Take instruction from the planner, and ask questions up front if you're confused. It's certainly reasonable to ask for a deposit to secure the date, as many of these events are booked far in advance. Naturally you should be reliable—show up on time, perform the songs you promised you'd perform, don't make jokes at the bride's expense (or at all), and do your best to stay away from the spiked punch. The best thing you can do to prepare is rehearse, rehearse, rehearse—work out the kinks in Nat King Cole's "Our Love Is Here to Stay" so you aren't frantically catching up on the big night.

The Least You Need to Know

- Even before you become a professional—which is to say, you get paid for a gig—act like one. Be on time, rehearse well, and, if the occasion warrants, wear formal outfits.

- Before venturing out into professional-gig territory, seek criticism from someone outside the band (or the band members' families). Learn from constructive comments and ignore jealous or snobbish ones.

◆ The local party, wedding, and bar-mitzvah circuits can be great opportunities for solid money. But they're hard work, and you'll have to prepare.

◆ Weddings are more regimented than most gigs, so get as much instruction as you can up front.

◆ The usual rules of making contact and networking—send a press kit, be persistent without being a pest, follow up politely and regularly—apply for weddings and parties as well as clubs.

◆ Will you get paid? Yes, but work out the details in advance, preferably in writing, but at least with an oral agreement.

Chapter 10

What Music Fits Where?

In This Chapter

- Finding the right place to play
- How to know if you're in the wrong place
- Where rock bands play—parties, dances, clubs
- Where country bands play—clubs, fairs, rodeos
- Where hip-hop and techno bands play—dance clubs
- Where blues and jazz bands play—clubs, weddings

Once your band settles on a style (or styles) of music, finding places to play will seem natural. Or rather, finding places *not* to play will seem natural. If you're a kids' party band, you know to avoid the heavy-metal head-bangers' gig. If you're a country band that covers Faith Hill and Vince Gill hits, you should probably avoid the gothic alternative-rock theater where everybody wears black and smokes clove cigarettes. If you're an "originals" rock band that prides itself on writing new songs, don't bother playing the venue where only Doors, Led Zeppelin, and Radiohead tribute bands have sold out on recent weekends.

Of course, when your band is just starting out, it may have to play any available venue and adapt its style of music and set list accordingly. But in time, the band should develop an identity—and will likely pick gigs that fit the style. This is a natural development, and finding your niche will improve your business. In this chapter, we'll help you determine which genres fit in which venues.

How Do You Know If It's the Wrong Gig?

The audience will tell you if it's the wrong gig. If you're playing middle-of-the-road pop standards to a crowd wearing leather and studs, it's probably the wrong gig. If you're performing the Pras/ODB/Mya funk-and-hip-hop hit "Ghetto Supastar (That Is What You Are)" to a crowd in cowboy hats and boots, it's probably the wrong gig.

In the early 1970s, an agent booked Mark's band Humpback Whale into a theater gig. The band hadn't done any advance scouting. It loaded in, set up the equipment, the curtain opened, and the band began its regular rock set. Within seconds Mark and the rest of the group realized the audience was not only completely silent, but they were signing to each other. The show turned out to be an evening's entertainment for a deaf school. To avoid such "Spinal Tap moments," scouting the venue is important.

Before accepting any job, if possible, attend several shows at the venue in advance. Check out the size and composition of the audience. If the club caters to a particular crowd, and your music doesn't exactly go with that crowd, you may be on course for a disaster. Ask the club owners, bookers, and bartenders for insight into the club. Giving up a gig can be a tough decision, but far tougher is performing to people who wish that they—or you—were somewhere else.

Rock Venues

In most cities, rock bands are the standard. They'll have clubs, parties, and dances to play as long as they can keep the crowd dancing and (depending on the type of venue) the beer flowing from the bar.

The same venue often caters to different audiences on different days of the week. A typical rock club might host a traditional, Elvis-style rockabilly band Thursday, a Kool & the Gang–style funk band Friday, and a Guns N' Roses cover band Saturday.

Don't give up if a club doesn't usually hire bands playing your brand of music. Sometimes it's possible to convert a club—or one special night at a club—to your style of music. For example, if the local club specializes in rock music, and your group is inclined toward bluegrass and acoustic folk, and if you're able to draw a crowd, you may be able to pioneer a "folk and bluegrass night." Just know what you're getting into before you do it, and publicize accordingly. (See Chapter 15 for more information on how to self-market your band.)

Cover Songs

Cover songs are an important concept. Some bands make an entire career of cover songs, taking the concept a step further and turning into cover bands. They'll dress up as Guns N' Roses, say, or Led Zeppelin or ABBA.

Behind the Music

One of the first cover acts was the Beatlemania stage show, which featured a quartet that dressed as the early 1960s Fab Four and faithfully performed Beatles renditions.

Other bands have become known for their cover versions of songs—the metal group Alien Ant Farm had a big hit with Michael Jackson's "Smooth Criminal," and the Counting Crows' "hidden CD track" version of Joni Mitchell's "Big Yellow Taxi" became a surprise rock-radio hit.

Still others create cover versions that trump the originals. After Aretha Franklin released her classic version of Otis Redding's "Respect" in the mid-1960s, Redding famously introduced his song onstage by jokingly accusing Franklin of theft. Jimi Hendrix made many rock fans forget Bob Dylan's version of "All Along the Watchtower." And Elvis Presley shook the foundations of American culture by speeding up Bill Monroe's bluegrass classic "Blue Moon of Kentucky."

Often, artists use cover songs as a gimmick or a way of galvanizing a crowd with a surprise. For the past several years, movie soundtracks have been filled with funny or unusual cover versions. Marilyn Manson covered AC/DC's "Highway to Hell" on the *Detroit Rock City* soundtrack, for example, and the Barenaked Ladies did Public Enemy's hip-hop classic "Fight the Power" on *Coneheads*. Christina Aguilera regularly performs Etta James's R&B standard "At Last" in concert, and the Foo Fighters salute 1980s hardcore band Hüsker Dü by covering "Never Talking to You Again."

Unless you're in a cover band, you probably won't want to cover too many songs by other artists, either live or on CD. But it's a good idea to prepare at least a few such songs for an emergency situation. If Limp Bizkit is performing across town the night of your show, consider a special "Break Stuff" as a tribute or satire. The punk band Coffin Break used to respond to fans' shouted requests for Lynyrd Skynyrd's classic tearjerker "Freebird" by playing a note-for-note version. And on a more basic level, it never hurts to pull out Chuck Berry's "Johnny B. Goode" if fans at a particular show aren't jumping the way you want them to.

Parties and Dances

Before your rock band hits the club circuit—see Chapter 11 for more details on how to do this—it will probably play its share of parties and dances. Your first dance gigs will probably be at high schools, although you can work your way up to bar mitzvahs and weddings. Early party gigs might be at fraternities or other college-campus events.

Almost without exception, crowds at these gigs will want to dance. So load your set list with upbeat numbers, including a familiar cover version or two, and throw in some ballads just to give the romantically inclined a slow-dancing break.

Parties and dances may not pay well, but they're excellent vessels for word-of-mouth exposure. If you play a killer version of The Velvet Underground's "Sweet Jane" in the basement of a packed fraternity party, some of the brothers of that fraternity—we guarantee there will be some Lou Reed fans among them—will almost certainly mention you to other houses. And once you latch on to the local fraternity circuit, you're all but guaranteed regular work. You may even be able to parlay the gigs to chapters of the same fraternity on other college campuses. In fact, this could wind up the basis for your first out-of-town gigs.

Battles of the Bands

Years ago, battles of the bands, in which well-known regional acts competed head-to-head in front of judges' panels, were hugely important for exposure and success. In the mid-1920s, bandleader Chick Webb's swing outfit defeated the likes of Count Basie and Benny Goodman en route to lasting national fame. In the early 1960s, surf bands such as the Del Rays, The Regents, and The Harmonics battled before 10,000 fans at the Waikiki Shell in Hawaii. Battles of the bands have since become fixtures in many different genres, from country to metal, in many different countries.

Backstage Insights

Battles of the bands have moved to the web, too: The song-posting website MP3.com sponsors battles in which users vote for winners online. The prominent Vans-sponsored Warped Tour annually allows online voters to pick from 2,600 punk-rock entrees; winners receive a coveted spot on the tour.

Although they're perhaps not as crucial now as they were in Chick Webb's day, battles of the bands are great ways to get exposure—especially if you win. The media invariably covers the events, record-label representatives sometimes attend, and local radio may be willing to spin your tune if you're the proven top band in the station's market.

Many such contests still exist: San Diego–area clubs Blind Melons and Winston's sponsor battle events every summer; Nishe, a British band, recently won a BBC Radio–sponsored contest in Wiltshire, England; and New Zealand has hosted a well-attended, countrywide contest for more than a decade.

In addition to the exposure, these battles are great opportunities for bands to gauge their progress vis-à-vis their contemporaries. You may not win, but the pressure of performing before discerning audiences, and your peers, is likely to give you focus and seasoning. It's also a way of getting crucial objective feedback from judges and expert bystanders. Also, battles may help your band set collective goals—beginning, perhaps, with winning the contest.

Country, Folk, and Bluegrass Venues

Regardless of which style of country-and-western music you play—flashy, mainstream ballads and rockers in the style of Tim McGraw and Darryl Worley, or alternative-country like Uncle Tupelo, Old 97's, and the Waco Brothers—you'll probably play venues very similar to rock venues. And no matter the genre, the bands' purposes are the same—keeping the audience dancing and (in many cases) drinking.

For mainstream-style country bands, the performance opportunities are similar to those for rock bands. In addition to performing at a fraternity party, your country band might earn a side-stage slot at a state fair. And as with rock, keep an eye out for local contests.

Behind the Music

When singer Clint Black was 18 years old, he played a version of The Eagles' "Desperado" that his friends and family enjoyed. They encouraged him to enter a corporation-sponsored Country Star Search the next time it arrived in the Houston area.

"The producers provided a backup band for everybody—a really good band—and I said, 'OK, I'll go do this,'" Black told Steve for a 2002 interview with the *Milwaukee Journal Sentinel*. "I sang 'Desperado' in the contest and I won. Then I went on to the next contest for the state level—from Houston to San Antonio—and won runner-up. 'Desperado' got me a big cash award of about $500 when I was about 18 years old and really had a good use for $500." It also helped Black take his first steps toward superstardom.

Alternative country bands, the kinds who record for Chicago's Bloodshot Records and get written up in *No Depression* magazine, play venues much like independent rock bands. They often start in small clubs and, in the cases of successful artists like Wilco and Ryan Adams, wind up in bigger theaters or opening for major rock acts.

Words to Rock By

The strict definition of **singer-songwriter** is an artist who writes and sings his or her own songs. But over the years, stars such as James Taylor, Carly Simon, and Jackson Browne have given singer-songwriters an image of gentle, self-aware sensitivity. That's not always the case, as performers from rocker Bruce Springsteen to mopey indie-rock hero Elliott Smith have demonstrated the breadth of singer-songwriters.

Folk and bluegrass bands progress in slightly different arenas. Because they're usually acoustic, they tend to start out in coffeehouses or other venues where fans are more inclined to listen than party. Talented *singer-songwriters* often emerge from this environment, and go on to become solo stars.

Open-Mike Nights

Generally held at coffeeshops, but sometimes at certain bookstores or clubs, *open-mike nights* are loosely organized talent showcases. Musicians usually put their names on a sign-in sheet and perform at the designated time. There's usually no audition or other weed-out process, and so the talent levels tend to vary widely.

Open-mike nights are great venues for singer-songwriter material. You, and perhaps one accompanist (but probably not the full band), will get to test your songs before an audience. The upside: Attendees will be able to scrutinize your material with minimal accompaniment—there will be no drum or guitar solos to fall back on. The downside: If your songs aren't yet worthy of an audience, it will be quickly, painfully obvious. Open-mike crowds are generally polite, but you can learn a great deal from awkward silences.

No matter what the crowd's reaction is to your songs, try to learn from it. Did a word, phrase, chord change, or chorus make attendees particularly excited? Did they get up to buy more coffee or hit the bathrooms during the bridge? If possible, ask people afterward what they thought.

Note that open-mike nights, while lower-key than regular band gigs, can be more stressful. If you make a mistake, your guitarist won't be there to cover it up with a solo. Before signing up for an open mike, make sure that you're prepared and confident.

Street Performing

Street performing, or *busking*, has a long tradition in music performance. The great blues singer-guitarist Muddy Waters (among many notable bluesmen) sang for change at Chicago's legendary outdoor market Maxwell Street in the 1940s, before he became widely known. Before selling out theaters around the United States, rock band Sonia Dada sang a cappella songs at Chicago subway stops. And Irish singer-songwriter Damien Rice performed for months on the streets of Europe—in Paris, Hamburg, Rome, Madrid, London, and Edinburgh—before putting out his debut CD.

Behind the Music

Many famous musicians started out at coffeehouses. Bob Dylan performed open-mike nights at Café Wha?, Kettle of Fish, and others in New York City's Greenwich Village in the early 1960s. (Much of the folk movement revolved around this scene.) Other clubs at the time, such as Memphis's Bitter Lemon, gave crucial exposure to folk and blues artists such as John Fahey and elder statesman Furry Lewis. More recently, Jeff Buckley's famous gig at New York's Sin-é launched the singer-songwriter's career in the 1990s, before his death.

At one point, Rice had to compete with a guy in a red rabbit suit singing "Over the Rainbow." "We used to always stay on two different ends of the street—we'd always be able to see each other from a distance," Rice told Steve in a 2003 CDNow.com interview, after his *O* album came out. "I used to play my songs with just a little microphone. I remember a gent saying, 'Would you sing something jolly, there?'"

In many cities, big and small, busking is a fixture—even if the laws technically prohibit it. When Steve visited New York City, recently, a singer and guitarist in traditional garb entertained subway riders with mariachi songs. In London, busking in the "tube," or subway, has traditionally been illegal, but for years, singers have ignored the laws. (Some London tube stops issue buskers' licenses these days.) In Chicago, folk guitarists wear heavy gloves in between songs to stave off the cold in subway tunnels. And in Boulder, Colorado, weekend nights on the red-brick Pearl Street Mall are filled with buskers of all types, from singers to acrobats.

"The part about the busking that was the most interesting and valuable was the freedom I experienced on the street," Rice said. "There's no expectation for you to be good, so you've no pressure. You're totally free to just be yourself. Nobody really listens so you just get somewhat trained in listening to yourself, and that's been really valuable to me with the shows I've been doing."

Be conscious of street politics, though. Some buskers have occupied certain heavy-foot-traffic spots for weeks or months and won't appreciate it if a new performer takes over their turf. Sing where you want, and stand your ground, but try to be fair to potential competitors, especially if they have that crazed look of having performed too long on the streets.

If you're good, and have some talent for interacting directly with a crowd, busking can be profitable. One well-known singer-songwriter, Boston's Mary Lou Lord, has been playing her guitar on the streets since the late 1980s. She opens her guitar case and people throw money into it; although she scrounged for cash in the early days, she has been known to make more than $1,000 a day during peak periods. Her strategy is to set up down the block from "whatever's happening," as she told Steve in a 2003 *Chicago Tribune* interview, and simply ignore would-be hecklers. Making $1,000 a day is unrealistic for beginning buskers, but the experience of performing in public and getting immediate feedback is worth the long hours, weird weather, and crowd politics.

Guitar Pulls

Guitar pull is the music-insider term for "a gathering of like-minded songwriters on the same stage talking and singing songs." These pulls usually involve three to five performers, all sitting on stools, taking turns playing songs (well known and obscure) and listening to the others.

The Bottom Line, a well-known New York City club, turned this concept into a national tour. For several years in the 1990s, the club sent various configurations of singers, including James McMurtry, Marshall Crenshaw, Joey Ramone, and the Cars' Ric Ocasek, to perform on its "In the Round" tours. The shows were often terrific, with songwriters trading "how they wrote that one" stories and performing off-the-cuff versions of famous hits. These shows were built on the guitar-pull tradition. In many regional coffeeshops, listening rooms, and showcase clubs, singer-songwriters will converge for guitar pulls. (A cigarette company once sponsored Joe Ely, Guy Clark, Lyle Lovett, and other country singer-songwriters for a national tour of this type.)

For your purposes, guitar pulls are excellent opportunities for exposure, and for getting your name out to audiences who might not necessarily see your band otherwise. Your band's singer or songwriter will be the most likely candidate to participate.

Rodeos and Fairs

Rodeos and state fairs are traditionally venues for country music. But not always. Metallica once headlined the Illinois State Fair, and metal hitmakers Staind performed before thousands of people at Wyoming's Cheyenne Frontier Days. Hundreds of thousands of people often attend, from all over the state, and promoters can sell a lot of corn dogs and cotton candy if they bring in well-known acts.

Even though your band is unlikely to get top billing at such an event, opportunities might exist for some sort of exposure. Most fairs and rodeos have more than one stage, with performances in time slots throughout the long weekend. Depending on how established you are in the region, you can possibly snag one of these slots—though don't expect it to be prime time. Generally, the later the hour, the bigger the crowd and the more prominent the band. Friday and Saturday nights are usually reserved for headline acts.

Backstage Insights

Casinos aren't just in Las Vegas anymore. There are tons of legal, well-established gambling dens all over the country, from Native American-run gaming houses in northern Michigan to Harrah's chains in the Mississippi Delta. Usually the big showrooms are reserved for big-time acts, but lesser-known bands often play on smaller stages throughout the casino. In Vegas, lounges are still popular.

Contests

Battles of the bands, as we mention earlier in this chapter, tend to be geared toward rock performers, but in some regions you can find country versions as well. In addition, contests are everywhere—the Topanga Banjo Fiddle Contest, in Topanga Canyon, California, has been drawing steady crowds since its 1961 inception. The New England Fiddle Contest runs every Memorial Day in a Hartford, Connecticut, park.

Songwriters' contests are prominent, too, in many genres. The American Society of Composers, Authors and Publishers (ascap.com) sponsors events in several different parts of the country. The U.S.A. Songwriting Competition (songwriting.net) offers a $50,000 cash prize and radio airplay to the winner, with sub-winners in various genre categories. *American Songwriter Magazine* (americansongwriter.com) gives away airplane tickets to Nashville for winners of several different annual contests.

Backstage Insights

Contests are popular in other genres, too, depending on pop-cultural tastes of the times. Rapper Eminem's movie *8 Mile* brought hip-hop "cutting contests" out of underground inner-city clubs and into the mainstream. During the Jay-Z/50 Cent/Snoop Dogg concert tour "Rock the Mic," aspiring rappers insulted each other onstage between the headlining performances. Prominent local radio DJs announced their names, offering exposure whether they won or lost.

In addition, scour the web for online contests. MP3.com, GuitarGirls.com, and many other websites offer sporadic competitions if you're willing to send in recordings.

Hip-Hop, Dance, and Techno Venues

If you're in one of these electronic genres, you're probably going to wind up in dance clubs or special events. No matter where you play, your music, but not necessarily the band itself, will be the crowd's focus. Often, the DJ sets up in a booth above or to the side of the dance floor. Lights and other effects tend to be the focus, rather than the DJ, who is usually sequestered behind his or her gear wearing huge headphones.

Bands with prominent DJs, no matter what genre they play, have a chance to become as big as Moby, Fatboy Slim, or OutKast. But their most reliable gigs, at least at first, will be dance clubs, raves, and house parties.

How to Be a DJ

We give more specific information about DJing in Chapter 3, but basically a *DJ* is a disc jockey whose primary function is to play recorded music to a dancing crowd. Such crowds are different from standard rock or country crowds—their collective goal is to dance, so they flock to particular types of clubs with nonstop dancing. Major metropolitan cities have literally dozens of these kinds of clubs, and experienced DJs can make a decent living on this circuit. Smaller cities often have one or no dance clubs, so competition for the few available DJ slots may be tough.

Dance-club crowds can be as straightforward as a bunch of classic-rock fans who want to hear Beatles, Righteous Brothers, and Elvis Presley hits all night long. But more often the crowd will consist of arty hipsters who want to hear creative DJs mixing a loud, rhythmic blend of trip-hop, drum 'n' bass, jungle, dub reggae, and ambient sounds.

Remember that being a DJ, whether on your own or as a member of a broader electronic band, you're probably going to stay anonymous. (Moby and Fatboy Slim are among the rare exceptions.) Most club DJs hunch behind their gear in booths to the side of the stage, and dancers rarely see their faces. Clubs will almost certainly have a designated area, separate from the dancers, where the DJ performs. If you have alternative needs, such as a larger amount of space than usual, be sure to contact the club owner or manager well in advance. You may have to negotiate.

Another kind of DJ buys amplification equipment and CD players and rents services to parties, weddings, and other functions. If you're experienced at gauging crowds' moods and talented at picking the right songs for various situations, this business can be quite lucrative. In most cities, you can find several successful DJs of this kind in the phone book. Unlike techno-music and electronic DJs, who perform mostly at dance clubs, these record-spinners set up their gear in all kinds of places, from private house parties to wedding-host churches.

No matter which kind of DJ you want to be, you'll need a certain amount of gear. Check musiciansfriend.com and local music-equipment stores for deals, but wedding DJs can find a combination of mixers, PA systems, and microphones from $500 to $1,600. (They may also need their own lighting systems, in case certain wedding or party venues don't have them.) Club DJs will probably need turntables, mixers, and samplers to better manipulate their electronic music. Be sure to check in advance with the venue to make sure it can accommodate your equipment.

Blues and Jazz

Decades ago, blues and jazz artists represented popular music, and they played the hippest clubs and the largest theaters. In most cases, however, today's established blues and jazz artists play a national circuit of specialized venues, from the blues-dominated Kingston Mines, on Chicago's North Side, to the tiny, legendary piano-jazz bar El Chapultepec, in downtown Denver.

If your idiom is blues and jazz, your career path, at least locally, will probably begin at one of these types of established clubs. Then again, many artists break out of this pigeonhole—the Chicago rock club Empty Bottle, for example, regularly sponsors experimental-jazz nights, and many blues acts on the harder electric side of the spectrum can play higher-profile rock clubs. No matter how you define your music, it behooves you to make connections at the widest possible range of clubs, for maximum gigging options. What if you play every night at the local jazz club for three years and the club goes out of business? Diversification is something many acts ignore at their peril.

Weddings

Blues and jazz performers may be a little more accomplished and versatile than their peers in rock or country. So they can adapt reasonably well to certain steady-paying situations, such as weddings and corporate parties. A conventional rock band may not have the chops to perform Glenn Miller's complex big-band standard "In the Mood," for example, whereas accomplished jazz bands may find it simple compared to the complex bebop they do at clubs.

Backstage Insights

Blues and jazz acts—or at least members of such acts—might find additional work playing part-time for other bands. For some gigs, bands may find their standard configuration—usually guitars, drums, bass, and vocals—isn't enough. So they'll have to hire additional musicians on a temporary basis.

What Next?

Now that you have a general sense of where your band might find work, it's time to start identifying such venues in your area. Ask friends in other bands where they play and how they got the gig. Check the local alt-weeklies and newspapers for club listings, and pinpoint upcoming bands that roughly match your style. Go to the club. Once you've identified appropriate venues for your act, it's time to determine who books the club and make contact. Lucky for you, that's the subject of the next chapter.

The Least You Need to Know

- Once you've figured out the type of music you'd like to play, find the venues that specialize in this area. Often, your band will get hired based on its genre.

- If you're at the wrong gig, the audience will tell you. A gentle folk band may not be perfect for the headbanger set. But consider working up emergency songs for various situations.

- Rock bands tend to start out at dances, parties, and clubs. In many cases they'll have to play familiar "covers," or other people's songs, to get the crowd going.

- Most country bands follow the same career progression as rock bands—parties, dances, clubs. But they may have extra opportunities at state fairs and rodeos.

- Hip-hop, dance, and techno bands will likely wind up in dance clubs. And they'll need at least one DJ.

- Blues and jazz bands are often limited to playing in specialized venues. But they should try to diversify their bookings to land a wider range of gigs.

Conquering the Club Circuit

In This Chapter

- How to join your hometown club circuit
- Doing your best in an audition
- Winning over club owners, bookers, and concert promoters
- Putting everything in writing
- What to do if you get stiffed

Unless you specialize exclusively in parties, weddings, and bar mitzvahs, your band's primary live-concert outlet will be clubs. In any town, the club circuit can be intimidating—the people in charge, owners and bookers, often have little time for small talk. The clubs themselves can be claustrophobic, with many loud people crammed into a small area and, often, an abundance of alcohol and cigarette smoke. And there's not exactly a *Rulebook for Clubs*, so while you can ask managers and bartenders questions, you may have to figure out where to plug in your own amps.

In big cities, especially music-heavy ones such as New York and Austin, Texas, many different clubs have music five or more nights a week. In smaller cities and towns, though, "clubs" may mean local bars—even VFW and Elks lodges—that push aside a few tables on Friday and Saturday nights to make room for the band. No matter what your club options are, it's your job to find the venues where you can play, make contact with the people in charge, and pass the audition.

Types of Clubs

There as many types of clubs as there are styles of music: *supper clubs*, popular in Las Vegas, catering to the older, Frank Sinatra–loving crowd; *youth clubs*, where underage high school and college students congregate when they can't get in anywhere else; *dance clubs*, which blast thumping electronic music well into the night; *live-music clubs*, your band's most likely outlet; *bars*, large and small, which often have all-ages nights or rope off a specific area for nondrinkers; and others catering to many different clienteles.

Some live-music clubs serve alcohol; some don't. Some, like the House of Blues, are run by national corporations; others, like Emo's in Austin, are run by local business-people. Some in your hometown may be so small they can barely fit a dozen or two people. Some may even have ties with church groups or community organizations. Don't exclude any type of club from your list of potential gigs.

Backstage Insights _____

If a club won't let you play, or your area doesn't have a club, consider inventing your own. In the mid-1980s, alternative-rock band Jane's Addiction rented Los Angeles's Black Radio building and promoted its own concert. The band didn't make a lot of money—and unexpectedly rowdy fans destroyed the tables and chairs—but found their eventual guitarist and drummer in the audience. To avoid problems, get permission first from local police and zoning boards.

Cracking the Code

Jumping onto the club circuit isn't as easy as merging onto the freeway. You'll have to send *demos*, follow up with regular-but-not-*too*-regular phone calls, make personal connections with influential people, and try not to get bamboozled in the process.

There's a certain romance to music nightclubs. From Mississippi *juke joints* to New York City's legendary punk-rock venue CBGB, smoky, dingy, crowded clubs have given bands a chance to grow in public before becoming famous. Lately, although there still are rough clubs out there, the business has grown up, too. Everything is more professional and less like *The Blues Brothers* movie scene where rednecks throw beer bottles at chicken wire surrounding the band. Many clubs now sponsor all-ages, non-drinking shows earlier in the day, and some Christian and youth clubs offer alternative music venues as well.

Meeting the Right People

Who books the club? How does that person prefer to be approached? Once you identify the booker, manager, owner, or promoter, generally, you shouldn't just "drop in" to say hello and ask for a gig. Your contact is probably busy with other important jobs, like mopping the bathroom or listening to the daunting stack of demo CDs on his or her desk.

So it's time to follow the *pitch* routine (which we discuss further in Chapter 14). In short, you'll send a demo recording and press kit through the mail, and then wait a week or two before following up—briefly—by phone. The key is to be persistent without being a pest.

Words to Rock By

One of the earliest types of American music clubs was the **juke joint.** Loosely derived from a Scottish word meaning "bend the head," juke is a slang term for dancing in a funky way. Southern blues artists played such ramshackle joints, mostly in African American communities in the early twentieth century, to rowdy crowds of dancers and partiers. They still exist today but are rare.

Words to Rock By

A **pitch** is used to solicit media coverage, record-label interest, and perhaps radio play.

Next, you'll call to make sure that the right person received the package and listened to your demo. When you talk to them, club bookers might say, "Yeah, it's around here somewhere, call back next week." Follow instructions and call back next week. When you call again a week after resending the material, they might say, "I can't find it, send another." Do it without complaint. These people are your band's lifeline, and you don't want to anger them. Or even mildly annoy them.

Backstage Insights

Your most important network at this stage involves friends in other bands. They'll know the names of the important local club people and can answer questions about the club scene in your area. Maybe they can put in a good word with the owner or booker. (Or they might allow you to "drop their names" when sending your demo.)

In addition, many cities, local music organizations support and advise band members and sponsor networking opportunities such as seminars, jam sessions, and contests. Take advantage of these organizations if they exist.

Auditions

If they like what they heard or saw on your demo CD or video, an interested club booker will probably want to see you play live, so you may have to participate in an audition. Don't worry, you won't have to memorize any lines or recite Shakespeare to a panel of directors. You'll just bring your key gear—guitars, drums, amps, and a sound system (if the booker tells you the club doesn't have one)—and play your best stuff.

Often, clubs will audition bands on slow evenings, like Sundays, with two or three different acts playing for free. You won't want to get in the habit of giving free gigs, but as you're essentially a nobody on the club circuit, it's probably your only option at this point.

An audition is like doing a truncated show, and you should treat it as such. Do some scouting in advance. Is there an adequate PA system in the club? Will it be available on audition night? Where can you plug in? How big is the stage, and can all the band members fit with their respective gear? How much time will you have to set up and play? (Don't worry, the people hosting the audition probably won't surprise you by pulling the plug early or letting you go on extra long.)

Plan to perform your best (or best-rehearsed) songs. And remember, you're auditioning for a job, so be presentable. If it's a fancy supper-club type of place, wear a tuxedo, or at least a suit. It's acceptable to wear T-shirts and jeans if it's that kind of joint, but make sure that you and your clothes are clean. (Nobody wants to smell the band from the front row.) And leave the ironic "This Club Stinks!" caps at home.

Depending on the club's management, you might find out whether you got the gig within a few days or a few weeks or months after the audition. Some club owners are amazingly efficient, and when they audition bands for a certain upcoming night, that's the night the winning band can expect to perform. Other bookers may be less decisive, and could sit on your name for weeks until another band's singer catches cold and needs an emergency replacement. Either way, be ready—don't berate the club booker if you don't hear back within a few days of your audition; and if you get the gig, even if it's that night, be ready to clear your schedules.

Backstage Insights

Don't be alarmed if the booker or owner—the very person you're trying to impress—walks out of the room during the audition to answer phone calls in the back or attend to other business. He or she is probably still paying attention. More important, the bartenders, waitpeople, regular clientele, and many other influential characters are paying attention. Later, the owner or booker may solicit everybody's opinions. So work to win over everybody, just as you would on show night.

Important Characters—and How to Deal with Them

Once you walk through the door of a club, whether it's for an audition, rehearsal, or gig, everybody is important. Bring your own door-stopper so the ID-checking bouncer doesn't have to hold open the door for every patron. Tip waitresses and bartenders. It goes without saying that you should be courteous and professional toward the people who are considering you. You want everybody in the club to think you're the best band they've ever heard *and*, equally important to landing a future gig, the easiest one to work with.

Club Owner

You probably won't see much of the owner during your audition, unless the club is so small the owner has to do the band-booking himself. Generally, the club manager conducts most of the day-to-day business, while the owner makes appearances just to make sure things are running smoothly. If you do encounter the owner, treat him or her with respect—this person could become your boss, even if just for one night. Don't complain to him about the stinky toilets, crappy sound system, or flat beer.

That's not to say you should allow the boss to take advantage of you, either. You're the entertainment, not the help, and should firmly but politely protest if somebody asks you to sweep up before the show.

Club Booker

The booker, unlike the owner or manager, is your direct contact person. He or she will review your demo and determine whether you're worth auditioning in the first place. The booker will arrange the details of the audition and decide whether you pass or fail. If you get the gig, the booker will hammer out the details—where you set up, whether you should bring your own sound system, what time sound check takes place, and how long you'll be playing.

Club bookers, to make a sweeping generalization, tend to have similar personalities. They're often hyperactive, kinetic music fans whose primary concerns are packing the rooms with fans. (And usually, selling drinks.) Learn to deal with this personality type. Rather than wasting time with sweet talk, take actions—like going onstage exactly when you agree to go on—that make his or her job easier.

Money

When money enters the picture, your band automatically changes—it becomes, by definition, professional. It also means that you have to deal with new problems. When money is involved, relationships and responsibilities have a way of shifting.

Playing music in exchange for payment doesn't have to be a negative process. If the band agrees on its expected fee, and the "money guy" (or maybe someday, booking agent) does his or her best to negotiate with the club, everybody should be happy in the end. (Unless somebody drinks too much "on-the-house" beer at the gig, but that's a different story.) See Chapter 8 for more details about contracts and negotiating.

Will You Get Paid?

You may not get paid at first, even when you start to inch onto the club circuit. Remember: Auditions don't pay at all. And the first time you play a particular gig, depending on a club's policy, you may have to deal with a "pay to play" or free-night-on-a-stage situation. At this point in your career, it's almost certainly worth the exposure.

At some point, though, you'll probably land a paid gig. Some clubs have rigid pay scales, and it'll be difficult for you to negotiate. Others may have "wiggle room," so ask for another $25 or $50 depending on your negotiating confidence.

Be flexible during the negotiations. Landing the gig and getting the exposure may be at least as valuable as the extra $50 or $100 you wanted to receive. It's not that you should never walk away. But you don't have a lot of leverage at this early stage in your band's career.

Beyond the actual gig payment, you may have to hammer out some other details with the club booker. Will you get paid by cash or check? (You'd prefer cash, obviously.) If you sell T-shirts and CDs during the show—or the club sells merchandise for you—does the club take a percentage? When will you get paid? Clubs usually have standard procedures for these issues, but be sure to answer these questions in advance so nobody springs a surprise later.

Do You Need a Contract?

Most clubs, especially small ones, work on a handshake basis. This is probably sufficient for your purposes, unless the club has only been in business a short time or you've heard from other musicians that the club managers have a reputation for swindling bands.

Some clubs, especially those owned by national chains such as the House of Blues, will have standard contracts. (See Appendix C for a sample contract.) If you don't want to play by their rules, you won't play for them at all. Often, however, clubs won't want to deal with contracts at all. Although you can try to draw one up to protect the band, be prepared to simply accept the handshake. Just make sure you spell out all the details verbally so there's no confusion afterward.

Backstage Insights

The American Federation of Musicians (afm.org) helps members on a number of issues, such as providing basic contracts. The union will help members fight for money they're owed. Depending on which local of the union you join, membership dues can be somewhat expensive, however, so you're probably on your own at first.

The Basics of Contracts

When dealing with a small club, or a wedding or party, all you'll need to prepare is a simple one-page letter. (And yes, prepare a laser-printed copy with some kind of band letterhead to make it look professional. Handwriting on napkins won't establish your credibility.) When you become more established, and start playing larger gigs, this one-page letter will expand to a more elaborate *rider*, usually a standard American Federation of Musicians contract. Many of its points will be negotiable.

In your letter, include the following details:

♦ How much will you get paid?

♦ When and how will you get paid?

♦ How long will you play? What times will you start and stop?

♦ Do you get a break and, if so, how long is it?

♦ Who provides the sound system?

♦ Will you play indoors or outdoors?

Words to Rock By

Although a **rider** is a general business term meaning "addendum to any contract specifying extra details," it has special significance in the concert industry. For band performances, a rider can deal with details ranging from particular food requirements to transportation to and from the gig. Famously, Van Halen's rider demanded the removal of brown M&Ms from backstage and Christina Aguilera's rider insists on Flintstones vitamins.

What Will You Have to Sign?

If the venue gives you a contract, you'll have to sign it in order to secure the gig. If the contract is at all complicated, consider asking for extra time and showing it to a lawyer (or even a friend or family member whom you trust). In the end, though, if you want the gig, you'll have to sign. Just remember to keep a copy for your records.

Getting Stiffed

At the small-club level, you probably won't deal with a lot of scams, save for *pay-to-play*. Some musicians consider this long-standing system, in which performers have to reimburse club owners for a certain percentage of the proceeds, to be a scam. Unfortunately, pay-to-play is somewhat common at clubs these days, and you may have to put up with it to get ahead.

Behind the Music

"There was the whole pay-to-play plague that was happening [in Los Angeles], where bands couldn't get a gig on Sunset without paying for rental of microphones and pre-buying the tickets," singer Perry Farrell, recalling the early days of Jane's Addiction, told *Spin* in 2003. "We said, 'Screw you all. Let's go find a warehouse. Let's go to the desert! We would rent boats in San Pedro and rock out there."

Generally, however, people keep their words, and if you play to the specifications outlined in advance, you'll get paid without much trouble.

But even after the most detailed advance work, occasionally a buyer may refuse to pay you. A club booker may tell you up front that you haven't lived up to the terms of your (written or handshake) agreement. Maybe the manager feels you didn't play long enough. Or maybe the club owner got up on the wrong side of the bed that day. Or maybe the bartender's significant other thought you stunk. The reasons range from the sublime to the ridiculous.

There may be nothing you can do about it. But don't give up without trying some of the techniques that we suggest in the next few sections.

Small Claims Court

Every state has a small claims court, which basically means you don't have to hire a lawyer to file a claim. Every state has a different limit, but if your claim is for more than $3,000, you probably won't qualify. If it's for a one-night club gig worth $200, it's probably a matter that can be resolved in small claims court—if you decide it's worth it.

Always make a final attempt to reason with the club people before taking them to court. Go back the next day, after the crowds have left and the alcohol has worn off. You may find more conciliatory people. If you have to, threaten to take your grievance to small claims court. But you don't want to get the reputation of being unnecessarily litigious.

If the club continues to stonewall, contact the court (most have websites) to learn the procedures. Pursuing a case in small claims court will take up several hours of your time, so make sure that it's really what you want to do.

Behind the Music
The American Federation of Musicians union (afm.org) publishes a "defaulter's list" in its members' newspaper. Check it before every new gig to make sure your club is on the level.

Lawyers and Lawsuits

Small claims court cases don't require lawyers. If your case gets to the point where you're considering a lawyer, be aware lawyer bills could suck up all of the money you stand to receive. Before taking the step of hiring somebody, contact a lawyer friend who may be willing to send a threatening letter to the club. Often, this can be just intimidating enough to get the money owed to you.

If the amount of money, or just the principle, is significant enough to you, then, yes, hire a lawyer. Again, start with friends and family—will somebody take your case *pro bono* (which is to say, free)? Can you get a recommendation for a cost-effective lawyer? The last resort is picking a name randomly from the phone book—but remember, lawyers are capable of swindling you at least as harshly as the club owner.

Avoiding Bad Notes

Once you start to draw crowds on the club circuit, sharks may show up asking you to sign a "production deal" or even a record-label contract. These scammers may, for example, promise to get you a record deal, but they retain 50 percent of whatever profits you make in the next seven years. Sleep on any such offers and reconsider them the next morning, after the gig adrenaline has worn off. If you're tempted to seriously consider such an offer, call a lawyer first.

When to Walk Away

You're in a perilous situation. There are never enough clubs to play, no matter how great the scene is in any given city. You don't want to be taken advantage of. But you don't want to limit the playing field, either. If the club is prominent, and the exposure is worth playing there again and again, consider giving up your grievance. When you've played a few more gigs, and your audience begins to grow, you'll probably have more leverage to get what you want.

The Least You Need to Know

- To find out which local clubs might hire your band, network with other bands. Find out which gigs they've enjoyed and which gigs they never want to play again.

- The club booker is your main contact person. He or she will decide to hire you and deal with most contractual and monetary issues.

- Be nice and professional to everybody at the club—you never know when you'll need a manager, bouncer, bartender, or waitperson to bail you out of, say, a rowdy-fan situation.

- Most clubs have honest reputations, but if you encounter one that doesn't, return the next day to negotiate with a clear head. In worst-case situations, you may have to send a threatening lawyer's letter or take the case to small claims court.

- If you've been bamboozled, you may have to grudgingly walk away. Especially if you hope to play at that club in the future. Early in a band's career, exposure can be more important than money.

I've Got the Gig! Now What?

In This Chapter

- ◆ Important equipment to bring with you
- ◆ What songs work—and don't work
- ◆ Broken strings and other pressure situations
- ◆ Dealing with hecklers and stage fright
- ◆ What to wear onstage
- ◆ Basic stage moves: leaping, talking, soloing

Finally, after months of basement rehearsals and badgering nightclub owners and wedding planners for opportunities, you have a gig. It's Friday night at 8 P.M., which gives you a few days to fine-tune a few songs, load your stuff into the drummer's trunk, and get set up. But hold on—there isn't as much time as you'd think. The small details, from protecting your equipment against theft to buying extra guitar strings, can be overwhelming. In this chapter, we help you plan ahead and build a "gig routine."

Scouting the Venue

You already know to case the joint first. If it's a restaurant or bar, you can probably drop by a day early for the scouting report. If it's a wedding hall, open only on Saturdays, you may have to call and schedule an appointment several days in advance.

If time permits, plan to attend another concert or two at the same venue. See a band that plays music roughly like yours. Approach that band between sets and ask questions. Befriend the bouncer, bartender, and waitpeople in advance. Tip well!

Make sure you know the answer to the following questions:

♦ Where are the power outlets, and how many does the club have?

♦ Where can you park while loading your equipment?

♦ Where can you park during the show?

♦ How big is the stage, and will it fit all your musicians and respective gear?

♦ Is the club generous about sound-check time?

♦ Do you need to bring your own PA system?

♦ What nights have the rowdiest crowds?

♦ Are there certain influential "regulars" you might need to win over? If so, what songs do they like?

♦ Are the venue managers prompt about payment?

Backstage Insights

If there aren't enough electrical outlets to plug in several amplifiers and microphones, you need to bring extra power strips.

The booker can answer some of these questions, but it never hurts to get a second opinion. While scouting, it probably can't hurt—if it's okay with the club—to pass out a few fliers announcing your gig. Finally, don't forget to figure out where the bathrooms are.

What to Bring

As a rule of thumb, plan to arrive two hours before your show at a familiar venue. If the club is out of town, or you've never been there, give yourself three hours. We also recommend compiling a "gig sheet," including the club manager's name and contact information, numbers for other bands on the bill and so on. This will help if you arrive early to find the door locked.

Also, ask in advance when the venue's doors are open to the public. If you arrive two hours early, and the club is already filled with people, it'll be hard to walk through the club, let alone conduct your business.

Finally, unless you're meticulously organized (most musicians aren't), prepare a checklist before every gig. Include preshow packing details on the list: Do you have transportation? Gas money? Does the equipment fit? And don't forget to account for the equipment: Include check boxes for guitars, amps, gaffer tape, set list, props, and a clean T-shirt.

Backstage Insights _____

A trip to the hardware and music-supply store before your first gig can save the show. A sturdy metal "band tool kit" should contain the following items:

- Soldering gun
- Gaffer tape
- Wing nuts
- Two or three spare packages of guitar strings, extra picks, and extra drumsticks
- Pliers
- Socket wrench and appropriately sized sockets
- Sturdy rope
- Aspirin
- Earplugs
- Small bottles of water
- Rubber "feet" for onstage equipment
- Small fire extinguisher

Transportation

Multiple guitars, amps, drums, and microphones—not to mention the musicians themselves—probably won't fit into the bassist's Yugo. Generally speaking, each band member will need a total of one car for himself and his equipment.

Consider borrowing a truck or van from a friend, or finding a cheap one-day rate at U-Haul (uhaul.com) or Rent-A-Wreck (rentawreck.com). Have everybody meet at the rehearsal space, several hours before show time, to load up and caravan to the concert. Allow extra time for crises and van breakdowns. And be especially kind to the drummer, who has the most stuff.

Sound and Lighting

At this stage, it usually won't be necessary to buy your own PA system (short for public-address system). If you regularly play at weddings or venues lacking their own such systems, consider investing in one—musiciansfriend.com lists two-speaker-and-amp systems for less than $300. At most venues that feature music regularly, however, the club's PA system is likely to be better than yours.

Feel free to scout the club's sound in advance, by checking out a band on another night, or simply contact the sound engineer and ask questions. You can almost always bring your own stuff—a singer's special microphone, for example—and mix it seamlessly with the existing system.

> ### Words to Rock By
>
> A **sound check** is the performer's pregig rehearsal, usually at the venue a few hours before the show. Ask the concert promoter or club owner for times and setup details. Even if it's just a few minutes, sound check is an excellent opportunity to test your gear, go over tricky musical chord changes, and generally get a feel for the stage and sound of the room.

Depending on the venue, you might not need to bring your own sound engineer. As with PA systems, the venues that specialize in music probably have their own sound people. Be nice to the club's sound person—a little rapport might make him inclined to tweak your sound so it sounds great. Also be sure to ask the sound person whether a *sound check* will be available.

As for lighting, cheap rigs cost $500 or less, but who has room for all that stuff in the van? If the venue has even a few lights, ask for permission to aim them on certain musicians. Some clubs will let you affix colored plastic paper over an existing light for maximum psychedelic impact.

Extension Cords and Gaffer Tape

Everything you need at rehearsal, you'll almost certainly need at the show. But this depends on the size of the venue. If you practice in a warehouse and the gig is a party, you'll need less stuff; if you practice in a walk-in closet and the gig is a banquet hall, you'll need more stuff.

And although most nightclubs are equipped for live music, a wedding hall or friend's party may position you far from the electrical power source. A 50-foot extension cord and power strip can't hurt.

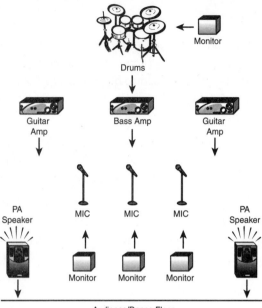

Set up onstage roughly the same way you'd set up in rehearsal—depending on the space you have at the venue.

Backstage Insights

Gaffer tape is a show-biz word for plain old duct tape. (Gaffers, like grips, are errand runners on movie sets.) You can solve a surprising number of problems with gaffer tape, as the following examples demonstrate:

◆ You can identify certain pieces of equipment by sticking distinctive pieces of tape on the bottom. It's your microphone, and not the opening band's, if it contains two pieces of blue tape marked with your initials.

◆ A small square of tape affixed to a drumhead can mute nasty ringing sounds.

◆ If you break a guitar stand during the show, you can fasten the pieces together with gaffer tape.

◆ The tape makes great reinforcement for the sides of drumsticks.

◆ Tape power cords to the stage so the band doesn't trip over them.

◆ If your borrowed van's tailpipe drops off, stick it back on with—you guessed it—gaffer tape.

Protecting Your Gear from Theft

While the driver for System of a Down was on a coffee break, thieves once stole an entire truck full of the heavy-metal band's equipment—guitars, drums, and amps. Around the same time, alternative-rock band Sonic Youth lost several expensive, classic guitars (including one with a Snoopy sticker on the front) after somebody made off with its rented Ryder truck. Thieves are everywhere.

Use common sense, a Chicago sales manager for a Guitar Center store tells us. Engrave serial numbers into every piece of valuable equipment. Don't make a point of showing off your fancy guitars and drums, especially near a club. Never leave anything in a car trunk. And be careful of "fans" who ask probing questions about where you rehearse or load.

Such advice may be harder to follow than you think. Say you're the third of three bands playing at a club one night, and the owner lets you stash your stuff near the stage. The easiest way to set up is to leave everything hours in advance, and then drag it to the stage just before show time. Unfortunately, that's also the easiest way to advertise "we have nice, unprotected gear!" to an entire crowd for hours.

As best you can, keep everything with you—tuners, guitars, even cymbals. Legends persist that famous rock guitarists such as Bill "Rock Around the Clock" Haley and Deep Purple's Ritchie Blackmore slept with their guitars. Now you know why. Also, it can't hurt to bring a large tarp to keep everything out of sight.

Avoiding Bad Notes

Beware: Your standard homeowner's policy probably won't cover your musical equipment.

Backstage Insights

Most bands play two or three 45-minute sets with 15-minute breaks. Advance planning avoids the "should we take a break in 10 minutes?" discussion while you're onstage performing.

For your own protection, prepare a postgig checklist, as well-wishers and adrenaline tend to distract you from the packing task at hand. The Nitty Gritty Dirt Band's former road manager, Lenny Martinez, *always* did a postshow venue walk-through. And sure enough, he always found something, whether it was a tuner kicked to the bottom of the stage or the singer's T-shirt left on the dressing-room floor.

What to Sing

A wedding crowd will want to hear Etta James's "At Last" and Hootie & the Blowfish's "Hold My Hand." A high-school dance crowd will demand upbeat rockers—and mostly hits of the day. Certain songs work in almost every setting. Others, such as the traditional Jewish dance tune "Hava Nagileh" or the Italian "Tarantella," will be requested only under very specific circumstances. You'll learn more songs with experience, obviously, but try to be prepared for anything.

Create your *set list* long in advance, and tailor it to the gig. If it's a bar or club, you'll want to fill the dance floor as quickly as possible, so stack the beginning with upbeat numbers. If it's a wedding, where you're on after the cake-cutting, start with slow, romantic stuff and build up to the rockers. With experience you'll develop several set-list variations—"party set," "bar set," and so on.

> **Words to Rock By**
>
> A **set list** is the band's master list of songs for an act, negotiated long in advance and affixed to the stage so everyone can refer to it. When preparing one, remember pacing—follow up several sweaty rock 'n' rollers with a cool-down ballad.

Are you lucky enough to have a signature song, whether it's an original or a cover? If so, play it as often as you can. Twice in the same night, sometimes! Frequently, attendees at the beginning and end of the show won't be the same people.

Songs That Always Work

One generation's dance-floor-filling "Macarena" may be the next generation's cringe-inducing old-fogy anthem. But we consider these selections to be fairly reliable and timeless (and easy to learn!):

- ◆ Chuck Berry's "Johnny B. Goode"
- ◆ Etta James's "At Last" (especially for weddings)
- ◆ U2's "(Pride) In the Name of Love" (especially on St. Patrick's Day)
- ◆ Van Morrison's "Brown Eyed Girl"
- ◆ Hoagy Carmichael's "Stardust" (as interpreted by Willie Nelson)
- ◆ Robert Johnson's "Sweet Home, Chicago" (especially at blues bars)
- ◆ The Isley Brothers' "Twist and Shout"
- ◆ Whitney Houston's "I Will Always Love You" (but only if you have a *great* singer)
- ◆ The Backstreet Boys' "I Want It That Way" (but only if you have *several* great singers)
- ◆ The Kingsmen's "Louie, Louie"

Songs That Never Work

You never know what's going to grab people until you try. Dethroned "King of Pop" Michael Jackson seemed like the epitome of cornball in 2001, until the metal band Alien Ant Farm took his "Smooth Criminal" to the top of the charts. Still, we recommend avoiding these clichés at all costs:

◆ USA for Africa's "We Are the World"

◆ Eric Carmen's "All by Myself"

◆ Billy Ray Cyrus's "Achy, Breaky Heart"

◆ Lynyrd Skynyrd's "Freebird" (no matter how many smart-aleck fans shout for it toward the show's end)

◆ Peter, Paul & Mary's "Puff the Magic Dragon"

> **Behind the Music**
>
> You can learn a lot in advance about the audience by determining what food will be served. If it's beer and barbecue, line the set list with honky-tonk songs like Hank Williams Sr.'s "Settin' the Woods on Fire" or rockers like Smash Mouth's "Walkin' on the Sun." If it's $500-a-plate *foie gras* and salmon, be sure the band knows plenty of Nat King Cole ballads.

Know Your Audience

Band and audience communicate with a sort of telepathy. If people at a high-school dance are having a great time rocking out, leave your hand-holding ballad for later. You can't always rely on your standard set list. At a wedding, for example, determine special requests in advance.

Being Prepared

Whether you're playing before 10 people or 100, at a bar mitzvah or a hip downtown nightclub, you want your first performance to be professional, flawless, and riveting.

So for the love of Axl Rose, be on time! In advance, get directions to the venue, figure out where and when you can load in equipment, and show up several hours early to deal with various small emergencies.

And don't let the small stuff become overwhelming. You want to channel all your energy into the music, not into changing strings, fixing microphones, or worrying about whether you should have brought a spare guitar.

Changing Strings Under Pressure

Strings break. Almost always at the wrong time. So guitarists should keep at least three or four sets of extra strings within striking distance. Bassists rarely break their much-thicker strings, but they should follow the same advice just in case. In a perfect world, a drummer will carry at least an extra snare drum—but if that isn't possible, consider keeping an extra "head" for the snare, the small tom-tom, and other most-frequently whacked drums.

Should you have the misfortune of breaking a string midperformance—and you will—let the crowd in on what's going on and perhaps take a five-minute break. Jokes and stories are dangerous, but certain well-rehearsed shticks can work. Steve once saw the great folk-rock guitarist Richard Thompson break a string and, during the change process, lead the crowd into a sing-along to "Twist and Shout." It was amazingly effective, but Thompson is a seasoned pro.

> **CAUTION** **Avoiding Bad Notes**
>
> If it's at all affordable, we highly recommend bringing a second guitar (even if it's a junky one) to gigs. That way, you don't have to waste time changing strings or tuning if something goes wrong.

As for tuning the guitar, an electronic tuner with little LED lights is a lifesaving investment. (For more details on tuners, see Chapter 5.) Fans usually understand short breaks for tuning—but they'll get impatient if they drag on too long.

Onstage Safety

When hundreds or perhaps thousands of people are packed into a small space, and nobody can hear each other, it's a potentially dangerous situation. So it behooves you to take basic precautions: While loading in before the show, locate all the exit doors and figure out how to get in and out.

The stage, too, can be a dangerous area, given all the cords and wires connected to high-power sound equipment.

Electrical Shocks

When you have equipment plugged into electrical outlets, shocks are always a possibility. For this reason, avoid stepping in puddles onstage, and always try to clean up any spills immediately. Never, under any circumstances, set drinks on top of amplifiers. And always take your hands off a guitar's metal strings before grabbing the microphone.

General Fire Prevention

Always pack a fire extinguisher in the aforementioned band tool kit. And locate the venue's extinguishers before you play. Even without performance experience, you'll be able to gauge the club's physical condition just by looking at the outlets—are plugs dangling off frayed wires? You don't want to squander an opportunity, but it's not worth your life. You can always wriggle out of a commitment if the situation is unsafe.

Other fire-prevention tips: Don't overload an electrical circuit (thus, the extra extension cords); don't confine amps and other quick-heating sound gear into small spaces; and never place drinks on top of electrical equipment.

Crowd Control

Fans are your friends, not your adversaries. They probably spent good money to hear you play. So don't abuse the crowd with obscure or difficult material. In that spirit, try to accommodate shouted requests; if you absolutely can't play it, kindly say so. "We don't play that—it's a stupid song" is unacceptable in every situation.

Occasionally, though, you'll wind up with an unruly crowd you can't possibly control. If that's the case, often your only choice is to rely on the club manager and bouncers on hand. Befriend these people—and bartenders—long before the show begins. In extreme situations, you can ask for assistance from the stage, via microphone.

The Alcohol Factor

As we already mentioned, on the club circuit you'll encounter *a lot* of alcohol— probably more alcohol than you've ever seen in your life. The primary aim of beer-serving clubs is to sell beer, and more often than not live entertainment is an afterthought. Or, in business terms, a "loss leader" to lure patrons into the club so they can buy more alcohol.

> **Backstage Insights**
>
> Your best offense against a heckler is simply starting the next song. If the heckling persists after every song, consider enlisting club staff for help. (This is one reason it's important to make friends with bartenders and bouncers in advance.)

You'll know instantly, upon playing for a crowd, whether people have been drinking. It's a totally different atmosphere, with normally shy people willing to shout all kinds of things and perhaps become physically abusive. You may run up against a character who has spent the day drinking in the bar and isn't particularly enamored with your distracting loud music. You may also find fans who pester you with requests or don't mind telling you exactly what they think of your music. It's always best to ignore these patrons.

As for your own level of alcohol consumption, flip to Chapter 7 for more insight. Although Jimmy Buffett and Mojo Nixon seem to get away with it, getting so drunk that you're unable to properly perform isn't good for you or the band. Just because fans are acting stupid doesn't mean you should.

Finally, keep in mind your underage band members may not be allowed to perform in alcohol-serving bars. Watch for all-ages venues, or venues that put on regular all-ages nights.

Hecklers

Again, ignore hecklers and move on. The fastest way to drown out an obnoxious fan is to count off the next song and plunge right in. Resist the urge to counterattack. The heckler's friends may make up half the audience, so once you've responded, you may have put off half the crowd. And be particularly sensitive at weddings—that drunk guy who keeps interrupting your set with profane toasts may just be the father of the bride—the same father of the bride who is supposed to hand you a check at the end of the night.

Stage Fright

Even successful performers experience stage fright on a regular basis—Barbra Streisand, Cher, Rod Stewart, and Chicago rocker Liz Phair had to overcome serious afflictions on the way to fame. (It's said Sonny Bono went onstage with Cher because she was so nervous he felt that she needed company; shortly thereafter they formed Sonny & Cher.)

The only cure for stage fright is to get on stage. Being well-rehearsed is a big help. Another effective strategy is closing your eyes, or focusing your attention on your bandmates, for a few seconds before the show begins. Trust the music to carry you through. If the problem is so crippling you're unable to endure it, this may be time for a different kind of career.

Excellent Rock Hairstyles—and Other Looks

Remember our suggestion, in the "Know Your Audience" section of this chapter, that scouting out the food in advance might help you determine the set list? Same goes for what to wear. A beer-and-barbecue crowd will be more than happy to see you in jeans and work boots. A high-end wedding crowd will want nothing less than tuxedos and other formal attire. If you're really the prepared type (and you sweat a lot), an extra shirt may save a lot of aggravation.

Costumes are occasionally effective—early in their career, The Beatles looked even more striking than usual when they donned matching gray suits. You can do this in a simple way, with color schemes: Just arrange for everybody in the band to wear something with, say, red and black on it, or green and yellow.

In 1986, when Mark was managing Lyle Lovett, who was just starting to tour with his Large Band, the musicians didn't have a look. They were a collection of guys with different senses of dress and presentation. So before a pivotal gig in Los Angeles, he took the band to thrift stores to find suits that looked like Lyle's. "It made a big difference in the presentation—all of a sudden they looked like a *band*," he recalls. "From that day on everybody in that band looked like they were there to do business. And people took them more seriously."

Be careful not to overdo the costuming, however. The last thing the beer-and-barbecue crowd—or the fancy-wedding crowd, for that matter—wants is a band dressed in elaborate "glam" regalia. Again, know your audience.

Before uncorking any sort of "look," check with your bandmates, who may not appreciate looking like normal people while the bassist with Marilyn Manson platform shoes upstages them.

> **CAUTION**
>
> **Avoiding Bad Notes**
>
> If you're a guy, you probably don't need makeup. The only scenario under which to consider it involves massive stage lights that are likely to wash out your features. Also, if you're a male in a cross-dressing band (The New York Dolls, David Bowie, Poison, Mötley Crüe), makeup is an imperative.

Women, of course, have much broader rock-history fashion precedents, from the close-cropped Pat Benatar 1980s look (although we recommend against the Spandex tights) to R&B singer Patti LaBelle's elaborate, sculpted hair creations. There are many music picture books available at the local bookstore, and a good stylist can match your vision.

Stage Moves

If you're an Irish folk-music trio, skip the next few paragraphs—all you need, presentation-wise, is strong music and an occasional rambling story to tell the crowd. If you're a bombastic rock 'n' roll quartet, some choreography may be appropriate. Generally, the larger the stage, the more physical space you have to fill, so it may be worth practicing your James Brown knee-drop in the mirror at home.

It's no sin to steal from the masters. Prowl the stage like rapper LL Cool J. Conduct an arm-flailing guitar "windmill" like Pete Townshend of The Who. Maybe even figure out a few basic group dance moves, like The Temptations or *NSYNC.

Backstage Insights _____

The primary way to look cool while playing a solo is to play a great solo. The crowd will know if you're overacting, especially if you aren't that good (yet). But especially if you're the lead guitarist, you may be the primary or secondary focal point onstage. So during the big solo, move away from your microphone, walk to the center of the stage, and stay in the spotlight (if you have one).

As for talking onstage, some performers have a gift for it. Early in his career, rocker Bruce Springsteen was a master at telling long-winded, personal stories and making them seem universal. Punk rocker Patti Smith effectively reads poetry between songs. In his solo shows, The Eagles guitarist Joe Walsh tells jokes.

You won't know for sure if you're good at it until you try. At first, avoid this stuff during key moments of the show—if you've finished one rocking song and the crowd responds enthusiastically for the first time, don't destroy the momentum with "so this guy walks into a bar …" But if things are going well, and the audience seems responsive, a joke, a story, or even "Hello, Cleveland!" (which is funnier if you're not in Cleveland) can be effective.

Props and Special Effects

Pyrotechnics are probably out of your price range at this point. And they're dangerous: Although rock stars such as KISS and Rob Zombie continue to blast them at arenas, many major acts are starting to worry about safety. In early 2003, more than 100 fans died at a small wooden nightclub in West Warwick, Rhode Island, because of fireworks set off in a claustrophobic, unsafe situation. So for many reasons it's best to keep your effects simple.

Props can be an easy band-marketing device—as simple as hanging a banner behind the stage with your name, logo, and website. (This can be tacky at weddings and bar mitzvahs, however.) If you're invited to perform an outdoor luau, try spending $20 at Paper Warehouse on palm trees, leis, and other inexpensive decorations. Your efforts could very well impress the people who hired you, which is a sure way to get recommendations for future gigs.

The easiest stage decoration is putting the band's name and logo on the bass drumhead—using paint or stencil or taking it to a professional sign store. Anything you can do for "brand identification," as they say in business, helps.

Working Together Onstage

A band in many ways is like a sports team. Some members might be superstars—the primary reasons fans arrive at the gigs. Others are team players, who solo when it's their time, but more often stay in the background and prop up the music. Unless you're the designated front person, resist the urge to grandstand. The bassist and drummer, first and foremost, are there to drive the rhythm.

Will Anyone Be Listening?

Your band is responsible for doing what you can to pack the place. That means alerting everybody you know—family, friends, co-workers, classmates, other bands. It also means putting up fliers, sending out mass e-mails, making website postings, and trying to get some publicity via local newspapers, alt-weeklies, and community radio stations. And ask the club booker how you can help with the advertising and promotion.

If, despite these efforts, you wind up with just a few people at the gig, don't get discouraged. You've just started, and nobody knows your name—yet. A small audience may seem awkward and humiliating, but it shouldn't deter you from performing really, really well. If you impress those five people, they'll tell five other people. And remember, the bartenders, bouncers, and wait staff are always listening. They may be your most influential audience. In short, make every show your best show, because you never know what it could lead to.

The Least You Need to Know

- Everything you need at rehearsal, you'll need at the gig—and more. Bring a band toolbox and gaffer tape. And don't leave expensive gear out in the open.

- Learn as much as you can in advance about the audience. Rehearse songs that are likely to work with this crowd.

- Shouting down hecklers isn't the most effective way of dealing with them. Let your music do the talking.

- Costumes, hairstyles, and basic props can be more effective—and cheaper—than you think.

- Prepare a few things to say onstage, but you're there to play music, not talk. Too many jokes are a risk.

Taking It on the Road

In This Chapter

- ◆ When to leave home—and how to do it without endangering your day job

- ◆ The romance of the band van (if you don't have to replace a fan belt in late-summer Phoenix)

- ◆ Carving out an itinerary

- ◆ How to build a crowd away from home base

- ◆ Where and how to set up the mailing list

- ◆ The basics of merchandising

Getting big in your hometown is a wonderful thing. But it has its drawbacks. If you play too often at local clubs, "familiarity breeds contempt" syndrome may creep in and promoters, bookers, and even fans may decide they have other things to do than hear your band once or twice a week. That's when it's time to travel.

Taking it on the road is perhaps the best investment you can make. It can be grueling, and costly, but if you do it right you'll immediately see growth—perhaps the kind of growth that attracts managers, booking agents, radio stations, and even prominent record labels. Once you've established a home base, it can never hurt to develop several satellite bases.

Before You Make the Plunge …

Before setting up a trip, consider the realities of taking the band on the road. Yes, travel can be a blast—rock history is filled with outrageous road stories—from dramatic accounts of The Who wrecking hotel rooms during all night bashes to those guys from the movie *Almost Famous* singing along happily to Elton John's "Tiny Dancer." What all such descriptions leave out are the countless hours of driving and waiting. Hours and hours of each.

So make sure you're ready. Is this the right time? Are all the band members emotionally—and physically—prepared for a grueling trip? Are you sure you've exhausted your local options? And perhaps most important, will the trip be a boost, from a financial or emotional perspective, for the band? If the answer is yes, or if you can find a quick out-of-town gig perfect for a short, nothing-to-lose road trip, it's time to deal with transportation.

The Van

The car (or cars) you've used to shuttle between rehearsal and gig will probably work for shorter trips, but when it comes to more elaborate road trips involving significant distances or several gigs, you'll need to find a more practical means of getting around. Vans tend to be the vehicle of choice for bands on the road, as they can haul a lot of gear with room to spare for several people.

Choose the van carefully, as you'll spend long hours in it.

Behind the Music
Vans have a romantic place in rock history. Punk singer Henry Rollins titled his on-the-road memoirs *Get in the Van*. Rock trio Big Head Todd & the Monsters bought a van just after high school, nicknamed it "The Colonel" and took off from Boulder, Colorado, to Chicago, to play impromptu happy-hour gigs for $50 a pop. More than 300,000 miles later, they secured a major record-label deal.

Buy or Rent?

When you're just getting started, it probably makes more sense to rent a vehicle rather than to cough up the cash to buy one. Besides, until you've tried a couple out-of-town gigs, you won't know whether you'll want to keep doing them. U-Haul and Ryder both rent cargo vans. They are the major truck-rental companies in most markets, and their rates aren't terrible: roughly $20 a day (plus about 60¢ a mile) for a cargo van, or $20 to $40 a day (plus mileage) for a larger truck. Shop around at smaller, local companies for better deals.

Read the fine print on the rental-insurance policy. Often it won't cover specific types of property damage or will charge a prohibitively high deductible. And check with your regular auto-insurance policy, which may not cover some trucks. You never know what kind of mishap will happen while maneuvering an unknown highway at 2 A.M. in the middle of a thunderstorm.

Once your band starts making road trips a regular part of its schedule, buying a truck or van may be more cost-effective than renting. Check the classifieds and visit used car lots for the best deals. And don't forget to comparison-shop.

The Ford Econoline has a certain romantic reputation in rock history. (Neil Young enshrined it in his dark classic "Tonight's the Night.") But vans are more or less interchangeable, and plenty of auto dealerships will be happy to try to meet your needs. Unless your band has three tuba players and a string section, a 15-passenger van works just fine.

The idea is for you and your gear to fit in a reasonably comfortable way. Be ready to make easy compromises: Do you really need the gigantic Marshall amplifiers? Consider taking smaller amps and, at the gig, hooking them up to the club's PA system using microphones. (Call ahead, of course, to make sure you can do this.) Downsize. Sleeping bags may be handy if you're planning to camp out or crash on a friend's floor—but they might take up crucial space.

> **Avoiding Bad Notes**
>
> Don't be too stingy—although a $1,500 junker may get you there and back, long-term repair-and-maintenance charges may wind up costing far, far more. Best to spend a bit more—$5,000 to $7,500, say, if you have the time and inclination to scour the classified ads—for a reliable set of wheels.

> **Backstage Insights**
>
> Road-trip entertainment is not a trivial consideration. Bring handheld video games and extra batteries. While the band may want to designate a few group CDs for sing-along (or musical study) sessions, headphones are a must for bands whose members have different musical tastes. If you really want to get fancy, battery-powered TVs and DVD players can suck up long hours on the road.

Do-It-Yourself Repairs

The van will break down. Inevitably, the radiator hose will blow out when you're late for a gig. The best way to deal with this is to have a band member who knows the basics of auto repair. He or she can recognize the problem, take a quick trip to an auto-parts store, and have the van running again in no time.

Of course, music and auto repair aren't always compatible talents, so somebody in the band may want to invest in *The Complete Idiot's Guide to Car Care and Repair Illustrated* or take a maintenance course at the local community college. At the very least, this knowledge will prevent you from getting taken at an out-of-town garage.

With the help of your mechanically inclined bandmate, or a friend or family member who knows the rudiments of auto repair, prepare a van toolbox. Screwdrivers, ratchet wrenches, soldering iron, and an extra tire or two are all crucial. But if your van has a unique mechanical characteristic, like an oddball-size fan belt, stuff a spare in the toolbox, too.

The Road Ain't Cheap

Once you all pile in the van and head down the road, your costs run up tremendously. Besides the cost of the van, you'll probably have to pay to sleep in hotels and buy your food from restaurants. When you're far from home, you're constantly handing money to somebody. The trick is to plan for those costs and to do what you can to keep them down.

Estimating Costs

We recommend setting up a tour budget before you even start. Typical costs on the road include the following:

- Food—three meals a day for each person, plus plenty of snacks and drinks
- Parking and tolls
- Hotels
- Gas
- Cell-phone bills, phone cards, or extravagant pay-phone long-distance rates
- Emergency van maintenance (Yes, you will break down on occasion; and even if you're lucky enough to have a mechanic in the band, you'll still require garage service.)

- ◆ Entertainment, including books, magazines, CDs, video games, and batteries

- ◆ Extra health and auto insurance if your usual policies don't cover road trips (Check first.)

- ◆ Medicine, from basic aspirin to a doctor's appointment if somebody gets sick in an unfamiliar city

Obviously, there are ways to keep these costs down. Bringing a cooler and buying bulk supermarket food is cheaper (and healthier) than eating at Taco Bell three times a day. Rather than paying $50 to $100 a night for even the cheapest hotel, perhaps a friend will let you crash on the couch in exchange for free access to the gig or some other favor. Check the map to see if you can avoid the toll roads, and bring lots of quarters to park at meters rather than paying for an expensive garage.

Can You Afford It?

Once you've determined the potential costs, it's time to figure out whether you can actually afford to take the trip. You'd be surprised by how many bands fail to take this extremely important step. Maxing out credit cards will only hurt you in the future, and possibly break up the band someday.

The fairest, most democratic method is for everybody to chip in—but that may not be feasible given certain members' financial situations. Maybe three musicians can split the costs, and the other can sign a payment plan involving future gig proceeds. But proceed with caution: If one musician is financially beholden to another, this can mess with fragile group dynamics. And if one musician winds up quitting (or worse yet, getting fired), the last thing you'll want is for that person to owe money.

Planning the Trip

Where do you go? The easy answer is, "Wherever you can get a gig." But there's more to it than that. The process can begin in two ways: You can pick a city within driving distance (which may be just a few hours for some bands with families and day jobs, or a longer summer adventure for band members with no such commitments) and find a club at your level in that area. Or you can find the club first, through connections or simply locating it on a map, and market yourself to that club. (See Chapter 11 for more information on conquering the club circuit.)

Some bands use an "exchange system" to broaden their markets to other cities. Bands outside your hometown might let you open for them in one of their strong markets.

In exchange, you'd let them open for you in one of your strongholds. Although competition among bands can be healthy, cooperation is often far more effective.

> ### Behind the Music
>
> Every state in the country is packed with weird or poignant roadside attractions, from the Mitchell Corn Palace in Mitchell, South Dakota, to the Iowa cornfield marker where Buddy Holly's plane crashed in 1959. Many travel books tell you how and where to find these tourist stops, but we highly recommend *The New Roadside America: The Modern Traveler's Guide to the Wild and Wonderful America's Tourist Attractions* (Fireside) and its frequently updated website, roadsideamerica.com.

It makes sense to plan a few "fill gigs" on the way home if schedules permit. (For example, if you live in Denver and have a gig in Omaha, contact a club in Lawrence, Kansas, about playing on the way home.) This can be an excellent way to spread the word and generate extra cash.

But be realistic. If the trip is a weekend quickie, you may not have the time or energy to play more than one or two gigs. And study the map carefully—don't make a side trip to St. Louis if you're making the Denver-to-Omaha trip. That can take you hours out of your way and drive everybody crazy.

Roadside Service and Maps

Joining the American Auto Association (aaa.com) is an excellent investment for many reasons: Roadside service is available in almost any city, and you can buy reasonable, reliable travel insurance if your own policy doesn't cover certain key areas.

But the main reason for a $60-or-so yearly membership is for the maps. They're all free. (Consider also buying a copy of *The Musician's Atlas* [musiciansatlas.com], which lists clubs, promoters, radio stations, and media outlets.) Before planning any trip, drop by the local AAA bureau to get state guides (listing hotels, prices, and recommendations, among other things), city and state maps, and maybe a TripTik, which is a specially prepared map charting the fastest route.

Online map resources are also invaluable. The maps feature of yahoo.com will diagram your entire trip in seconds.

Surviving the Road

Jack Kerouac's classic Beat Generation novel *On the Road* notwithstanding, the road isn't as romantic as you might think. If rehearsal spaces and local stages seem cramped, imagine stuffing all the same people and gear, plus luggage, into a small van. And on the road, you'll have very little leisure time (aside from long hours staring at the white lines of the highway). The whole experience can make it difficult to keep a positive attitude.

To survive, perhaps the most important thing is to maintain a sense of humor and perspective. Your band is doing a good thing! The out-of-town gig can easily pay off in terms of exposure or even money, but regardless, going on the road with your band is an experience you'll always remember.

Many musicians treat traveling, even the grueling road kind, as a romantic adventure. "I kind of read too many Jack Kerouac books and heard too many Woody Guthrie songs and started looking at the road not as a means of getting somewhere but as a means of finding where songs come from," Texas rocker Joe Ely recalls of his late-teen years, in an interview with Steve for the *Chicago Tribune*. "I'd hear Chuck Berry singing about Route 66 and I had to go to Flagstaff and all those towns in that song. At that period of my life the road was kind of my university."

It's fine to look to the road as your route to adventure, just don't neglect your health and safety. Shuffle drivers regularly—on a long trip, one driver's shift shouldn't go more than three hours. Night shifts are sometimes inevitable, and someone should always plan to ride shotgun, helping the driver not to fall asleep at the wheel. Make regular stops, not only obvious ones for gas and restrooms, but also for the occasional leg-stretching "Chinese fire drill."

It's hard, especially for young road-trippers, to avoid a steady regimen of junk food. You'll encounter every conceivable fast-food chain and gas-station food store at road-side exits, and it's tempting to load up on tacos, cheeseburgers, chili-flavored corn chips, and Mountain Dew. Occasional indulgences are okay—even good for morale— but you'll be better off if you make salads and grilled-chicken sandwiches the main-stay of your diet.

"Eat properly on the road!" sounds like the ultimate bossy-parent advice, but it'll pay off for everybody in the long run. If you're in your mid- to late-20s, just as your body's metabolism is starting to change, a steady regimen of French fries will fatten you up in a surprisingly short period of time. (It's also hard to exercise on the road—try to squeeze in short runs at rest areas and use hotel workout rooms when they are available.)

Backstage Insights

Rather than stopping at the first gas station after the freeway exit, go a little deeper into town and hit the supermarket. You'll have access to deli sandwiches, fresh fruits and vegetables (always good for snacks), juice, nuts, and spare toothpaste and razors—all much cheaper than you'd find at the average truck stop or restaurant.

Make a game of eating healthy. "I've developed an art of eating at a truck-stop café in 5 or 10 minutes. I'll have a full salad while everybody else is [using the bathroom]," Luther Dickinson, lead guitarist for the blues-rock trio North Mississippi Allstars, told Steve in a *Chicago Tribune* interview. Yes, truck stops are filled with big-bellied customers loading up at the Hardee's, but salad bars and healthy snacks are available if you look for them.

Building a Base Away from Home

It's crucial to get people onboard early. A fan who faithfully comes to your shows during the band's formative years will be a fan forever. And building a base at home is nice, but being a "local band" forever will take you only so far. If you have aspirations to sign with a record label someday (see Chapter 22) or get your songs on the radio, a broad geographic base will give you credibility and ultimately help sell your band.

Big Head Todd & the Monsters, one of Mark's management clients, began in the late 1980s by picking out-of-town cities where they knew people. Then they expanded to those markets, playing low-paying bar gigs at first and developing a small but loyal audience. Their first "conquest" was Chicago—they played for just a few people the first time, returned to a few more people and, after several regular visits over a period of years, played large theatres.

When Mark started "shopping" the band to major record labels, he was able to say, "They're selling out 500-seat clubs in Chicago, Minneapolis, and San Francisco in addition to their hometown." That had tremendous impact.

Return to a receptive city as often as is economically and physically possible. Treat each "satellite city" like you'd treat your home base—contact the press, be nice to club owners, distribute fliers, and generally make friends and contacts. It'd be ideal if you could play the city every month, but try to go back every two or three.

The process of building a significant out-of-town base is slow and steady. Make sure your expectations are realistic: Unless you're an MTV "buzz band," which most bands aren't, you probably won't blow into town the first time and play to hundreds of people. Win over the clubs, owner by owner. You might lose money on the first trip, or you may have to do something such as play a Sunday-night "open mike." But these are all tiny steps on the big ladder to success.

The Mailing List

A fan is a terrible thing to waste, and once you've developed one it's important to start communicating with him or her. In the old days, before the Internet, bands would ask people to sign up on a pencil-and-clipboard mailing list, and then send upcoming-concert and CD-release updates via snail mail. Fan clubs, which gave exclusive materials to fee-paying members, were an effective way to build an underground support network. Today you can do most of this stuff online.

But let's back up: The information you want on a mailing list is name, address, and e-mail address. Once you get that, enter the data into your e-mail program's address book, create a user group, and send regular updates to fans. (Occasional snail-mailings, like CD singles or logo stickers, are costly but effective.)

How do you get this information and make these connections with fans? It all starts at the gig. Your job isn't just to play, it's to network. And sell merchandise.

How to Sign Up People

Don't just put your mailing list on the bar and hope people will sign up. Take the mailing list to the crowd. If somebody in the band isn't willing to do it, maybe a significant other or a new fan might have the time to ask people to sign. In our experience, you'll get easily double or triple the number of signees than you would with the clipboard-on-the-bar approach.

Backstage Insights

Most of our advice in this chapter is geared toward night-club bands. Wedding, party, and bar-mitzvah bands may want to take care not to sell merchandise or even pass around a mailing list. When the crowd is wearing formal attire, people may consider these marketing efforts the epitome of gauche.

Merchandise and Where to Put It

Selling merchandise on the road can make for lucrative side income. At the very least, it's a potential way to pay for gas.

Before heading out, check into local T-shirt silk-screening companies. Contact printing companies or local copy shops about stamping your logo onto a sticker, button, or, more creatively, a container for earplugs. Laser printers and graphic-design software such as Adobe Illustrator can also generate professional-looking artwork in bulk.

Then pay a T-shirt company to copy off a dozen or two. When choosing the number of designs, determine how much space you have in the van. Twelve T-shirt designs becomes "stuff you have to carry," which means a bigger van and a bigger expense.

Keep prices as low as you can to cover your costs. Stickers might go for $1. It's better to sell all your T-shirts for $10 rather than having to lug half of them back because you stubbornly kept the price at $18.95. (Yes, Aerosmith can get away with $33 T-shirts, but you're not Aerosmith. Your fans may be loyal, but they aren't stupid.)

Backstage Insights _____

If you happen to have a CD for sale, use creative marketing techniques. Denver musician David Booker, for example, recently tried—without great success—to sell $12 individual discs to his fans. Then he got the idea to bundle three of his CDs together as a $27.50 "box set." Fans said, "It's the whole thing!" and bought tons. _Value-added_ is the big buzzword these days, as record companies bundle bonus DVDs and free online knick-knacks with standard artist CDs.

Placing merchandise at a gig is an art. During a break, one band we know stacked its merchandise at the front of the stage—a smart move, because people's eyes naturally gravitate to the stage when they're not looking anywhere else. Bring the merch into fans' fields of vision.

Using Your Web Page

We'll get more into the specifics of websites and how to use them in Chapter 16. For now, though, consider designating your homepage as the "meeting place" for your fan club. Pearl Jam, like many bands, uses its online "Ten Club" to distribute special ticket offers and offer various kinds of Internet-only merchandise. Many bands put up bulletin boards for fans to interact—and, sometimes, offer useful advice.

Make sure upcoming-gig information is accurate and timely—and consider using a special design to advertise certain important gigs. Again, be creative with links. When pushing a gig, link to a MapQuest or Yahoo! map site giving explicit directions to the club or to the club itself, and be sure to inform the club that you've done so.

The Least You Need to Know

- ◆ Road trips are great fun, but they're costly and grueling—know what you're getting into before embarking on one.

- ◆ Depending on the number and type of trips, either rent or buy a van.

- ◆ Repairs will be necessary. Consider taking an auto-mechanics course or reading a how-to book to avoid costly out-of-town repair bills.

- ◆ Budget and plan your itinerary long in advance.

- ◆ Put merchandise and your mailing list at the gig where people can seem them. Interacting with out-of-towners is an excellent way to build your base.

Part 4

Getting the Word Out

What good is a performing band if nobody ever goes to its shows? You can be the best musicians in the world, but almost as important as improving your songs is drawing fans to your venues. The main tools for this task are publicity and marketing—start contacting local media to push for free advance stories, and create fliers, handbills, posters, online ads, and mailing lists to help spread the word.

At first, the band members will handle these jobs themselves, unless they have friends or relatives with the time to call newspaper music critics. But as the crowds grow, and it becomes too cumbersome to focus on the business and the music, consider hiring a publicist. Sometimes, the jump from somewhat popular to really huge requires an exposure boost that can only come from an experienced professional.

Chapter 14

The Importance of Media

In This Chapter

- ◆ Why media coverage can help your band
- ◆ Publicity and how it works
- ◆ Types of media, from alt-weeklies to local dailies
- ◆ Making connections with busy writers and editors
- ◆ How to conduct press interviews

Word-of-mouth is a great way to get people to your shows. Not only is it effective, it will establish your reputation as a "street-level" or "grassroots" band that hasn't yet registered on the public's radar screen. But eventually you'll want to expand your audience, even if it's just from 10 people to 50, or from the tiny suburban coffeehouse to the hip downtown night-club. One excellent way to do this is by landing articles—or even brief mentions—about your band in the local media. The process can be intimi-dating: Busy music writers have eight zillion CDs stacked on their desks, and the last thing they need is another local band pestering them. Don't get discouraged! We'll help you master the art of publicity, so you can create some hype and expand your reach.

Why You Need Coverage

You can be the best band in the world, but if people don't know about you, they won't come to your shows. The more people hear about you, the more people will assume you're worth watching—or hiring. To expand, and spread the word, the local media is an invaluable tool.

"Media coverage" is a broad term—for your purposes, it can mean a glowing review in the local newspaper trumpeting the band's talents and achievements. It can also mean a tiny-type listing in the local alt-weekly stating the time, date, ticket price, and location of your upcoming gig. Any mention of your band is valuable. At the very least, it might encourage music fans to come hear your show. But it has the potential to create the kind of *buzz* that leads to a sold-out show.

> **Words to Rock By**
>
> **Buzz** is the intense interest that results from aggressive media coverage and word-of-mouth publicity. It's a lot like *hype*, only much more intense. Buzz can't be bought, and if you're lucky enough to get it, sell as many concert tickets, CDs, and T-shirts as you can until it (inevitably) disappears.

> **Words to Rock By**
>
> **Publicity** is basically free media coverage. It can lead to all sorts of valuable things—more people to buy concert tickets, CDs, and T-shirts and a general enhancement of your image and reputation. It's the antidote to being ignored.

Publicity and How It Works

There are two kinds of media: paid and free. Your band can easily take out a paid advertisement in the local newspaper or arrange for a pop-up ad on a web page. But paid advertisements aren't generally persuasive to fans—savvy readers know paid ads have more to do with how much money the musicians have than how good they are. *Publicity*, the free kind, usually has much more credibility than paid ads.

Getting People to Shows

When planning a show, it's important to do some advance research—several weeks in advance, if possible—and determine how many people you'd ultimately like to attend. If it's 50, and your family and friends total just 25, you'll have to do some publicity legwork.

Ask other local bands to quantify the benefits of certain types of press. Perhaps a short "critic's choice" article in the newspaper's weekend preview magazine can generate about 15 ticket buyers to a small club. Perhaps a calendar listing means five.

Do the math and figure out what you need, and what you realistically can get at this stage. Target those publications that will lead to the attendance you seek.

If the press doesn't bite the first time you contact them, don't be discouraged. For the next gig, maybe the writer or editor will remember your name and be more generous.

Local radio stations, especially the big ones, are publicity machines. You may not have a chance at the nearby, corporate-owned KISS-FM, which plays exclusively well-known pop artists, but there's probably at least one community or college station in your town. Call the program director and offer free listener tickets to the upcoming gig; you may get crucial DJ mentions on the air. Or offer to play in the station's studio—or hallways—the day of your show. Such radio networking can also help you build contacts for future publicity; you never know which student station manager will land a job at the KISS-FM.

Once you've received a taste of publicity, you can use it for many different things. Save the article for your press kit. (We'll get to press kits later in this chapter.) Then mail the new material to more publications, perhaps in different cities or states. Such clippings can also be a huge help later, if you decide to plan a tour.

Buzz and positive publicity (or even negative publicity, if you spin it right) will attract even more fans—and maybe even the attention of important people in the concert industry. Nightclub owners constantly scan publications for hot new ticket-selling acts, as do record-label representatives, record-store managers, and even other media writers and editors.

"Oh yeah, I think I saw that name" is a great thing for people to say about you. This feeling creates demand for your product, which is to say, live concerts, and helps solidify your status as a working band. It's an investment in your future and, at the very least, a way to ensure you'll get more shows in the short term.

Types of Media—and Their Influence

Both of your authors live in Denver, which, with a population of 470,000, is the twenty-sixth-largest city in the United States. It's no New York or Los Angeles. But it has two daily newspapers, *The Denver Post* and the *Rocky Mountain News*, with a combined Sunday circulation of almost 800,000 Coloradoans; several alternative weeklies, including *Westword* and the *Boulder Weekly*, a prominent alternative weekly; nearby regional papers such as Boulder's *Daily Camera*, Longmont's *Times-Call* and Vail's *Trail*; a glossy monthly magazine, *5280*; and several tiny specialty publications such as *Riff*. All of them cover music. You can find outlets in your city, big or small, too.

Alt-Weeklies

Alt-weeklies, short for alternative weeklies, are tabloid-format newspapers that print many local features—heavy on the entertainment, and music in particular. They can be the key publicity source for your band.

Before tackling the daily newspaper, where writers are often obsessed with covering the Céline Dion show at the basketball arena, try the alt-weekly. Publications such as New York City's *The Village Voice* and the *Chicago Reader* often hire critics and writers to scope out the "underground"—which, at least for now, is where you live.

It sounds strange, but if you play up your obscurity, you might be able to talk a writer into attending your concert or reviewing your CD. Just be sure to study the publication before making contact: Classical combos, for example, are less welcome in these pages than hardcore-punk bands or jazz saxophonists.

Behind the Music

Although alt-weeklies are famous for printing stories that mainstream newspapers won't touch, very few are truly "independent" anymore. The national New Times chain, for example, owns *New Times* publications in Dallas, Phoenix, and Miami, plus *Westword* in Denver and many others. Village Voice Media owns New York City's influential *The Village Voice* as well as other cities' alternative weeklies. Nevertheless, the writers and editors remain open-minded to new ideas and local phenomena and may still pay attention to your band.

Local Newspapers

Almost every daily newspaper has some music coverage. If you live in a small town, that may simply mean a nationally syndicated update on Jennifer Lopez's upcoming wedding (or divorce). But many papers have at least one writer who covers the "music beat," and they're often looking to cover a local story. That's you. Pay attention to the long, wide, daily pages of newsprint and all the nooks and crannies that fit music coverage. The tiny-print calendar listings are great for announcing concerts, and if you're creative (playing a charity event for the crumbling local library, say), you might even land on the front page, or in a prominent writer's column.

Although rock critics are usually on the prowl for something new and different, for various reasons they may not be responsive to your pitches. Do a little research to determine who else writes about music—maybe an editor's specialty is bluegrass, or a feature writer branches out into country, or a local freelancer is just looking for good ideas to pitch. Besides music critics, newspaper writers who might cover your band include the following:

◆ **Feature writers.** Although they don't necessarily cover music full-time, feature writers may detour into a profile of a local record label or a trend story on clubs or like-minded bands.

◆ **Calendar compilers.** They don't write articles, but they are crucial for providing information about upcoming shows. Usually, all you have to do is provide these people with the information on your gigs several weeks in advance. Check the listings pages for guidelines, or call the publication.

◆ **Freelancers.** Freelancers are writers who sell stories to multiple publications. Find their contact information on the web (they often have homepages) or in the phone directory. Freelancers thrive on good ideas, especially those that haven't been covered. If your band has an angle—the singer is a dot-com millionaire, for example—a music freelancer will be happy to pitch the idea. Short of an angle, your band just has to be good; many freelancers look to break talented bands nobody has yet heard of.

◆ **Editors.** The writer's boss often has distinct musical tastes of his or her own, and if you pay attention to bylines in the publication you might suss some of them out. If you see the editor's name on numerous blues articles, for example, and your band has a blues edge, consider playing up this aspect of your music in a press release and sending it directly to the editor.

◆ **Business reporters.** Do you run your own record label out of a former eye doctor's office in the middle of downtown? The business section may be interested in publishing a feature.

Backstage Insights

One way to land a feature story in a prominent newspaper or magazine is by coming up with a unique angle about your band. Is your drummer an aspiring NASA astronaut? Maybe you could pitch a profile to the local daily's science reporter—or even the glossy magazine *Popular Science*. Also keep *trend stories* in mind. Are your singer and guitarist husband and wife? Declare yourself part of a trend, including established husband-and-wife rock bands such as Sonic Youth and Yo La Tengo—and, in the press release, make the happy rocking couple "available for interviews."

Other Free Publications

Go to the local record store and check out the publications—the freebies and the ones that cost money. You'll find a wide variety of local publications, some you probably didn't know existed. In larger cities, you might find trade publications, such as *Music Connection* in Los Angeles, which has a large classifieds section. (The Exies, a southern California punk-rock band, found replacement drummer Dennis Wolfe in 2000 by reading the ads. He turned out to be their final ingredient before they signed to a major record label, garnered lots of media coverage, and landed on the pop charts.)

You might also find a variety of 'zines, or homegrown magazines, that have a rich history in rock 'n' roll. They began in the 1960s and 1970s as individual fans' labors of love, usually mimeographed and distributed by hand. Some, like the still-punking *Maximumrocknroll* and the late, great *Trouser Press*, have become widely influential. (Often, these days, you'll find them on the web.) Don't ignore these often vibrant, hard-to-find publications—if they like you, editors might write about your music with thoughtful enthusiasm. Take them seriously.

'Zines are almost by design hard to find. Ask at local record stores; some carry them in racks near the door. Other stores, such as Quimby's on Chicago's north side, display them prominently among the latest issues of *Time* and *Newsweek*. And search the web for "zines"; once you locate the home page, e-mail the editor and ask him or her for a copy.

> **Behind the Music**
>
> Some calendar editors are aspiring music writers or enterprising freelancers, and they may relish the opportunity to "discover" a good unknown band.

> **Behind the Music**
>
> A *blog*, or web log, is one person's online diary. Some of these sites, such as nycbloggers.com, have distinctive regional identities. They may be interested in a band like yours and might have a loyal readership. This is a nontraditional but possibly lucrative publicity opportunity. (To start your own blog, check out blogger.com.)

Calendar Listings

As noted previously, newspaper and alt-weekly, and many magazines, publish tiny-type calendar listings of upcoming events. These are free advertisements for your gig—usually, all you have to do is provide the information several weeks in advance. Check the listings pages for guidelines, or call the publication.

Online

"Online media" is a wide category, ranging from a fan's electronic 'zine to the influential, arts-and-entertainment-heavy online magazine Salon.com. Every little bit of exposure helps. Web publications, obviously, aren't always located in your hometown, so consider sending your press releases via e-mail—with a friendly message suggesting a story. (Almost every website contains an e-mail address, and don't feel shy about sending a well-focused note.) Again, reading the publication is key; Microsoft's Slate.com might run a "trend" story about political music, for example, while Popmatters.com posts lots and lots of CD reviews.

Contacting Writers and Editors

On a basic level, to obtain publicity, all you have to do is call a local publication and ask for it. Often, this is an easy way to wind up in a calendar listing. It's much harder to place a big story or review about your band. To do this, you'll need to sell yourself.

Ultimately, your music is your most effective sales tool. If your band is the second coming of The Rolling Stones, the selling-yourself-to-writers process won't be hard at all. If you have that kind of confidence, and fans are packing your shows and giving great feedback, let the music speak for itself.

No matter how good you are, though, always send material to journalists *early*—three or more weeks in advance of the event. Writers can't stand desperate last-minute sales pitches—and will probably remember you, for the wrong reasons, afterwards. As the old saying goes, lack of preparation on your part is no reason for an emergency on my part.

Behind the Music

David Menconi, pop-music writer for the *Raleigh News & Observer*, makes this style suggestion for bands trying to catch on with print reporters: "My only piece of advice to bands is to avoid hype/overselling. They are far more likely to turn me off than win me over. Humorous self-deprecation is a better tactic. If someone can write in an amusing or engaging way, that's more likely to get my attention than yelling at me about how great they are."

Using Your Press Kit

The press kit is the leading punch of your promotional efforts. (See Appendix F for sample press kit material, including bio and press release.) You'll want to send one to every music writer or editor at every publication you're trying to crack. We recommend calling the publications in advance to double-check the recipient's spellings, job title, and address.

A press kit should contain the following three basic elements:

◆ A **biography** ("bio," for short), which gives a brief history of the band. It should include members' names (spelled correctly!); year and place the band formed; a pithy quote or two from band members; and relevant or unusual trivia such as an explanation of the band's name.

◆ A **press release** or letter announcing the band's upcoming gig, including time, date, and place—and, of course, a contact e-mail address or phone number.

◆ An **8×10 photo,** black and white or color, clearly depicting all band members with their names underneath. Don't forget to print contact information on the photo paper!

Timing is important. Send the package at least three weeks, preferably four or more, in advance of the gig. Sometimes you won't nail down a show date until it's too late for press. If that happens, feel free to send the package, but don't be surprised if you get a cool reception—editors may have already determined what's going in the paper at that point.

Words to Rock By

An **electronic press kit,** or EPK, is a high-tech version of the press kit discussed in Chapter 14. Rather than sending the traditional photo, press release, and bio to a media outlet, you'll provide a website containing a bio, digital photos, MP3s, and your video. These press kits can also be a high-tech, professional way of capturing a record-label scout's attention.

Sometimes, in your press kit, you'll want to include a demo. Later in your career, you might wind up recording a professional demo in a studio as an audition for a record deal. But for now, all you need is to communicate to a writer what you'll sound like at the show. (We discuss creating demos in Chapter 19.)

When Mark drummed in cover bands, they would record demo "medleys," or four or five snippets of songs linked into one block. "We'd do a few seconds of Beach Boys, a few seconds of Beatles, rather than the whole 3 minutes and 52 seconds of 'baby, you can drive my car,'" he says. That way, busy writers can get the idea quickly and your hour-long CD won't have to compete for attention with new releases by Bruce Springsteen and The Red Hot Chili Peppers.

Phone Manners and Following Up

Be persistent—without being a pest. It's a fine line. Wait at least a week after sending the press package. Then call the writer's direct number. Rehearse what you plan to say—your name, the band's name, the name and date of the upcoming concert, and a contact number—in case you get voicemail. If the writer or editor answers, be polite and respectful and try to end the conversation before wearing out your welcome.

Sometimes it's effective to learn a little background about the writer or editor you're calling. If the writer does a regular column, you can learn biographical tidbits just by reading. If he or she skis, for example, you can mention the "great snow pack we've been having." But again, don't go overboard. You don't want to waste the writer's time with rambling anecdotes about your own life.

After reviewing concerts all night, music writers tend to straggle back to their desks around midmorning. Then they need about an hour to drink coffee, talk to their editors, and catch up with phone calls and e-mails. Mondays are particularly stressful. Tuesdays (before deadline crush sets in) and Fridays, around 11 A.M., are often phone-friendly times.

If a writer or editor answers the phone when you call, introduce yourself quickly, and immediately ask, "Do you have time to talk?" If they say yes, be brief. If no—a distinct possibility, no matter how rude it may seem—politely ask for a better time to reach them. The "down period" is good information to have. And a journalist is far more likely to remember you the second time.

> **CAUTION**
>
> **Avoiding Bad Notes**
>
> The easiest way to get on a writer's bad side is by stalking. Leaving a voicemail or e-mail once a week (or, preferably, every other week) is polite and reasonable. Anything beyond that is irritating. Calling several times a day, and hanging up on the voicemail, is risky indeed in the caller ID age.

Finally, e-mail is convenient and cheap. It's also easily deleted. And pitches from bands can look suspiciously like spam. (You know, the annoying form-letter advertisements that clog up your inbox.) We suggest sticking to more personal snail mail, then following up with e-mail only after you've made personal contact with the writer. Even then, keep it short.

Interviews and How to Conduct Them

Congratulations! You've "sold" a writer on your music and the publication plans to print a big preview story. They'll run your band's photograph and include lots of quotes from the musicians.

But wait … quotes? Can't they just use the ones in the press release? Nope. Writers need new, fresh quotes, to distinguish their stories from any other story run in any other publication. Which means it's time for an interview.

Interviews are very, very good for your band. They're also fun—who wouldn't like spending a half-hour talking about himself? But you have to do some preparation, or the interview process can be very, very bad. And no fun at all.

Odds are the writer won't come armed with probing Mike Wallace questions. But a good interviewer probably won't ask for the basic facts, which can be gleaned from your press kit. (So don't expect "Where does the name Slobbering Death Monkeys from Venus come from?")

You'll want to provide colorful, long-but-not-*too*-long answers, which means anticipating the questions. A writer will probably ask about your influences, or other artists who've inspired your music. Other common questions include the following:

♦ Where do you get ideas for your songs?

♦ What are your long-term goals?

♦ How did you meet the other band members?

♦ Why did you choose to play this type of music?

♦ Do you prefer playing live or making music in the studio?

No matter what, always have something to say—politely—even if the question is awkward, poorly worded, or even under-researched. And avoid answering simply "yes" or "no," even if it's in response to yes/no questions.

Finally, as a new artist, your message may be as simple as "we want people to come to our show!" But if your singer is charismatic and sexy and gets a lot of attention on-stage, you also may want to highlight your underrated bassist and drummer. During interviews, you can direct writers to your message in subtle ways. When they ask about how your singer overcame stage fright, you can say, "It was difficult for him, but our rhythm section is so solid and professional that they give the whole band confidence."

The Least You Need to Know

♦ You can be the best band in the world, but until people start to hear your music, you'll inevitably starve. An effective way to spread the word is through the media.

♦ *Publicity* is another word for free advertising. In addition to steering people to gigs, it generates buzz, which expands your base and builds your reputation.

♦ Alt-weeklies and newspapers cover music in entirely different ways. The more you study the nuances, the better equipped you'll be to achieve preview stories and reviews.

♦ Your press kit includes a short bio, a photo, and a press release. Send them far in advance to writers and editors, then follow up by phone or e-mail when you're pretty sure they're not on deadline.

♦ Be prepared during interviews. Anticipate the questions—"what are your influences?" for example—in advance.

Chapter 15

Handbills and Other Guerrilla Techniques

In This Chapter

- ◆ Using handbills, posters, and fliers to spread the word cheaply
- ◆ Getting the tools you'll need
- ◆ Taking advantage of another concert's success

Professional advertising and stories in the local paper are well and good, but rock fans have been trained over the past 40 years to pay attention to lampposts, telephone poles, kiosks, and coffeeshop bulletin boards for their concert information. With posters, handbills, and fliers, you can publicize a show inexpensively—and use some artistry and imagination in the process.

From the swirling, Day-Glo, psychedelic posters announcing San Francisco bands in the 1960s and the more ominous, choppy, and defiant imagery of late-1970s punk to today's raves and festivals, rock posters have become an art form. But for your purposes, they're an immediate way of reaching your audience (or potential audience), containing simple messages (time, date, location, contact number, and website address) and imagery you design. Your image can be postcard-size, perfect for distribution at clubs and under windshield wipers; letter-size, for stapling onto bulletin boards and kiosks; or poster-size, for papering at the place you're playing or a prominent wall in your city. "Postering" can be a credible way of circumventing other media, spreading the word to regions and audiences newspapers don't traditionally reach.

Making the Perfect Flier

A *flier* is usually an 8.5-by-11-inch piece of paper containing your band's name, photo, website address, and information about an upcoming gig or CD release. Like everything else involving your band, you'll want it to fit into your musical scheme and reinforce your image. A genteel Irish folk band, for example, probably shouldn't borrow from Iron Maiden's classic googly-eyed-skeleton artwork.

At the very least, you can simply print the name and contact information in block letters and laser-print a solid page. For this, all you need is a word processor and printer—if you don't have one, local copy shops often offer printing resources, and you can usually rent a computer there, too. More sophisticated graphic artists use software such as QuarkXPress, Adobe Illustrator, and Photoshop to lay out their designs. You can also search for an interesting, offbeat image on the Internet and import it into your graphics program—just make sure it's in the public domain. Otherwise you'll need permission to do so. Learning to do this stuff yourself can be fun, and a way for the band to bond collectively.

If somebody in the band has graphic arts or computer skills, consider delegating the poster duties to him or her. Or if you have some spare cash after a gig, contact a local artist for consultation. Sometimes people at the local copy shop will help.

Getting the Most out of Your Local Copy Shop

Unless you own a copy machine that prints in bulk, you'll probably spend a lot of time in the 7¢-per-page copy shop. It sounds easy enough, but you'll have to make many important decisions: What color paper should you use? (Color is almost always more expensive than black and white.) What type of stock? (Thickest is most pricey.) What colors reproduce the best? How can you lay out the artwork in the straightest, most professional way?

Copy-shop employees will (usually) be glad to help answer these questions. But if not, we'll note that white is the most professional color if you're snail-mailing fliers or sending out small handbills as postcards. An obnoxiously bright color like Day-Glo

pink or orange is effective if you're posting a flier on a bulletin board and want to
distinguish your concert from the garage
sales.

If there's a good chance your poster will
hang on a kiosk or bulletin board for weeks
or months at a time, go with heavy paper stock.
Small handbills, which you might hand out to
fans after concerts, should be thin and cheap,
because they're likely to be quickly thrown away.

Backstage Insights

Print several posters with a rec-
tangular area of blank, white
space at the bottom. Every
time you have a new gig,
CD release, or other event,
simply write the new information
in the box.

You can also spread the word using business cards. If you order them from a professional printing company, cards will cost in the range of $9.99 for 250, or you can get
a bulk rate of roughly $29.99 for 1,000. You might be able to shrink your handbill
design and print it up in a business-card format. Or you might opt for something
more simple—just the band name, one phone number, one e-mail address, and perhaps your type of music. It's just as professional and less expensive, of course, to print
off sheets of business cards via your own laser printer.

Stickers are also effective in the rock world. You won't have to worry about using tape
and staples, and the designs and logos are yet another way to express your originality.
They are, however, very difficult to scrape off—and as we note in the upcoming
"Observing Local Laws" section, they might rack you up a hefty fine.

Designs and Slogans That Work

A good slogan is an indispensable tool in rock music. The Sex Pistols, The Clash,
and other famous punks were notorious for their slogans, affixing fliers all over
London reading, "White Riot!" and "Hate and War." One of the Pistols' revolutionary, military-lampooning gems was "Be a man. Be someone. Kill someone. Be a man.
Kill yourself."

The alternative-rock trio Primus got a lot of mileage out of the sarcastically self-
deprecating chant "Primus sucks!" The Fluid, a great Denver punk band, arranged its
name inside a familiar car-company logo and, on the back, printed, "Volume Is Job
One." (Volume, volume … get it?) The Boulder jam-rock band Leftover Salmon has
earned quite a lot of mileage with its musical self-description "polyethnic Cajun slamgrass." Printed in big letters on posters and fliers—so they're readable from some distance away—these slogans can be incredibly effective.

Note: Be careful not to infringe on a copyrighted logo or slogan. "Soup is good food" might seem hilarious on a rock-band T-shirt, but the Campbell Soup Co., which owns the slogan, won't find it so amusing. Then again, if your band is still relatively unknown, it's unlikely a major corporation will notice this kind of thing.

A slogan isn't a requirement, of course. You can make a perfectly fine poster with just the band's name, time and location of gig, and website address. But if you're stapling a poster to a telephone pole, construction site, or other widely papered location, you'll want to stand out.

Bulletin Boards

In Chapter 2, we brought up bulletin boards—in coffeeshops, record stores, bookstores, and campus activity centers—as an excellent networking device for meeting potential new band members. But the boards are excellent forums for lots of other band-related activities, too. At the very least, you can post your upcoming-gig flier or handbill.

Just be respectful of the bulletin-board owner (and other users). Don't plaster your material blithely over the flier begging for the whereabouts of a lost 15-year-old Labrador Retriever. And while you may be tempted to preempt a rival band's flier in the same location, try to resist. This kind of activity can start a long-term war that will ultimately upset the bulletin-board owner. Be courteous. Look for an open spot and don't jam in so many staples or string up so much tape that it's impossible to remove later.

Also, ask for permission first, even if it seems obvious that everybody gets to post whatever they want. In a location without a bulletin board, use one small, not-too-sticky piece of tape so as to not leave gunk on the window or wall.

Working the School

Bands in college towns face heavier competition than bands in rural or out-of-the-way areas. But they're also blessed with far more promotional opportunities, from (usually) receptive campus radio stations to prominent banner-placing opportunities.

Whether or not you're a student, go on a few exploratory missions around campus. Where are the bulletin boards? What publications exist with prominent classified ads? Is it a grassroots "tradition" that people chalk or spray-paint the sidewalks in certain areas? At the University of Michigan in Ann Arbor, for example, there's a huge rock at a major intersection that students have spent the last several decades spray-painting. One week, it's filled with fraternity-rush graffiti; the next, "Go Blue," in honor of an upcoming football game. Why can't your name—and, perhaps, slogan—appear there on certain occasions?

Also, study the other band fliers that seem effective on campus. Were they laser-printed? Designed by hand? What works and what doesn't? What information appears most prominently? How do the artistic designs of posters, fliers, and hand-bills differ? Learn from these artistic and informational decisions and copy the best ideas.

Finally, your campus probably has some kind of graphic-design or general art depart-ment. A student looking to stuff his or her portfolio may be willing to design a flier or at least consult on one for little or no fee. If this person is imaginative and reliable, you could wind up employing him or her again later for CD covers and videos.

Posters

Some bands simply design a small handbill and, when it comes time to hang up a poster, enlarge it several times. This works, but on super-size posters you may want to take advantage of the extra space and add more art and perhaps written information.

When using a poster as a canvas, you have more space for imagination and creativity. Consider turning the poster into a mini-billboard—and for inspiration, check out cor-porate highway billboards to see what works and what doesn't. (*Hint:* Short, terse, and funny or colorful messages are incredibly effective for pedestrians rushing past the posters. The National Dairy Council's "Got Milk?" campaign managed to turn stodgy milk into a hip, desirable product.)

No matter what else you decide to put on your poster, the following information is essential, but feel free to arrange it in an unusual way: band name or logo; time, date, and location of gig, CD-release party, or other event; contact information; band photo; and website address.

Observing Local Laws

In some parts of certain cities, tacking your posters on lampposts or the wooden areas surrounding construction sites is an even more effective way of spreading the word than local newspapers. In many ethnic neighborhoods where English is a second lan-guage, for example, it's more likely people will watch the phone poles than English-language local newspapers for upcoming events. In urban areas where people are far more likely to ride the bus than commute on a highway, lamppost-type messages can be effective. But in some areas, litter-law enforcement may be so intense that you never see posters at all.

> **Words to Rock By**
>
> **Guerrilla marketing** refers to untraditional means of gaining exposure for a business. Whereas a traditional music marketer buys advertising on a local radio station, a guerrilla marketer might set up his own soapbox in the middle of a crowded street and loudly act out the reasons why his product is worth buying. This approach can be valuable for developing rock bands.

Posting a concert announcement on a lamppost isn't the ultimate act of rock 'n' roll rebellion, of course, but it's a small form of *guerrilla marketing*. Although the term has become part of corporate strategy over the past 20 years—meaning, loosely, "spreading your message with your own hard work rather than spending tons of money"—it's still effective for grassroots bands. Depending how extreme you want to get, guerrilla marketing can involve everything from spray-painting graffiti at a subway stop to shouting the band's name via bullhorn on a crowded street.

Before indulging in guerrilla marketing, it's best to have a working knowledge of local laws. In some cities, including New York and Los Angeles, stickering and postering private property is illegal; if you do it, you could receive a fine or even jail time. (The penalties tend to be even stricter for more permanent street displays such as graffiti.) Rock marketing has a long history of rebelling against these laws with defiantly underground poster and handbill displays. However, in no way do we condone illegal behavior.

Leafleting

Unattached handbills, posters, and fliers can be used as leaflets. Some merchants will let you drop off a stack of them at the front counter, near the cash register, or at the front door, near the alt-weeklies and classified-ad rags. But as this can lead to an unruly mess, many merchants prefer people to post fliers to central bulletin boards. (If a merchant is generous about leaving stacks of fliers around, be sure to keep the area neat and return frequently for cleanup.)

A more effective way of dispersing leaflets involves standing in the street outside a club or theatre. When a band finishes playing, approach everybody in sight to hand out fliers. This is especially effective if you're playing the same venue later—and if you are, you'll win points with the owners if you stick around to clean up the fliers fans inevitably toss on the ground. Also, it helps to get permission from the club booker in advance.

When should you hand out the fliers? Definitely as fans are leaving the concert. If you hand out leaflets on their way in, fans will invariably drop them in the first garbage can they see and focus on more important tasks such as buying beer or staking out a seat. On the way out, however, fans are idle, walking leisurely to their cars, and talking about the show they just saw. They'll be more receptive at that time, for sure.

Backstage Insights _____

When deciding where to hand out leaflets, find a like-minded band's gig and park yourself there after the show. If you play funk and rock, for example, hit The Red Hot Chili Peppers show at the local basketball arena. The risk is that fans will perceive you as a cheaper version of the band they just saw; the potential reward is that they love this type of music so much they'll want to hear more.

Don't be insulted if your fliers wind up on the ground. If you hand out 200, and 190 people drop them and 10 decide to attend your show, that's a half-hour (or so) well spent. But again, clean up after yourself so the club will let you hang around with the handbills on a future date.

You can also stick handbills under windshield wipers, although many fans find this a nuisance. Annoying advertising can be effective—take television commercials and pop-up ads on websites, for example—just be aware you risk alienating potential fans.

When handing out fliers, you don't have to say anything, of course, but consider these (somewhat tongue-in-cheek) suggestions:

- "Hey, come to the show."
- "Please excuse me, I'm spamming you in person."
- "We're way better than the knuckleheads you just saw."
- "If you drop this flier on the ground, you break your mother's back."
- "This will be the best concert you've ever seen in your life."
- "Guess who's opening for us? The Rolling Stones!"
- "Cheaper than a movie."

Street Teams

Street teams, or platoons of volunteer fans dispatched to spread the word about a particular band via posters and fliers, caught on as a corporate marketing device in the late 1990s. Artists such as Chicago metal band Disturbed and R&B singer Willa Ford became popular, in part, because their respective record labels gave fans free promotional stuff (like cassette tapes and stickers) to spread around schools, skate parks, and, yes, the streets.

Since then, this approach has become big business. Mega-companies from Sprite to MTV have tried it with much success. "The way that street teams are being used in hip-hop adds a whole new element to the promotions game because the street is an open market," Dan Seliger, head of marketing for the hip-hop label Rawkus Records. "When you are promoting to the streets, you don't have to worry about some out-of-touch [music director] or promotions director making a judgment on your music. You have the real critics—the fans—choosing for themselves. It's the best place to go if you want to see where you stand on a rap record."

Street teams are especially effective because the fan deputized to disperse the promotional materials gets an added "cool boost" among his or her friends. In addition to spreading the word to many different people, this fan will almost certainly became loyal to the artist for a long period of time.

The concept has become so ingrained in the music industry that entire companies, including Bandbitch, Cali Kings, and Metro Marketing, have begun to specialize purely in street-team marketing. Check out some of their websites, including Bandbitch's streetteam.net, to learn how major bands such as KISS, Powerman 5000, and Queensrÿche use the street-team concept. Street teams are usually assembled via online bulletin boards, website announcements, and e-mail lists.

What does the street-team concept mean for your band? At this point, unless you have corporate backing to assemble such teams and send out large quantities of promotional material, probably not a lot. But you can learn from corporate success, and assemble a smaller, more local version of a street team on your own. The kids down the block who have nothing to do over the summer might be willing to help spread the word if there's something in it for them (read: free T-shirts or tickets).

The Least You Need to Know

- Posters, fliers, handbills, and leaflets are an effective and cheap way of spreading the word about your band. You can print them up quickly and easily via computer laser printer, but try to be as imaginative as possible.

- Every variation on your band's poster should contain a few basic pieces of information: band name or logo; time, date, and location of upcoming gig or other event; contact information; and website address.

- Use local coffeeshop and record-store bulletin boards, but clean up after yourselves. And check college campuses for quirky places to spread your message.

- Slogans can be an effective way to supplement your band name and photo in a poster, flier, or handbill.

Chapter 16

Using the Internet

In This Chapter

- ◆ Registering a URL and setting up a web page
- ◆ Stuff to put on your band's website
- ◆ Should you post MP3s? And if so, how?
- ◆ Marketing the band online
- ◆ Generating hits through links and promotions

In addition to revolutionizing everything else in the world, the Internet has vastly improved the way bands network with their fans. The Internet—specifically, bands' websites—has replaced the old-fashioned fan club.

Some bands, such as Pearl Jam, still run fan clubs the old-fashioned way—but they do everything through their websites. Metallica, to name one prominent example, runs a bulletin board so fans around the world can talk to each other. Weezer, Zwan, Wilco, and others post live or rare music files directly onto their sites. At a minimum, a band can provide basic information and spread the word about upcoming gigs or CD releases. Learning to do this is a huge marketing and promotional leap forward.

Creating a Homepage

Check out some existing homepages. Metallica.com: logos everywhere, big news headlines, leering photos of the band. Eminem.com: animated color photos of the rapper posing with a microphone, as news "tickers" float by at the top. Phish.com: pictures of the band enclosed in a graphic "honeycomb," with news items and merchandise links popping up as you move the cursor around the page.

These exact descriptions may not be up to date by the time you read this, but you get the point. Like a CD cover or a promotional photo, a homepage should be an extension of the band's personality. Beyond that, it should provide solid, straightforward information. And maybe it should try to sell stuff—without coming across like an annoying salesperson.

Registering Your URL

But let's back up. First you have to find a *domain name*, or World Wide Web address. A URL, or Uniform Resource Locator, is the high-tech way of saying metallica.com, phish.com, or any other name you type into a browser to call up a page. URLs usually end in an extension such as ".com," but many use ".net," ".org" and ".edu" for various reasons not worth going into here.

The first thing to do is determine whether anybody else has your name. (The easiest way is to use your browser, probably Netscape or Internet Explorer, to see if anything's posted to that site.) Go to networksolutions.com, the website for the Internet's most popular registrar, and plug your band's name, followed by ".com" into the box. If nothing pops up, you're free to register your name. We'll get to that in a minute.

If somebody else owns "your" URL, it's time for a few decisions. Maybe your band is called Slate—in that case, you're out of luck, because Slate.com has existed for years as a Microsoft online magazine. If that happens, and if your band isn't attached to its name (see Chapter 3 for more advice on finding a band name), consider changing the name to something else.

If the site in question is more obscure, e-mail the owner to see if he or she will relinquish the domain. (If the e-mail address isn't on the site, you can often find it through the "Whois" link at the top of networksolutions.com.) In rare cases, people will agree to do this for free. More likely, they'll ask for money or another favor. (Free band CDs?) Still others will be completely unreceptive.

Yes, you can attempt to displace people from their domains by declaring a copyright infringement in court. But this process is complicated, costly, and probably not the way you'd like to spend your time and resources. Also, if you're a new band, odds are that another entity beat you to the copyright, so you're bound to lose the case. Fortunately, theslate.com is almost certainly available. Or the-slate.com. Or slate.org. Or slate-the-band.com. A simple URL coinciding with your name can be a valuable thing, but with a little "branding" you can alert fans to the alternative.

Once you settle on a name, go back to networksolutions.com—or any other Internet registrar, from domainmonkeys.com to catalog.com—and follow the site's instructions. Prices vary, but it usually will cost about $75 a year to register and maintain your domain. Depending on how you ultimately use your website, this is pretty much a bargain.

Do It Yourself

The great thing about the Internet is, like rock 'n' roll, anybody can use it. Sure, you can hire a fancy web designer, but learning HTML code, the fundamental language of the World Wide Web, is easier than you'd expect. People who are terrified of computers in general may want to avoid this duty, but there's bound to be someone in the band, or a friend or family member, willing to delve into the project.

Once you've registered a domain name, you need to follow three basic steps to building a homepage:

1. **Find a web server.** You'll need an Internet service provider to provide space on the World Wide Web for "hosting" your page. Many companies, like Geocities, Earthlink, AOL, and Angelfire, offer this service, usually for about $8 or $9 per month plus a small setup fee. To avoid these costs, find a friend or family member who has a server. Prominent service providers often include web hosting as part of the regular Internet subscription fee.

2. **Learn the language.** Server sites such as Geocities (geocities.yahoo.com) provide easy-to-read, not-overly techie steps for posting basic content on your site. *HTML* is pretty simple, although it looks complicated, with lots of strange less-than and greater-than symbols; you type it in via Microsoft Word or another word processor. To learn from or copy what others have done, using Netscape or Internet Explorer, go to a web page you like and

Words to Rock By

HTML, or hypertext markup language, uses text commands to tell web browsers like Netscape or Internet Explorer how to display a file online. A typical HTML layout might look like this:

```
<HTML>

<HEAD>

<TITLE>The Fabulous Dogs
Official Homepage</TITLE>

</HEAD>
```

under "View" in the toolbar at the top of the page choose "Source" or "Page source"; this shows you the codes used to construct the page.

3. **Post content on your web page.** For this step, you'll need FTP, or file transfer protocol, software. On the fancy side, Microsoft's Front Page will run $160 to $200, and HomeSite costs about $100. But you don't need these all-purpose, user-friendly programs if you're willing to put in a little technological legwork on your own. On a more basic level, Cute FTP (about $40) simply transfers the Word file you've created onto your site.

These steps are usually enough to give you the basics. Eventually you might want to expand to fancy graphics and animation. To do that, you'll need more expensive software, like Adobe GoLive or Macromedia Dreamweaver.

Hire a Webmaster

Far faster and easier than learning HTML on your own, of course, is finding somebody who already knows how to do it. Even better, find a fan who has time and the knowledge. Consider this bluestraveler.com biography of Gina-Z, a diehard Blues Traveler fan who developed into the rock band's "mom," fan-club president, and eventually, webmaster:

> She was a Deadhead who got stranded in NYC and happened into the Nightingales bar one night. She instantly fell in love with the band she heard and started bringing her friends down … She had no title other than "band mom." She washed and folded laundry, saw to it that the band was eating as well as they could and kept the places as clean as four completely disgusting slobs would allow …

> As success created new jobs, Gina continued her greatest talent which was understanding and acting as liaison for the ever-growing fan base. When the Blues Traveler mailing list was established she took that role in hand.

Every band can use a tech-savvy Gina-Z.

What to Include?

The short answer is, "Whatever's in your press kit" (see Chapter 14). Post your clearest and most up-to-date group photos, with band members' names and corresponding instruments underneath. Post your bio. And create a "news" page containing press releases about upcoming gigs, CD releases, and other band developments. An up-to-date tour itinerary, with contact information and directions to the club, can never hurt.

How to Buy Your CD

The easiest way to sell CDs over the Internet is by posting a link to the corresponding page on Amazon.com or CDBaby.com. (Of course, first you have to contact those companies and make the sales arrangements; instructions are available on both websites.) You can also provide a mailing address (preferably a PO Box, if you don't want Internet creeps knocking on your door) and send CDs via snail mail.

Or you can set up a "store" on your web page. Usually your Internet service provider will be happy to take care of the details—sending you the HTML code and the graphical "buy me" buttons. They'll also help you accept credit cards, as long as you have a business account at a bank. The money from buyers' credit cards will get deposited directly to your account.

Also consider posting a discography, including any CD or tape releases you've offered to the public, even if they're demos, singles, or EPs. Lyrics to songs are always handy. And stamp your band's logo on every page. A web page is a lot like an ad.

> **CAUTION**
>
> **Avoiding Bad Notes**
>
> Radiohead, the super-arty British rockers, can get away with web page index categories such as "escape" (links), "waiting room" (message board), and "spin with a grin" (press resources). You can't. Title the news page "NEWS" and the band-bio page "BIO." At this stage, if people arrive at your web page, they want basic information. Make it easy for them.

Journal Entries

In some popular bands, certain members periodically post their own diary entries. This is an excellent way to create your own "news," and sometimes, as when Limp Bizkit singer Fred Durst described his alleged relationship with singer Britney Spears, may generate publicity through print or television media outlets.

For example, when The Who's bassist, John Entwistle, died, guitarist Pete Townshend was able to communicate to large numbers of fans and media by posting tributes and updates on his website. And New York City techno star Moby posts a daily "Moby Journal" at moby.com with scintillating tidbits such as: "All of this conflict about the state flag in georgia has made me realize that i don't even know what the new york state flag looks like. is it a dancing pigeon? a stripper standing by niagra falls? a pretzel?"

Keep in mind that the Internet is supposed to be interactive. The more you communicate, and demonstrate there's no snobbishness between artist and fan, the more people will relate to you.

Bulletin Boards

Many bands have their own online bulletin boards, which allow fans to post and read each other's public e-mails. The "bulletin board" concept is almost as old as the Internet—check out the Usenet newsgroups, indexed on the search engine groups. google.com, for conversational "threads" on an infinite number of subjects.

To run your own bulletin board, contact a third-party company such as UBB.threads (infopop.com) or phpBB (phpbb.com) to set up the software and servers. (Doing it yourself can be a little complicated.) Some of these services are expensive, however—UBB charges $229 a year, plus more for technical support, upgrades, and consulting fees. It's far cheaper and easier to sign up for Yahoo! Groups or (for free) create your own Usenet newsgroup at groups.google.com.

Once you've established a band-focused bulletin board, it's fun to jump into the fray and converse with the people who come to your shows. (At first, this may just be a novelty for a handful of people, but you'll be surprised at how fast it grows the more popular you become established and maybe even release a CD or two.)

Keep in mind bulletin boards can be addictive—and especially so when the subject is *you*. Consider "lurking" without posting responses, or using a pseudonym. Of course, early in your band's career, the discussions will probably take the tone of "what time does the show start, again?"

Words to Rock By

MP3 is short for MPEG Audio Layer 3. It's an audio-compression technology many people use to distribute digital songs over the Internet. Developed in 1991 by the Fraunhofer Institute in Germany, MP3s approximate CD-quality sound and are easily played with software on your computer (or various portable players).

MP3s

MP3 is an abbreviation for an invisible computer file, yet some people believe it will destroy the music industry as we know it. In short, MP3s are digital music files you can trade, through e-mail, websites, or software programs such as Napster (now defunct), Kazaa, and Morpheus.

The music industry—specifically, the "Big Five" record labels, including Sony and Warner Bros.—has been fighting MP3s since they first became popular in the late 1990s. It's easy to "rip," or convert, a CD into an MP3 using cheap software such as musicmatch.com. And it's easy to "burn," or copy, MP3s to cheap recordable CDs known as CD-Rs. And because it's so easy, artists, songwriters, and record labels worry people will trade these songs online for free rather than paying for them in music stores. Thus, the debate.

The labels consider this type of "file-sharing" to be piracy—especially when millions of people use software like Napster to exchange copyrighted songs for free. And the Recording Industry Association of America has taken aggressive steps to stamp it out. The organization successfully sued Napster, forcing it out of business. It also sued four college students for $98 billion, in early 2003, after they had run elaborate file-sharing networks.

Someday, the music industry will probably find a way to sell MP3s online without worrying about piracy. (As of this writing, Apple Computer had just begun collaborating with the big record labels to sell songs online for 99¢ a pop.) Until then, the debate continues.

At this stage in your band's career, you likely won't have to worry about the piracy implications of posting your music online. But it's something to be aware of—if you record a version of Elvis Presley's "Jailhouse Rock" and post it on fabulousdogs.com, this could conceivably infringe the copyrights of songwriters Jerry Leiber and Mike Stoller. You don't want to receive threatening letters from faraway lawyers, so be careful about this.

Posting original songs, if they don't belong to any recording or publishing company, shouldn't give you any legal trouble. Have fun with the process—post your special Christmas song (recorded at the last gig) in December and your spooky song just before Halloween. This is the place to stick rare or weird tracks you don't want to release on a professionally made CD.

Once you've actually produced the music, to create original MP3 files and post them to a website, follow these rough steps (which vary according to your software and hardware):

1. Record a song as you usually would onto a compact disc.

2. Using a rewritable computer CD drive, *rip* the song onto your hard drive with software such as MusicMatch. (Some versions of the software are available for free at musicmatch.com; instructions are on the website.)

3. Contact the people who run your server—sites like Geocities (geocities.yahoo.com) include instructions—about uploading an MP3 to a web page. You'll need a server that supports FTP (file transfer protocol) and login information from your server administrator.

4. Use HTML code to link to your files. A music file on your computer labeled "mysong.mp3" will be accessed via the web page code <a href="mysong.mp3">Download mysong here</a>.

5. For more information on this process, check out *The Complete Idiot's Guide to MP3: Music on the Internet.*

> **Backstage Insights** _____
>
> Ripping and burning are slang expressions for transferring songs between compact discs and your computer hard drive. To rip, put the original CD in your computer's CD-RW drive and use software such as MusicMatch JukeBox Pro (musicmatch.com) to copy a song onto the computer. To burn, put a blank CD in the drive and use MusicMatch to copy it onto the CD.
>
> There are plenty of other available ripping-and-burning applications. Apple Macintosh owners have it especially easy, as they can use the built-in iTunes system without having to worry about downloading extra software.

Beware of technology, though. Once your song is on the Internet, it can potentially travel endlessly all over the world. Usually this won't matter; only your family, friends, and fans will want the music. But if your song is titled "Saddam Hussein Is My Favorite Friend," it may creep onto the media's radar and give you the wrong kind of publicity—not everybody shares your sense of humor.

Streaming Audio and Video

Another option that's far less controversial than an MP3 is *streaming audio*. This concept is similar to a radio station. If people listen to streaming audio on your web page, it's a one-time thing. They can't download it and therefore can't "own" the music or easily trade it to anybody else.

But creating audio streams and posting them to your website is a fairly involved process. To do so, you need special software such as Radio Broadcaster 2.0 or DMP 2002 Radio Automation 2.0. Many of these applications are available, for free, at download.com. Keep in mind, though, even streaming-audio "Net radio stations" have been under fire for copyright-infringement reasons. You'll be safe if you post your own original compositions, as long as no publishing company or record label owns them.

Finally, to generate streaming video from a digital camcorder, connect your video hardware to your computer using an interface cable. (As of this writing, Apple's

FireWire is the industry standard.) Then, using software like iMovie, you can call up a video file on the screen with the Import function, then export it to a QuickTime streaming-video file. Once there, you can use the video file in all sorts of ways, including posting it to your web page.

To post streaming audio or video to your web page, use the instructions in the previous MP3 section. For more information, contact your server administrator, a how-to website such as ZDNet.com, or a tech-specialized reference guide.

Words to Rock By

Links are a great way to connect your web page to other popular websites. It's fun to link to pages you like, and exchanging links with other sites is a great free tool for marketing and networking. Do this often: Link to musical equipment manufacturers, other bands, clubs you've played, and especially places where people can buy your CD.

Getting Hits

"Hits," or the number of people who surf to your page on the web, are always desirable. You want lots of fans to buy your CDs, T-shirts, and concert tickets, and the more people who reach your homepage, the better. To get a lot of hits, you need to make a lot of *links*.

Driving Traffic

You're not the first webmaster to worry about hit counts. Marketers have developed some savvy ideas for generating sky-high hit numbers. Here are hit-boosting suggestions from Peter Geisheker, who designs Mark's web page bandguru.com:

- Have an electronic newsletter to which fans can subscribe.

- Submit your website to search engines and search directories. Check out searchenginewatch.com for more information.

- Consider using pay-per-click search engines like Google's AdWords, Findwhat.com, and Overture.com to purchase keywords and direct visitors to your site. This form of marketing will cost you money but it works wonderfully.

- Tell everybody about your website. When giving concerts, tell people to go to your website to download new songs and learn more about the band. When promoting your band with posters and fliers, make sure to list your website address.

- Make sure your CDs have your website address listed on them.

- Have contests on your website to win free T-shirts, concert tickets, your CDs, and so on.

We would add: Seek out band-listing sites that will post your web page as part of a larger database. Allmusic.com, an online rock encyclopedia, is constantly being updated, and even if you have no music to review it might grant you a separate entry if you ask nicely. Many city-focused arts and entertainment pages, such as Chicago's Metromix.com, are hungry for new bands to chronicle. And if you're touring the country, e-mail the concert-industry trade publication pollstar.com about adding your upcoming dates.

Elements of an Effective Web Page

For this section, we yield the floor, one last time, to bandguru.com webmaster Peter Geisheker:

- Make your website easy to navigate. You want it to be easy for your website visitors to find their way around your site.

- Keep fresh content on your site. A site should have new content added a minimum of once per month to give your site visitors a reason to come back.

- Use HTML instead of Flash (a fancy, graphics-oriented web language) because search engines can't index Flash pages. Also, Flash is only cool the first time a person goes to your website. After that it's annoying.

There are situations where you'll want to beef up the look of your page with color, graphics, and animation. Kids tend to love this stuff, which is why the first thing you see on Nickelodeon's website nick.com (as of this writing) is a cartoon of a talking frog floating by on a lily pad. If you're a children's musician who plays a lot of parties, it can't hurt to have some entertainment for parents and kids looking to hire you (or buy your CD).

Otherwise, we recommend avoiding graphics and animation almost entirely. Post your band's logo, and that's it. Some fans will have broadband, or high-speed Internet access, and will be able to view the page quickly and easily. But many have archaic, poky dialup modem connections and will become frustrated upon pulling up your state-of-the-art page. The last thing you want to do is push away these fans.

E-Mail Spam—Does It Work?

We all check our messages regularly and, of the 146 we receive on any given morning, 143 of them are spam. Most spam, or bulk e-mail, is of the "enlarge your penis size!" or "refinance your mortgage!" variety. But to many record-label owners, writers, and radio stations, "come see my band!" qualifies, with equally annoying connotations.

E-mail networking is fine. As web guru Peter Geisheker suggested a few pages back, sending out an e-newsletter on a monthly basis is perfectly legitimate—especially if the news is relevant and well-written. But don't send updates every few minutes; nobody aside from your family and a few friends wants to read about how your guitarist overcame a broken string during last weekend's gig.

Besides, if people crave information about you, such as tour dates or members' names, they can surf to your homepage.

Using standard e-mail programs Eudora and Microsoft Outlook, or spreadsheets such as Microsoft Excel, maintain an electronic list of people who sign up at your gigs. (More on this in Chapter 13.) And every time somebody sends an e-mail to your website address, add their name to the list. Keep in touch with these people regularly—but as we've discussed, not too regularly. Again, be persistent without being a pest. It's a fine line, and you'll learn to walk it.

The Least You Need to Know

- Your band's web page is like a high-tech advertisement that can reach millions of people around the world. Post clear, easy-to-access information on it.

- To register a domain name (fabulousdogs.com, for example), use Network Solutions or another online registry.

- Boosting your hit counts can help bring fans to shows and encourage them to buy CDs. Online marketing "tricks," like paying for Google's Adwords.com, can help this process considerably.

- E-mail is an excellent tool for getting the word out, but don't be tempted to go in the spam direction. People hate spam, and your message will be ignored or taken as a hostile act.

- MP3s, streaming audio, journal entries, and bulletin boards are all excellent online bonuses for fans.

- Avoid graphics and fancy animation unless you have a specific reason for using them. More often than not, they'll just put off web-surfing fans who have slow dialup modem connections.

Paying for Publicity

In This Chapter

- What a well-connected publicist can do for you
- Using magazine and newspaper advertising to boost your exposure
- Considering billboards, community radio, and other marketing gimmicks
- The art of self-publicity

After you've figured out how to place stories in the media (see Chapter 14), flooded your city with fliers and posters (see Chapter 15), and even spread the word on the Internet (see Chapter 16), you may be ready for the next level of exposure. Which means it's time to hire a publicist. Although many of these professionals work for record labels or other artists, they're often independent contractors with computer databases or Rolodexes full of media contacts. They'll contact the media on your behalf in an attempt to place free, high-profile feature stories and reviews.

Because there are as many different types of publicists as there are bands and styles, it's essential to find one who understands your music and knows the appropriate terrain. How do you find—and afford—such a person? Read on.

Should You Hire a Publicist?

Until your band reaches a certain popularity level, you'll probably be able to handle the publicity duties yourself. Perhaps a band member is a "people person" who enjoys schmoozing with the media, or perhaps a friend or relative likes the band so much he or she is willing to help for free. See Chapter 14 for more information on how to contact writers and place prominent, free stories in publications.

What's a Publicist, Anyway?

We previously defined publicity as, essentially, free media coverage. A publicist's job is to try to get it. At the most basic level, publicists write up press releases, prepare press kits and send them, either via e-mail or snail mail, to newspaper reporters, alt-weekly critics, magazine editors, radio programmers, and even television producers around the country. After that they follow up by phone and attempt to connect with the media person personally. A good publicist will land strong feature stories or reviews in several publications.

Publicists operate on many levels in the music business. At the top you'll find people like Liz Rosenberg, who represents Madonna and is instrumental in helping the pop superstar create her *image*. With every album, Madonna changes her look and style and even the way she talks—sometimes she's a sex goddess, other times she's an elegant movie star. Either way, Rosenberg helps communicate Madonna's *message* to the press so the big feature stories in magazines and newspapers and on television reflect the Material Girl's latest persona.

A publicist can act as a *spokesperson* for a musician or entertainment celebrity. For example, British media speculated in early 2003 that Madonna was pregnant with her third child. Madonna wouldn't dignify the report with a personal interview, so Rosenberg spoke on her behalf. "It's not true, it's not accurate. She dyed her hair brown instead of blonde—that does not confirm somebody's pregnant," she told BBC News. "And she's been wearing baggy clothes for

> **Words to Rock By**
>
> In many other businesses, publicists are called public relations managers or communications directors. But in the music industry, where the idea is to expose artists in as much media as possible to sell records and concert tickets, publicist is the standard term. They all do similar work.

> **Behind the Music**
>
> An example of a recent successful publicity campaign is that of the big-time rock band U2, which for 1997's *Pop* CD and tour convinced the media it was entering a hip techno-music phase. In the end, despite the hype, *Pop* sounded like most other U2 albums.

20 years, so what else is new?" A publicist can act as an effective barrier between media and celebrity.

Often publicists create entire campaigns when a superstar artist is about to release new music or embark on an international tour. These usually begin with press conferences—or other events in which the artist answers reporters' questions—and continue with press kits and news releases targeted to various key publications.

High-powered publicists also often engage in *damage control*. When rap star Sean "P. Diddy" Combs was arrested, whenever pop stars like Britney Spears and Justin Timberlake break off their romance, or whenever Michael Jackson faces bankruptcy, publicists step in to try to convert negative media coverage into positive. (Or at least reduce the negative coverage to a manageable level.) This is similar to a White House communications director clarifying the president's positions and actions and keeping his daily newspaper photos as warm, cuddly, and patriotic as possible.

On a slightly lower star level, publicists simply try to give their clients access to prominent media outlets. This process may involve pitching an artist feature to a major magazine with plenty of time before the CD release, or promoting an upcoming concert to a newspaper writer. Publicists also try to expose their clients to different media outlets—if a rock star wants to act, for example, the publicist may try to place him or her in *Premiere*'s or *Entertainment Weekly*'s movie section.

Publicists may also help train less-experienced artists to deal with the media. Out-of-nowhere hit records generally lead to big stories in publications like *Rolling Stone* and *The Los Angeles Times*, and it's important for inexperienced musicians not to say anything mean or embarrassing to the press. (Unless, of course, an artist like Eminem has a heavy or mean reputation and wants to come across that way in public.) Publicists advise artists on how to articulate their life stories with some drama and charm—and answer more than "yes" or "no" to questions.

For a band that's just starting out and that doesn't have any hits to speak of, all publicity is good publicity. No publication is too small. And no publication, or TV or radio station, is so big you shouldn't try it. A publicist will find the right contacts and flood them (persistently but not too persistently, of course) with news about the band. The publicist will also set up interviews, patiently answer questions, and

> ### Behind the Music
>
> If a friend or relative is doing a good job as your publicist, you may not have to hire anybody else. In the early 1990s, Ambrosia Healy was a publicist at the Fox Theatre in Boulder, Colorado, before she hooked up with an up-and-coming act called the Dave Matthews Band. As the DMB grew famous, Healy stuck with them—and eventually became a top publicist at the major label Capitol Records.

drop timely bits of new information. So should you hire a publicist? Yes, if you've al-ready exhausted all the local media outlets—and those in cities where you play gigs. And if your budget accommodates it.

Standard Rates

Rates and pay structures vary wildly, depending on the publicist's reputation and client roster. Some will work one show or CD-release party for your band and charge by the event or even by the hour. Others may offer monthly retainer rates, which can range between $1,000 and $5,000. What you're paying for is a publicist's enthusiasm and contacts—although a friend may handle your publicity adequately for free, cer-tain Rolodexes are worth paying for.

Note that the smaller the event, generally, the less you'll have to pay to publicize it. A club show, for which you want to place preview stories in the local alt-weekly and daily newspapers, will likely be on the low-cost end. Trying to plunge into *GQ* or *Esquire* requires a savvy publicist with editors' and writers' names and numbers—and insight on selling them stories that they might otherwise ignore.

Finding a Good Publicist

In addition to asking local bands, managers, and agents you respect for recommenda-tions, many resources are available for finding good publicists. Billboard magazine puts out several referral publications, including *The Musician's Guide to Touring and Promotions* and Jim Pettigrew's *The Billboard Guide to Music Publicity*. How-to public relations websites such as publicityhound.com and 101publicrelations.com contain excellent tips—although they don't specialize in music or entertainment.

How do you know whether the publicist is any good? If he or she has placed stories you like about bands you like, the publicist probably has an admirable track record. Your contemporaries on the local music scene can also vouch for people. And once you've narrowed your list down to two or three people, check out the compa-nies' websites to see who else they represent.

Once you've signed with a record label, whether it's large or small, you often won't have to worry about doing your own publicity anymore. Record companies usually have their own publicity departments, staffed with (mostly) experienced professionals who know how to deal with media. But as with anything involving a label, be careful. Sometimes the company will try to hire an independent, nonlabel publicist for your band because its own people are "totally jammed." You could wind up paying the bill for this service later, and so ask questions up front. (See Chapter 22 for more on deal-ing with labels.)

Backstage Insights

On rare occasions, a local media reporter, from an alt-weekly or daily newspaper, will befriend the band and offer to do freelance publicity work. These professionals are invaluable resources who have experience with media from both the writer and editor perspectives. Note that in these cases, the writer probably won't be able to cover your band, maybe ever again, in his or her own publication. Many journalists, especially those who work for mainstream publications such as *The New York Times,* are very strict about conflicts of interest.

A Publicist Speaks

Lisa Shively owns The Press Network, a Nashville-based publicity firm that represents artists such as country singers Jim Lauderdale and Robbie Fulks and veteran rocker Nick Lowe. Over the years, she has worked with talents from country superstar Vince Gill to Austin, Texas, singer-songwriter Alejandro Escovedo. We asked her some publicity questions, and she was kind enough to answer:

How does a band know when it's ready to hire a publicist?

If you can come to me with a stack of clips from your local market, and your next record has some distribution behind it, and you've picked a market you're going to be touring in, maybe I can do something for you. But if you have no clips and you're just putting out a CD and the record's just available where you play, or on your website, it's not enough. You've got to prove yourself on your home turf.

When you get unsolicited material in the mail, what are some examples of red flags, indicating a band may not be ready?

I'll just get a CD in the mail and there's nothing with it—or they'll send me a press kit, but there's no cover letter and I don't know what it's for. I get a lot of those. There's no way for me to respond.

How much do you charge, and what's the pay structure?

The only way I've ever done it is monthly, plus expenses. Right now my bottom line is $1,500 a month, but it does depend what part of the country you're in. I know people doing publicity for bands at kind of a "baby band" level, and maybe they charge $500 [a month]. People can also do arrangements per gig.

What can a professional publicist do for a band that it can't do independently?

It's going out of their home markets to places they don't know. Then I've got the contacts and it adds a level of respectability. In your home market, a band member or significant other can make the calls. But when you're getting ready to go out into the rest of the world and you've got the means to hire somebody, basically what you're getting are the contacts—and going up to a different level of professionalism.

So why can't a band just handle its own publicity forever?

As long as they can feel comfortable handling it themselves, they should. Because it's an expense. To do posters and make merchandise—that's probably a better place to put their money until they feel they want to get into *Entertainment Weekly* or *USA Today* or something. Then they want to hire somebody.

Any other publicity advice you'd give to bands?

If you want to bump up [to a professional publicist] too soon, you miss out on developing relationships with the local writers. They can become your champions for a long time. And you can grow with that writer.

CAUTION

Avoiding Bad Notes _____

Remember that a media writer doesn't necessarily have the same interests as your band. Newspaper reporters may not see their jobs as "promoting the local scene," as some believe, but to cover news and inform the readers. So while it's frustrating that a paper pays attention to an artist only when bad things happen, that's the reality of the business. Magazines and television stations have similar agendas; a good publicist understands this and works within the system.

Setting a Budget

"Extra cash" may seem like an oxymoron when you're dividing dollars among the band members after a local club gig. But should you be fortunate enough to wind up with some money to spare, and you've already bought and maintained the proper musical equipment (not to mention adequate gig transportation), that's when to consider spending money on publicity or advertising.

Setting up a budget often works best when you divide it into small, manageable chunks. For example, if you know you'll get paid $300 for a show next Friday night, and the four band members can live with divvying up $250, consider spending $50 on an hour of professional publicity work. This may be just the boost you need to land a major newspaper preview and attract an extra 50 or 100 people to the show. But long-term budget planning is effective, too, if you're making enough money. Say you've set up a 10-city tour of the Midwest and club bookers have agreed to pay roughly $300 each. That's $3,000—deduct travel and equipment expenses of roughly $2,600 and you might be able to hire a publicist for a week or two. A publicist, of course, won't be able to guarantee you free preview stories in local publications, but at the least you'll probably make future contacts.

Newspaper and Magazine Ads

Advertisements aren't technically publicity because you're paying for the exposure, rather than trying to convince a writer or editor you're newsworthy enough for free coverage. Ads can be costly, but one advantage is you get to control the information and message presented in the publication. One disadvantage is most readers know you're paying for the ad yourself, rather than convincing a reputable writer or editor you're good enough to deserve coverage. But if the ad is big enough, most readers won't care.

Paid ads often work best in specific, targeted situations. For example, you can present a "two-for-one" or "ladies' night" coupon in an ad, while a newspaper story will almost never present this information. Also, if you've determined a week before a show that you've sold 50 tickets too few, a prominent ad in a credible alt-weekly might pack the place.

Ads can be as small as an alt-weekly classified or as large as a full-page announcement in a major glossy magazine. Your advertising options will depend on your budget, of course.

> **Backstage Insights**
>
> Ads are one way of circumventing the frustrating process of waiting for a magazine to write about you. The Samples, a veteran rock band with a large following, tried for years to draw coverage in *Rolling Stone* magazine. Eventually the band gave up and simply bought a prominent display ad in the magazine.

Following are examples of (black-and-white) ad rates for various publications. Note that discounts are often available and rates change from month to month.

- A quarter-page display ad in the New York City nightlife magazine *Time Out New York:* $952

- A one-column-inch (1 by 2¹⁄₁₆ inches) in Sunday's *New York Times:* $994

- A half-page display ad in the *Chicago Tribune:* $44,730

- A quarter-page display ad in *The Boston Globe:* $12,473

- A one-sixth-of-a-page display ad in *GQ:* $11,285

- A five-line classified ad in the Denver alt-weekly *Westword:* $20

- A quarter-page display ad in the *Chicago Reader:* $775

- A three-line classified ad in *Rolling Stone:* $585

There's an art to creating a great advertisement, just as there's an art to writing a great song. In fact, some say ads and rock music use similar artistic elements of economy and pop art. You'll need an eye-catching "hook line" and, if the ad is big enough, perhaps a gimmick, like a coupon or a photo of a very attractive person. At the bottom, include the band's CD cover (if you have one) or a band photo (if you don't have one, get one). Don't forget the club address, contact number, and—perhaps most important—your website address.

Finally, do a cost-benefit analysis before placing any ad. That $775 spot in the *Chicago Reader* might be eye-catching, but maybe the money would be better spent on two weeks of professional publicity. There's always the risk the publicity won't generate any press, but placing an advance review or feature in several different publications may be better than placing the one-time ad.

> ### Behind the Music
>
> Sometimes you'll want to avoid publicity—like if your upcoming show is totally sold out and you don't want to irritate fans who haven't yet bought tickets. On these welcome occasions you'll have to stop granting press interviews (and maybe come across more mysterious and desirable in the process) and pull any upcoming ads. (Sometimes you can also ask the publication to add the words *sold out* to the pre-printed advertisement.)

Other Types of Advertising and Publicity

Until you become a superstar, or at least have the resources of a major record label, billboards, radio spots, and television commercials are probably prohibitively expensive. But there are cheaper forms of high-profile advertising—get your band's name on a bus bench, for example, or on the bus itself. Hire a small plane to carry your band's name on a banner above the local football stadium. It's best to have a gig, CD, or something else tangible to sell when you try these approaches.

Don't forget to look into the web for advertising opportunities, in addition to the free message-posting techniques we've discussed. You may be able to buy a banner ad on a well-traveled music site like the All Music Guide (allmusic.com), an online magazine site like Salon (salon.com), or your local newspaper's home page. Less expensively, e-mail a well-known music weblogger such as Rock Critics Daily (rockcriticsdaily.blogspot.com).

Again, if you pay for promotion, it technically constitutes advertising, not publicity. (Publicity is the free stuff, remember?) But be creative with publicity, as well. If you can't afford to buy half a minute on the local KISS-FM, approach the college or community station with free tickets to your next gig. Usually they'll be happy to receive them, and perhaps put your name on the air in connection with a ticket giveaway.

Pick a worthy cause and put on a benefit concert—media are usually more enthusiastic about covering benefits than plain old gigs. Gimmicks, as we mention in Chapter 14, can also be effective, although for some reason they're not used very often these days. The Rolling Stones kicked off a 1975 tour by performing on a flatbed truck as it rolled through the busy streets of Manhattan. The manager for the great funk band Funkadelic and punk legend Iggy Pop once cooked up a marriage between Pop and Funkadelic's George Clinton. It never came to pass, to Pop's great relief, but Clinton reportedly said later: "He could have been my wife!"

DIY: What You Can Learn on Your Own

Don't rush to hire a publicist if (1) you're not ready for one; or (2) you or somebody in your band's "posse" is perfectly capable of handling publicity for free.

The more you can do on your own—from management to booking to promotion to publicity—the more you learn about the music industry. Yes, a professional publicist will have tricks and contacts you can't possibly match when you're just starting out. But a professional publicist may not share your enthusiasm about the band, and you may be able to attract reporters and editors with your personality. Eventually, if you keep up the amateur publicity work, you'll wind up with a fat Rolodex or database of your own. Some bands, as we've noted, never have to hire a publicist. You may be one of the lucky ones.

The Least You Need to Know

+ Publicists handle many tasks for musicians, from communicating new images to damage control. For a young band, a publicist's job is to contact media and attempt to place features and reviews in prominent publications.

+ Publicity rates range from very high to somewhat affordable. You may be able to hire some firms for $20 an hour. Others charge as much as $5,000 a month.

+ If you have extra cash—a big "if"—consider spending it on advertising for the upcoming gig or CD release. But keep in mind the money might be better spent on a publicist. Analyze your budget and see what you can afford.

+ Ads cost anywhere from $20 (for an alt-weekly classified) to tens of thousands of dollars (for a full-color ad in a major glossy magazine).

+ In the end, do-it-yourself publicity is the most affordable and perhaps the most effective. See Chapter 14 for more tips on "pitching" your band to the media.

Part 5

Making a Record

There are two basic reasons to make a record—one is to send a demo to record labels, managers, media, and radio stations; the other is to sell a compact disc directly to the fans. Both approaches are worth pursuing, especially after you've played a bunch of gigs and reasonably large crowds have started to pack your shows.

In either case, the band will have to enter the studio. You may be able to buy recording equipment and convert your rehearsal space into a studio. Or you may have to pay by the hour to rent local studio space and work with an engineer. Either way, the process can be costly.

Note that the record-making process has changed dramatically over the last decade, as software packages such as ProTools have become more affordable and easier to use. But there's no substitute for a great-sounding room and the experienced ears of an engineer or a producer. We encourage you to record your own music, but if your budget accommodates it, consider working with a professional as well.

Chapter 18

Live and Home Recording

In This Chapter

- ◆ Reasons to record: group critique sessions, boosting your songwriting, preparing for demos and CDs

- ◆ Recording live: bring your usual sound gear, plus recorder and mixer (or combination of both)

- ◆ What's a recorder? What's a mixer?

- ◆ Staying at home: where to put the microphones, how to get the best drum sounds, and laying down vocals in the bathroom

- ◆ Buying equipment—"cheap" stuff for less than $2,500, and when to spend more money

At some point, after mastering rehearsal and perhaps playing a few live gigs, you'll have the impulse to roll tape. Initially, at least for the purpose of critiquing playback and showing off to friends and family, this process will probably involve a cheap cassette recorder. But when you start envisioning a demo, or a for-sale CD, your approach will become costlier and more sophisticated. You'll have three choices: *recording live*, the easiest and fastest (but least polished) way of capturing the band's sound; *recording at home*, which is extremely practical as you have amps and guitars set up already; or *renting studio time*, a highly professional but expensive undertaking with a steep learning curve. In this chapter we'll focus on the first two options (we discuss buying studio time in Chapter 20)—both are effective and surprisingly affordable.

Why Record?

As we mentioned at the end of Chapter 5, rolling tape is an excellent tool for group critique sessions. It can also help sharpen your songwriting skills and give friends and family a sense of what you've been doing all those hours in the basement. Recording generally helps you grow as a band. The more you expose your music to other people, and open your work to outside criticism, the more it changes for the better.

Recording, like performing live, will also take you into new business areas. As we'll discuss in Chapter 19, you can record your music onto a brief *demo*, or demonstration CD, and send it to club bookers, media, record labels, and radio stations. You can also record onto a full-length compact disc and sell it at gigs. These ventures may make the band valuable connections or even a little pocket money.

Equipment You'll Need to Bring to the Gig

Although you'll have to purchase a certain amount of recording equipment no matter what, the least complicated approach is to simply turn on the tape machines at your live gig. This way, you won't have to play the same song 15 times in a row until you get it right, and the recording may contain a certain spontaneous energy. (Then again, it also may be filled with mistakes and unfortunate tuning incidents.)

You can generate a live recording in any of the following ways, all of which vary in sound quality and expense:

- Ask the sound engineer at the gig for a "house board" recording, which is a tape made directly from the venue's sound system. "They don't really sound that great," says veteran Denver engineer John Macy, "but generally, 'off-the-board' is great for studying your performances."

- Ask the venue to burn a CD of your performance at the end of the show. Some clubs are already equipped to do this and will produce the recording free of charge.

- Invest in a splitter, which will divert the sound from the live microphones into a mixer and recorder. Splitters can be cheap—a Behringer DI20 Ultra DI 2-Channel Active DI Box/Splitter costs $19.99 at guitarcenter.com—and you can rent them. (Check homerecording.com for rental advice.)

◆ Hire an engineer. Once you get to the "splitter" stage, "that's generally where you'd want to hire somebody," says Macy, who has worked on gold records with Gladys Knight and the Pips and other stars. He recently charged a singer $600 for one night to get her live show onto tape. (The *mixing* process, at the studio later, costs extra.)

Using a Computer Laptop

A tip about gear for recording live music: Pay attention to the people in your community who routinely tape concerts by big-time bands such as Phish, String Cheese Incident, and the Dead. Whether you like those bands or not, their fans have developed a sophisticated network of recording shows and distributing them over the Internet. "Tapers" are great resources, and if you can't find them at the shows themselves, ask around at local music-equipment stores.

Words to Rock By

Typically, bands record the vocals on one tape-recorder track, drums and bass on another, and guitar on a third. "Leveling" all these disparate elements into one cohesive sound is called **mixing,** and to do it you'll need a device called a mixer—and, depending on your preferred level of sound sophistication, a mixing engineer.

We're not necessarily suggesting you tape and "bootleg" major rock concerts yourself—some bands frown upon the practice, which is technically illegal, so be careful. But it's perfectly acceptable to record your own show, and why not learn how to do it from the experts? Some bands even buy or borrow live recordings from fans and use them for their own purposes—in exchange for letting the fans tape shows.

You can also search for taping advice via Google. A query for "Phish" and "taping" turns up more than 7,000 sites—check out a couple and e-mail the webmasters, who are often happy to help. Other useful online resources include etree.org, a meeting place and instructional site for the taping community; Usenet newsgroups such as alt.music.bootlegs and rec.music.dylan; and band-focused websites like livenirvana. com, phish.net, and stringcheeseincident.com.

Alexandria, Virginia, Internet technology consultant John Bartol, whom Steve once interviewed for *Wired* magazine, tapes shows using a computer laptop with portable recording hardware and mixing software. "It's certainly easier to slice it up and transfer it to CD and to the Internet, because it's already on your computer," says the taper, who focuses on Phish and Dead shows. "You run the risk of the computer dying during the show, but I'd say there's a better risk of tape failure."

This taper's computer equipment is as follows:

- A Nomad Jukebox 3, which, like an Apple iPod, is mostly used to store songs from your computer and play them back, Walkman-style. But the Nomad is also a high-level, portable recording device. You can plug it directly into the band's soundboard (if the sound people will let you) or use it in tandem with small, high-level microphones.

- A computer laptop with plenty of memory.

- Audio capturing software such as Cool Edit or SoundForge, which will "grab" the recording and allow you to edit it on many different levels. (Later, you can use this software to burn CDs at home.)

- Two to four tiny portable microphones.

- Some working knowledge of computer .WAV files and the patience to read a manual or two. Here's an excellent webpage with step-by-step recording instructions: electronics.cnet.com/music/0-1566077-7-3781159.html.

Conditions at the Venue

Can your band record at every venue it plays? Mostly yes, but ask first. Some prominent concert halls around the United States, including the House of Blues nightclub chain, New York City's famous Carnegie Hall, and San Francisco's Fillmore Auditorium, will make you sign a contract charging the band fees in the thousands of dollars to record.

As for acoustics and other audio issues, basically, if the room sounds good when you perform, it's probably worth taping there. If it's a horrible room where you always get bad sound and play mediocre shows, roll tape somewhere else.

To wind up with rough live recordings, you'll need the following equipment:

- All the gear you normally bring to the gig—microphones, amplifiers, gaffer tape, and the instruments themselves. You may want to include a special microphone for a certain sound or feel, as opposed to the usual "gig microphone." Same with amps and instruments if you have more than one.

- Recorder. Tons of high-quality recording devices are available in many different combinations. For less than $400, you can buy a Tascam cassette package, including microphones, headphones, blank tapes, and cords; for about $2,000, there's a far fancier, faster, and more reliable Alesis hard-disk recorder with sophisticated editing abilities. Either one will serve your needs at this point.

♦ Mixer. Most high-end recorders come with mixers as part of the electronic package. As with recorders, mixer prices range from $50 (Behringer Ultra DI, which accommodates limited amplifier power) to $2,500 (Roland VM-C7200 V-Mixing Console, with 94 channels and lots of cool sound effects). Ask at music stores about the best device to fit your budget.

Just remember to hit "record" when the time comes! And try not to worry about the blinking red light; low-pressure shows are usually the best shows.

Can You Make a Record at Home?

The advantages to recording at your rehearsal space, as opposed to taping your live gig, are numerous. The band's equipment is already there, positioned just the way the musicians like it, and it won't take much to set up a recorder and mixer. Also, you'll have the chance to perform several "takes" until the band is satisfied with the song.

When recording at home, you can also record tracks separately. "Tracking" is an old studio expression for recording individual parts at different times, then combining them later using a multi-track mixer. Although many bands insist on performing live, as a full unit, in the studio, because that's the way they rehearse and play at shows, at least as many use the "shift" system. For example, the bass and drums might play an entire song and record it on one track. Guitars might be on another track, vocals on a third and, say, handclaps on a fourth.

It's also easier, and much cheaper, to record in your rehearsal space than to rent time at a professional studio. We'll get more into the details of studio recording in Chapter 20, but suffice to say you pay—a lot—by the hour. Unless you're independently wealthy or a record company is willing to foot the bill, it's easy to dump a ton of money into studio time. And, at least at first, you probably won't be familiar with all the knobs and gadgets and may need an experienced (and costly) producer or engineer to help you figure everything out. Before plunging into the studio, we recommend hands-on experience by recording at the gig or, even better, during rehearsal.

Can you make a professionally sounding demo or full-length compact disc at your rehearsal space? Yes! Even cheap recording gear is good enough for a CD. The less-polished sound may even create a raw or intimate feeling, which can sound terrific depending on what type of music you play.

Advice from a Sound Engineer

We asked our sound-engineering expert, John Macy, to answer some questions about the home-recording process. An excerpt of the conversation follows:

Can any band record at home?

The price of technology is just falling so fast right now, it's amazing what you can do at home. But it still boils down to what you do with it. A really great engineer can go into a basement studio and make a phenomenally sounding thing and an idiot can use $3,000 gear and make a piece of crap.

> **Avoiding Bad Notes**
>
> Before purchasing sound equipment, a big group investment whether you have $100 or $100,000 to spend, set a budget. Recording is one of those things like remodeling a house—your original estimate can very easily double or triple. Stay within the budget, no matter how tempting.

Where do you stand on the "do-it-yourself" approach?

Well, a home studio is a really great place to work it out, and a lot of people use a home recording to build a demo. Great tunes and great performances are going to rise above any of it—if you've got "it," if you've got the tunes.

So what do you recommend, for a band that wants to make a CD at home?

Sometimes recording drums is tough. Something that's very common is to hire a studio for a day or two and record really great rhythm tracks. Then you spend three months at home doing the guitar and background vocals.

How much do engineers charge for that sort of thing?

Some people hire a pro for a day and help them get set up. Or we can spend three months. Engineers can cost $15 an hour. My minimum is $350 a day, and it runs to $500 a day.

Great Equipment for $2,500 or Less

Recording equipment used to be expensive, but technology has become amazingly cheap in recent years and you can get a full-functioning four-track recorder for less than $250. Mark recently came across a $99.99 cassette recorder, from the reputable Tascam brand, which will work just fine for a demo. (The list price for this recorder is $120, but a Musician's Friend catalog [musiciansfriend.com] will give you deals and shopping ideas.)

As with computers and basic band gear, the more money you spend, the less hassle you'll have. Cassette recorders are relatively cheap, although, as we'll discuss in Chapter 19, sending a cassette demo or selling a cassette copy of your work to fans is more amateurish than working off a CD. More expensive digital equipment will burn your recording directly onto a blank CD.

Similarly, the more you spend, the more tracks you'll be able to use. Basic four-tracks are useful when recording guitars, drums, bass, and vocals. But what if you want to add keyboards? Or "layer" several different guitar sounds on top of each other? This process is far easier on, say, a 96-track recorder than on a little four-track cassette. Finally, there's the analog (cheap) versus digital (expensive) recording debate, which we'll get to later in this chapter.

Behind the Music

In 1967, The Beatles recorded their masterpiece *Sgt. Pepper's Lonely Hearts Club Band* on a four-track recorder. This technology was considered state-of-the-art in popular music for years, until recorders expanded to eight, 16, and many more tracks, and from analog to digital. Today, *Sgt. Pepper's* recording technology is available for $400. Of course, the warm studio rooms, microphones, and producer George Martin's good instincts are not so easy to find.

Generally, in a rehearsal space, you'll need the same equipment we suggested you bring to record a concert: microphones and cords, a recorder or mixer, and the usual gear (drums, amps, guitars, effects pedals). If you're not plugging guitars and amps directly into the recording gear, soundproofing may become necessary. Foam strips are available at most hardware and music stores, or you can make a project out of it and rebuild the basement, garage, or warehouse room. Check out soundproofing.org if you're interested in a major soundproofing renovation.

Headphones are important in order to hear the other instruments more clearly than usual. They're also essential if you're performing late at night and don't want to disturb family or neighbors in the next room.

Backstage Insights

There are a million different kinds of headphones, ranging from the tiny, open-ear styles you'd use with your Walkman or iPod to the big "cup" headphones DJs use at dance clubs. You can buy them almost anywhere, from Target to Guitar Center, but keep in mind the sleeker, open-ear style may lead to "bleed-through"—in other words, the mike may pick up the sounds coming through the headphones in addition to your singing voice.

The local music store, or wherever else you buy your instruments and amplifiers, will have plenty of options for recording and mixing devices. Catalogs and websites may contain slightly better deals—we've found Musician's Friend (musiciansfriend.com, 1-800-776-5173) to be reliable and thorough. Big chains like Guitar Center (guitarcenter.com) and smaller shops like O. DiBella and Sons, of Bergenfield, New Jersey (odibella.com), are easily accessible via the Internet.

As for hooking these gadgets together in the studio, or onstage, the process is pretty simple. If you can set up a home stereo system, you can almost certainly arrange recording gear.

Microphones, amplifiers, and guitars will plug directly into the front of the recording device. To patch the recorder and mixer together, use the color-coded inputs and cords. Be sure to connect the red plug (usually "right") into the red hole and the white plug (usually "left") into the white.

Recording Techniques

Before you strap on the instruments and begin to play, listen to the room. Sing into the microphones in various corners, on different surfaces, next to a glass-exposed window, alongside thick curtains. Experiment. Play a few guitar notes in a room with thick shag carpeting. Prepare to sing in an echoey, tile-covered bathroom (and maybe fill up the tub for a deeper, more, uh, "wet" feeling). Different rooms lead to subtly different sounds.

When the folk-and-rock duo Simon and Garfunkel recorded their classic "Bridge Over Troubled Water," they tethered a microphone to the bottom of the elevator shaft to create an unprecedented reverb. When the record came out, tons of drummers scrambled to emulate the huge snare-drum sound. Of course, today, after decades of heavy metal, grunge, and alternative rock, that sound is like a coin in a well.

Behind the Music

"Magic" happens in certain warm studios where everything's set up just right. To record his worn-sounding 1975 classic *Tonight's the Night*, rocker Neil Young assembled his band in a nondescript black-and-gray Los Angeles building called Studio Instrument Rentals; the control room was the size of a closet.

Other magical rooms include Chicago's Chess Studios, where Muddy Waters and Willie Dixon recorded blues classics in the 1950s; The Beatles' Abbey Road; and Sun Studios in Memphis, onetime home of Elvis Presley and Jerry Lee Lewis, where a modern-day tour reveals plain, cushioned soundproofing.

Test and tinker with everything until everybody in the band is satisfied with the sound. Try positioning the microphones close to the guitar amp, then far away.

Feedback, or screeching electronic noise from electric guitars and other instruments, probably won't be a factor in this setting—unless you record at super-high volume. (And some guitarists who emulate Jimi Hendrix and The Who's Pete Townsend may actually try to incorporate feedback into the music.) If feedback does come up, sometimes the solution is for the guitarist to move two steps to the right, away from the microphone or amplifier. Or try turning around.

One method of recording a guitar is to set up a microphone next to the amplifier to capture the sound that comes out. This way, the general "feeling" of the room may wind up in the recording. But that microphone will pick up other noises, too, such as vocals or footsteps, and may be susceptible to feedback. To avoid these problems, plug the guitar directly into the recorder—or plug it into a special-effects box and plug that into the recorder. If you're hooked in directly, the dogs barking in the next room won't land on the guitarist's track. On the other hand, you might sacrifice that warm-room sound. Preparing to record is often a series of such small logistical and artistic decisions.

You'll sometimes get *amp buzz* if the guitars and amplifiers are too close too each other. In most cases, you can quickly fix the problem by separating the two pieces of equipment.

When you're recording frequencies above a certain level, you might end up with *tape hiss*. Often this general tape-recorder noise is something you can't do much about (short of buying a more expensive recorder, preferably a digital one).

Although positioning can be fun in a *feng shui* sort of way, try not to overobsess about the details. Outside traffic noises, a bassist's footsteps, laughter, "start again!" and "you kids turn that down!" can make for funny, spontaneous breaks from the music. Take recording seriously, but learn to laugh at the process, too.

Backstage Insights

Many recording machines, synthesizers, and keyboards contain built-in sound effects, from handclaps to gunshots, which you can use to create distinctive noises. But sometimes the old methods sound richer than the synthesizers—on one Beatles song, Ringo Starr tapped on a matchbox for percussion; Motown producers smacked boards together to approximate hand-clapping; some enterprising DJs scrunch up corn-chip bags to make sounds.

Be Prepared

Your first recording session generally won't have the crushing pressure of your first gig. For one thing, dozens of people won't be insisting that you entertain them on the spot. For another, if you make a mistake, you can just start over.

Nonetheless, preparation is still important. You don't want to find out at 9:30 P.M., after the local music store closes, that you broke a guitar string and have no replacement. You'll need almost everything at a recording session that you'd take to the gig—the band toolbox, plenty of gaffer tape, and so forth. You'll also need the manuals for the recorder and mixer, and maybe some extra soundproofing.

Getting More Sophisticated

There's a lot to be said for a "lo-fi" recording—in the 1990s, this was a sonic trend, as alternative-rock bands Dinosaur Jr., Pavement, and Sebadoh put out deliberately muddy, raw, bluesy sounding CDs. (The Rolling Stones' *Exile on Main Street* is a classic in this genre.) But at some point you may want to smooth out the edges and put out something a little more polished. This decision depends on your musical style—if your lead singer is Justin Timberlake, go for polish; if she's Courtney Love, keep it raw.

We'll delve into the studio—where, for a price, you can really buff the sound—in Chapter 20. Until then, fortunately for your band, fancy studio "toys" such as the popular software package Pro Tools are now available to the general public. Using this stuff properly will shine things up.

A Pro Tools Primer

Pro Tools has changed the music industry. On the plus side, it has generated millions of dollars for its creator, Digidesign, and placed professional recording tools into the hands of every aspiring musician in the country (that's you!). On the minus side, it has gradually made studios' roles less important in the recording process; *Rolling Stone* magazine reported in early 2003 that several, including New York's Greene Street Studios, had to shut down, in part, due to do-it-yourself competition from Pro Tools users.

Many popular musicians are among the legions of born-again Pro Tools users. The techno band Dirty

> **Behind the Music**
>
> Ricky Martin's 1999 Latin-rock smash "Livin' La Vida Loca" was the first number-one single to be recorded and mixed entirely on the computer. Producer Desmond Child used the computer system Pro Tools in his Miami studio.

Vegas and the hard-rock band Incubus told *Rolling Stone* they have the capability of making important records without paying for any studio time whatsoever.

Pro Tools essentially edits multiple vocal and instrumental parts like a word processor manipulates sentences and paragraphs on the screen. It also greatly facilitates the mixing process and allows a producer to quickly pick the best mix and add new parts at any point in the process.

Naturally, experienced musicians—especially those with money—have access to high-end computer software and hardware. Big-time producers will often use the Pro Tools system to record music onto many powerful hard disks at once. This level of gear can cost tens of thousands of dollars. Musicians on tighter budgets can improvise: Glenn Olander, a 42-year-old software engineer in Carlsbad, California, told the *Houston Chronicle* he used the less-than-$300 software program Cubase VST to record music to his 200-megahertz Macintosh computer.

Versions of Pro Tools exist for $495—and they work on any relatively strong laptop computer. (You can buy many plug-ins and extra gimmicks as you go along.) But before you go out and spend hundreds of dollars on software and equipment, consider this "sound" advice from Butch Vig, a member of Garbage and producer of Nirvana's classic pre-Pro Tools album *Nevermind*: "The Beatles recorded Sgt. Pepper's on four tracks," he told *Rolling Stone*.

Digital or Analog? (and Other Fancy Questions)

For most of music history, artists recorded with *analog* equipment. That basically means the sound signal comes from a physical encounter, like a needle hitting a groove on a phonograph record. (Thomas Edison first invented this technique in 1877, and it was the industry standard all the way until the early 1980s.)

Around the time compact discs became available to the public, the recording scene began shifting to *digital*. As with computers, digital recording involved unseen numbers. At first, the technique was to convert an analog wave into a series of numbers, then record the numbers.

For consumers, the digital transformation meant one CD could store many more minutes of music than a vinyl long-playing record. The CD was also far more durable than an LP, as the act of pressing a record-player needle onto the grooves of a record eventually wore everything out.

For producers, engineers, and musicians, the digital age meant recording could be more precise. Using old-fashioned analog technology, studio people had to edit by splicing physical bits of tape together. Using digital technology, the editing process is as easy as cutting and pasting text in your computer word processor.

For a while, in the 1980s, digital was the rage—to many ears the recordings sounded far more precise than old-fashioned analog. Then came a backlash, and gradually producers and musicians decided all-digital recordings were too tinny and not "fat" enough. So today, most major rock bands use a combination of digital and analog recording. They'll lay down the tracks using digital equipment, and copy those master sounds onto analog tape recorders. Naturally, there are numerous other ways to do it, too.

The Least You Need to Know

◆ Recording is an important step in a band's career; in addition to helping group-critique sessions, the process can lead to demos and full-length compact discs. These can generate crucial income and connections for the band.

◆ Taping your live show is easier and cheaper than you'd think. But keep in mind you'll have little opportunity to correct onstage mistakes or repeat a song to get it right.

◆ Recording at home, or your rehearsal space, is probably the best available option at this stage. The equipment is cheap and the gear is already set up.

◆ Experiment. Move a microphone into various rooms and spaces. Fill up the bathtub. Try different "feels" and sounds while setting up recording gear.

◆ As you get better at recording music, and your budget accommodates some extra gear, you may want to get more sophisticated. One easy, cheap way to do this is to jump on the Pro Tools computer-recording bandwagon.

◆ Digital or analog? Probably some combination of both.

19

Making the Demo

In This Chapter

- ◆ How to not go broke while recording a demo
- ◆ Sending demos to media, club bookers, record companies, managers, and agents
- ◆ Choosing songs and catching recipients' attention
- ◆ Navigating the formats: DAT, CD, cassette, or MP3?
- ◆ Brevity is a virtue

A *demo*, short for demonstration, refers to a homemade recording usually used for noncommercial purposes. Its purpose is to "pitch" your music to club promoters, wedding planners, media writers, radio stations, or even record labels. Although many famous band members use demos to sketch out rough musical ideas, a demo at this stage is your band's calling card, a way to introduce people to your music if they're unable to hear the show. It doesn't necessarily have to be pristinely produced—recipients aren't obsessed with fancy recording studios—but the music should be solid and designed to make a good first impression. Here, we help you purchase basic recording equipment, choose the songs, determine the format (CD or cassette?), and send it to the right people.

Why Do You Need a Demo?

At first, when you're trying to line up a gig or place a story in the local newspaper, your only weapon will be enthusiasm. You can write the most beautiful press release or pose for the most glamorous photo in the world, but if you have no music to send out, nobody will know what distinguishes your band from any other band. That's when a demo is crucial.

Behind the Music

The demo has an almost mythological standing in rock and pop music history. Bruce Springsteen originally recorded *Nebraska* as a set of homemade demos to present to his band; he eventually realized they were perfect as is, and released them as his landmark 1982 album. The Who's Pete Townshend has spent his career recording demos in his home studio—they have emerged on a series of solo albums called *Scoop*. And pop stars from the late folk singer Eva Cassidy to jazz pianist Harry Connick Jr. to rocker Dave Matthews have transformed their early demos into commercially available CDs.

Sending Out the Demo

We'll get into the specifics of presentation and how to formally send a demo later in this chapter, but for now here are some typical recipients of demo recordings:

♦ **The media.** A demo opens up potential coverage areas—you may be deemed worthy of a review in a writer's local-music column. Or you may get lucky and hit a reviewer whose favorite song is "Walking On the Sun" when you have a prominent version of that Smash Mouth hit on your demo.

Backstage Insights

Although many managers, record labels, booking agents, and even club bookers say they won't accept unsolicited materials, don't perceive this as a closed door. Good music will open that door almost every time. Often you can get around this barrier by calling or e-mailing in advance. Even better, find a well-connected attorney (or manager or booking agent) who can deliver the demo on your behalf.

♦ **Concert promoters (or wedding planners).** A demo will help distinguish you from other bands. If your version of "Hava Nagileh" sparkles while the other band's version falls flat (or worse, they have no demo), you may get the gig.

♦ **Managers.** Bands send Mark, a veteran rock-band manager, demos all the time. Although it's a long shot, you may make an important managerial connection—or even wind up hiring a manager—on the strength of your demo. Be sure to e-mail or call first before sending.

- **Booking agents.** Same with managers, and an equally hard sell—and you might not need a booking agent at this stage of your career. Managers usually come first.

- **Record companies.** Many of them won't accept unsolicited material, so you might need a connection, or at least some buzz from concert gigs or media articles, to wedge yourself into the door. Pick your shot: Often, when big-time record-label scouts reject submissions, they never want to hear from that artist again.

- **Radio stations.** This is almost always a waste of time, unless you're trying to get on a community or college station. Big radio programmers have strenuous weeding-out procedures and almost always pick songs that come from major record labels.

- **Friends, family, and other musicians.** Grandma may not be able to attend the gig, and rehearsal is closed, so send her the demo unless you're worried that banging her head to your heavy metal may present a health risk.

> **Backstage Insights**
>
> When you get around to selling your own CDs, you'll want to put lots of information in the liner notes. Not so with the demo—include only the band's name, members' names, song titles, contact information, and perhaps a few writing and production credits.

Posting Songs on Your Website

Although sending demos through snail mail remains your best chance of grabbing a club booker's ear, you can supplement these networking efforts by posting demo tracks on your website. Sometimes you'll be able to avoid the music-mailing process completely, and simply refer recipients to the website. In any case, fans love online freebies, and demo tracks (in the form of MP3 files or streaming audio, which we explain later in this chapter) are an excellent tool for your promotional arsenal.

If you post song files online, be sure to copyright them, even if it's just including the word "copyright" and the year in the text of your home page. (As we've mentioned in other chapters, instructions for the official copyright process are at copyright.gov/register/performing.html.) Once one of your songs emerges on the Internet, it can spread around fast, especially if it's posted in MP3 format. Make sure you're happy with it first. The only time it isn't appropriate to make your music available online is if you're under contract with a record label or publishing company; the company might consider it copyright infringement if you sell the songs online, or make them available for free.

What Songs Should Be on the Demo?

The answer to this question is "it depends." Know your audience. The demo you send to the club booker probably won't be the same demo you send to the record label. The club owner's agenda is to fill the dance floor and keep people buying drinks all night—so you'll need to stack your demo with upbeat, possibly even familiar, songs. The wedding planner will want a mixture of traditional ballads and upbeat hits, plus certain specialty songs. The record label scout will want to hear evidence of originality and talent, and may reject you upon recognizing a cover.

Demos should be brief: 3 songs, no more than 15 minutes total. (Certain bands, if they're playing for a hippie crowd that digs the String Cheese Incident and Phish, can get away with including 20-minute jams on their demos.) Rock bands should be upbeat; a cocktail-jazz band auditioning for a wedding should lean on pop standards like Nat King Cole's "Our Love Is Here to Stay"; a folk duo should consider Joan Baez, Shawn Colvin, Ani DiFranco, and original material in that vein.

Original material, in most cases, gives you credibility. You may not want to load your demo tape with original songs if you're auditioning for dance night at a high school or night club. But generally if you start moving in this direction, and you turn out to be good at it, new gigs and media coverage will open up to you. The demo tape is the perfect vessel for communicating this talent to the public.

When structuring a demo tape with original material, put the best song first. If you think a song is weak, and you aren't sure whether to include it, leave it off. There's no room for fat or filler on a demo tape.

Your original songs will probably be rough at first, but with time and practice you'll begin to get the hang of it—see Chapter 24 for more tips on writing songs. Melodies are key, especially if you're trying to sell the band for a gig or recording contract. We acknowledge the qualities of avant-garde or improvisational music, of course, but your first songs for this purpose should be straightforward, with strong melodies and lyrics to which people can relate.

Which Songs Work Before an Audience?

The only way to determine which songs work before an audience—and, to a lesser extent, which songs will work with your demo recipient—is to perform them in front of people. If your songs get a big reaction, you're probably doing pretty well. But this formula can be misleading: When your cover of 3 Doors Down's "Here Without You" gets a huge crowd response, it may just mean the audience loves 3 Doors Down. Generally, though, if you give a crowd a song, they'll give it back to you in such a way that answers your "what moves people?" questions.

Covers or Originals?

Whether to be a "covers" or "originals" band is part of your "setting the band's goals" discussion, which we've discussed in previous chapters. When choosing the songs for a demo, make them representative of the covers-originals ratio you perform in concert. The last thing you want to do is raise a club booker's expectations for a Coldplay cover band, then break out skronky-jazz originals during the audition or, worse, the show itself.

If you're the kind of band that plays occasional cover songs, consider placing one toward the beginning of your demo tape. New songs, no matter how good they are, take a few listens to sink in; a short, familiar song can grab the listener's attention just long enough to get to the first original on the tape. When sending the demo to a club booker, think about the way you'd structure a live set list—and make the demo tape a shorter, quicker version of that.

Some cover bands, of course, dedicate all their music to one particular artist—the most famous example of this is probably Beatlemania, four guys in mop top hairdos who do exclusively (what else?) Beatles songs. But in any given city you'll find similarly profitable tributes to Guns N' Roses, Radiohead, Mötley Crüe, and others. If you're that kind of band, the demo tape should include almost no originals.

> **Behind the Music**
>
> At this stage, royalty rates are probably not yet relevant to your band. But it's worth knowing how they work: If you write a song for a CD, you will receive "mechanical" royalty payments (usually about 8¢ per song) through international songwriter associations like BMI and ASCAP.

How Many Songs?

Put your best three songs on a demo tape—but save at least one good one in case you get the "sounds good, can we hear more?" call. At that point, send one more. This process is a fishing expedition—you have to bait the line, and slowly reel in the recipient, one song at a time. If you dump 24 songs on the first tape, even if they're good and find an enthusiastic audience, you'll have nothing with which to follow up.

What Format Should You Use?

Compact discs are the universal standard, and there's usually no reason to deviate from that. But other formats are appropriate in certain situations—specifically, if the recipient requests it that way. Here are some of the pros and cons of distributing demos in various formats:

- **Compact discs.** Everybody uses them. They're much cheaper and easier to produce than they used to be. It's the default standard, and even if you're in love with Digital Audio Tape, err on the side of recording on a CD.

- **Rewritable compact discs.** The blank CD-Rs you can buy, 50 for $7.95 at Target, are the standard for people making burns on their home computers. Generally, these are reasonable for you to send out, as well.

  Just remember to check the CDs after you record them—Mark has actually received blank CDs from aspiring bands in the mail. As unprofessional gestures go, this ranks with misspelling the recipient's name on the envelope.

> **CAUTION**
>
> **Avoiding Bad Notes**
>
> Sending rewritable or "burned" demo CDs is almost always acceptable. Just distinguish yourself by being professional. Scrawled Magic Marker labels on the top of the CD, like the ones you'd use for your personal bootleg collection, screams "amateur." Use simple, basic laser-printed labels and, if possible, sophisticated artwork for the cover.
>
> On the other hand, don't go too crazy with the artwork. Teachers never give better grades to students with fancy plastic binders around their term papers. What's important is what's in the grooves—make that your first priority.

- **Cassette.** Sending cassettes probably can't hurt, as anyone with a CD player probably has access to a cassette player as well. But CDs have generally displaced cassettes in the market, and recipients may be less likely to listen to them.

- **Other tapes, including reel-to-reel or 8-track.** Don't even bother. Nobody has these anymore.

- **Digital Audio Tape.** DAT for short, these high-tech tapes were sexy when they first came out and audiophiles love to use them. But CDs are almost as good, and since few people own DAT players, why take the chance?

◆ **MP3 and streaming audio.** You can't beat these formats for convenience, although, as we mention in Chapter 16, they're a little challenging to figure out. By posting them to a website or sending them via e-mail, you enable recipients to quickly and conveniently listen to your music on their desktop speakers.

Just beware: Big MP3 files can crash computers with slow Internet connections, and often people don't like to listen to music at their desks.

Whenever possible, ask the person to whom you're sending the demo about the preferred format. And while it's almost always acceptable to send a bio, press release, and photo, don't send a lyric sheet unless it's requested. This sort of gesture can come off as presumptuous without the right context.

A Few Words About Cost

To make a demo, you probably shouldn't spend a lot of money. Why exhaust your life savings on a pristine recording a record label is unlikely to accept? A demo can be as cheap as the cost of blank rewritable CDs at any local Target (a pack of 30, at, say, an OfficeMax, can run you $10.95—less if you can find a coupon or rebate deal). Disc Makers (discmakers.com), a CD copying service, will run off multiple discs for affordable rates. Remember that a demo isn't designed to recoup costs. The best-case scenario involves a record-label scout expressing interest, but even then, your big payoff is still months or years down the road, if ever.

Keep It Short

In a perfect world, everybody who receives your demo will spend quality time listening to it and, even if she doesn't like it, will respond with a detailed critique. In reality, not only will you not get that kind of attention, you may not get any response at all. Don't take it personally. And don't decide that your recipient is a big jerk and take it upon yourself to sully her reputation all over town. Just move on to the next person.

One of the reasons writers, club bookers, A&R reps, and radio programmers are so busy is because they listen to hundreds of CDs a week. For them, music-listening is work—fun work, but work.

Backstage Insights

Don't expect to get a response just because you sent something. In almost every case, you'll have to follow up—and even then, you might not receive a response. Be patient and persistent and take responses other than "no!" as encouraging signs. And make sure you have plenty of extra CDs available to send.

So your job is to catch their attention quickly. Again, keep the songs short and limit the demo to no more than three songs or 15 minutes total. If you have something they want—talent is often evident quickly—they'll respond. If not, try again later.

If you get no response, it's totally appropriate to follow up with a brief voicemail or e-mail to the effect of, "Wanted to make sure you received our demo." And, if you're feeling brave, "What did you think of it?" Such a message should arrive about 10 days after you send the demo. Any faster and you're at risk of being a pest. Any slower and they may forget about you. Again, don't panic if you get no response.

Taking Your Music to Key People

Obviously you can't set up a formal audition for every important person you want to impress. Sometimes club owners will ask for an audition, but people at record labels, newspapers, and even radio stations just aren't equipped to plug in your amps and listen to several songs in a row live. So send your demo to them instead.

Presentation—Including Your Bio and Press Kit

Remember the press kit—bio, contact information, and photo—from Chapter 14? It'll come in handy when sending out your demo as well. The recipient will likely have a short attention span, so your demo-supplementing material should be brief but meaty. Include a one-page bio with the band members' names, instruments played, and a brief description of the music, plus a photo and perhaps a press release announcing an upcoming gig.

Ideally, every item that comes out of your envelope should scream your band's name. If you have a logo, use it everywhere you can—as a letterhead, on top of the bio and press release, underneath, on the photo, and even on the envelope. Don't go overboard—resist the temptation to make glitter spill out of the envelope onto an irritated reviewer's desk. But visual themes, and packaging continuity, can make an impression.

Think of it this way: You have just a few seconds to get your message across to the person sitting at the desk. And then, if the effectiveness of your packaging coaxes that person into listening to the demo, your music has a few seconds, too.

Gimmicks

Gimmicks work on rare occasions. The Irish band The Boomtown Rats, in the 1980s, sent dead rats in bags of formaldehyde as promotional items to grab attention. Also,

Steve once received a large box from a Colorado band stamped "HUMAN HEAD ENCLOSED"—inside was a mannequin head and bits of brain candy, in addition to the demo, of course.

These amusing stunts can distinguish your band from the pack. Just put some creativity and imagination into them; clichéd gimmicks can earn you the label of "boring," which is worse than being ignored. It's important, however, not to rely completely on gimmicks. Your music should get the most attention. And gimmicks must be relevant: The band with the human head enclosed should be a head-banging heavy metal band, not a gentle folk duo.

Sending It Out

Even if you're not interested in creating clever packaging gimmicks, you still need to pay attention to how your demo is prepared for mailing. If somebody receives a CD jewel case crumbled into a thousand pieces, it's highly likely that person will not listen to the music, period. So buy a cushioned envelope, or bubble wrap, at the local Mailboxes Etc., UPS Store, or post office, and secure the CD so it won't wiggle around. The envelope doesn't have to be Fort Knox, but you get the idea.

Some people believe you'll capture more attention if you send the demo via Federal Express or UPS. Save the money. Unless it's time-sensitive—meaning you have a specific gig to promote or, even better, the recipient has asked for it by a certain date—First Class regular mail should be fine. If you must use FedEx, consider saving money by sending the package two-day rather than overnight—if you're sending it from one big city to another big city, the package will probably arrive within a day anyway.

The Least You Need to Know

- It's possible to record a demo fairly cheaply, if you know what equipment to buy.

- A demo is your musical "calling card"; send it to media, club owners, managers, record labels, and, if you're ambitious and have a tolerance for rejection, radio stations.

- Three songs or 15 minutes (or less) is the limit for a demo early in a band's career. Any more and recipients will get bored. Any less and they'll think you have no substance.

- CD is the acceptable format.

- Brevity, brevity, brevity.

Chapter 20

The Studio

In This Chapter

- ◆ How to use the studio—and to avoid being intimidated
- ◆ Engineers—learning from the experts
- ◆ Producers—what they do and how to get along with them
- ◆ How to record efficiently while the meter runs
- ◆ How much studio time costs
- ◆ Should you record separately or together?

The do-it-yourself studio band has experienced a renaissance in recent years—home studios have become more sophisticated, recording gear has become cheaper, and computer equipment such as Pro Tools has become easier to use. But many argue there's still no substitute for a professional studio and an engineer's well-trained ears.

If you really want to expand as a band—and you have the money—book professional studio time. If you prepare in advance, writing the songs and plotting out your general attack, the by-the-hour fees won't seem quite so intimidating. Then, once you get in, pay close attention to how everything works. An engineer will almost certainly handle the technical details your first few times, but eventually you may want to produce your own (or others') work. The studio is a sort of second home for musicians, so get comfortable with the place. In this chapter we show you how it works.

How to Use the Studio

The studio can be an intimidating place, and later in this chapter we cover a lot of equipment, from mixers to preamplifiers, that you may have never encountered before. Don't get overwhelmed! Fortunately, you won't have to pore through big, heavy user's manuals upon your arrival at the studio. The equipment can be complicated to learn, but most hourly rates come with the services of an engineer. Under most circumstances, you'll simply have to turn on your equipment and start playing—the engineer, and the producer if you use one, will handle anything requiring technical know-how.

But if you aspire to be an engineer or producer someday or simply want to speed up the studio process on future recording dates, it's worth figuring out how stuff works. "You don't have to learn anything. Of course, it'll go faster if you learn everything," says John Macy, a prominent Denver sound engineer. "Ask questions: 'How did you get that sound?' The more you can learn, the better it is in the long run."

So how do you learn? One way, as we suggest in Chapter 18, is by buying your own inexpensive home-recording equipment and teaching yourself how to use it. (Everything comes with a manual.) Far more effective, once you've decided to rent professional studio time, is by shadowing the producer and engineer.

Behind the Music

Five well-known musicians who've gone on to be reputable producers:

- Dr. Dre, rap star and former N.W.A. member, became almost as famous by discovering and producing Eminem.
- Ric Ocasek, former Cars lead singer, produced many future stars, including Weezer (the "green album") and Hanson (*Middle of Nowhere*).
- T-Bone Burnett, veteran rock singer-songwriter, produced Elvis Costello (*Spike*, among others), Counting Crows (*August and Everything After*) and the multiplatinum *O Brother, Where Art Thou?* soundtrack.
- Joan Osborne, blues singer who had a hit with "One of Us," produced the Holmes Brothers' *Speaking In Tongues*.
- Don Nix, former saxophonist with The Mar-Keys, Memphis' touring instrumentalists, spent the 1970s producing blues legends such as Albert King, Freddie King, and John Mayall.

To figure out how to do it yourself in the studio, try one of these books: *Recording in the Digital World: Complete Guide to Studio Gear and Software* (Berklee Press Publications, 2001), by Thomas E. Rudolph and Vincent A. Leonard Jr.; *Basic Mixing Techniques* (Sanctuary Press, 2000), edited by Paul White; or *Anatomy of a Home Studio: How Everything Really Works, from Microphones to Midi* (MixBooks, 1997), by Scott Wilkinson, Steve Oppenheimer, and Mark Isham. But again, once you're in the studio, your best resources are the engineer and producer.

The Engineer

The *engineer* is the recording-studio employee who's in charge of transferring your band's sounds onto the recording source (such as a tape or a digital console). Engineers don't have quite the sexy reputation of producers—they're in-the-trenches types who know what buttons to push at what times, and they rarely become stars in their own rights.

Some engineers, however, have become famous. Alan Parsons, for example, worked with The Beatles and on Pink Floyd's classic *Dark Side of the Moon* before forming his Project for rock-radio hits in the mid-1970s. Larry Levine helped create Phil Spector's famous "Wall of Sound" in the 1960s. Toby Scott and Bob Clearmountain have been Bruce Springsteen's studio wizards for years.

Backstage Insights

If you have any interest whatsoever in the big-time studio process, we recommend an anonymous website diary titled "The Daily Adventures of Mixerman" (prosoundweb.com/recording/mm/week1/mm.php). Mixerman is an unnamed engineer working with an up-and-coming rock band who notices every annoying detail of recording-studio politics, from the singer's egotism to the drummer's incompetence. Although the diary is a little profane and very cynical, it's a funny insider's look at how records *really* get made.

What Does an Engineer Do?

The engineer, simply put, is in charge of the technical studio details. He or she will work with you to get your sounds onto tape the way you like them. The first thing you do, upon arriving at the studio with your performance gear, will probably involve setting up microphones around the drum kit to capture the perfect rhythm sound. This process is an art, and it can take hours, but it's time well spent. The engineer will go through each of your band's instruments in this manner, ensuring that they'll sound reasonably good (and according to your specifications) when the record comes out.

A good engineer will know so well how to use the mixers, sequencers, and other equipment that you won't have to worry about that area at all. Your job will be simply to perform.

Getting the Engineer on Your Side

We can't emphasize enough how important it is to get along with the engineer. This person may hold the key to transferring the sound you want to a demo or for-sale CD. At the very least, he or she will be a central person from whom you'll receive advice, instruction, and insight. Develop a rapport with the engineer at the beginning of the process.

One way of doing this is through communication. Never, *ever* treat engineers as if you're the customer and they're the wait staff. Listen carefully to their suggestions— don't reject them simply because they're not your suggestions. Let the engineer eat the last chocolate donut—sometimes—in the studio reception area. Figure out what type of music the engineer likes and use that as a conversation piece.

The Producer

Although renting a studio means you'll get the services of an engineer, a producer almost always costs extra. Sometimes you'll get hooked up with a producer through a mutual connection, like a friend in a similar-sounding band. Other times, your record company will hook you up with somebody who fits. In any event, you should interview this person carefully and decide whether you can work with him or her before making the decision. The wrong producer can wreck an album.

What Does a Producer Do?

Here's how Steve Albini, the barrier-breaking Chicago hard-rock producer who has worked with Nirvana, the Pixies, Nine Inch Nails, and others, defines the traditional role of a producer:

> In band-centric music, the producer can be anything from a fairly innocuous "nodder"—someone who sort of proffers ideas and offers commentary—to fairly heavy-handed, directorial people who will think nothing of replacing a band member or hiring outside musicians to replace the band members to improve the end product.

Behind the Music

Ten famous producers and the artists they've worked with:

- Phil Spector (The Ronettes, Ike and Tina Turner, The Beatles, many others)
- George Martin (The Beatles)
- Sam Phillips (Elvis Presley, Jerry Lee Lewis, Roy Orbison, Johnny Cash, others)
- Butch Vig (Nirvana)
- Phil Ramone (Billy Joel, Bob Dylan, Frank Sinatra, Elton John, Tony Bennett, others)
- The Bomb Squad (Public Enemy)
- Brian Eno (U2, Talking Heads, Roxy Music, others)
- Lee "Scratch" Perry (Bob Marley, Junior Murvin, The Upsetters, others)
- Sean "P. Diddy" Combs (The Notorious B.I.G., Lil' Kim, Mase, Faith Evans, others)
- The Matrix (Avril Lavigne, Jason Mraz, Liz Phair, others)

It should be noted that Albini, who spoke with Steve for a 2001 *Chicago Tribune* article, doesn't consider himself a producer in the traditional sense. "I basically provide the technical knowledge and experience to get done whatever the band wants to get done," he says. "If a band says, 'All right, this song needs to have a really distant ghostly feel,' for example, I have to insert that into a technical menu of things that you have to do. I'll need ambient mikes in the distance and make sure it's kept in balance."

Conversely, Phil Ramone, who has helmed hits for Billy Joel, Frank Sinatra, and many others, believes the producer must be assertive and provide direction even if it makes things awkward for one of his superstar clients. "They look to you at the right moment and you say, 'The picture is pretty perfect, but it needs this or that.' It takes a lot of courage to say those words at the right time and not try to impress anybody," he told Steve for the same *Chicago Tribune* article. "It's the oldest joke in the world: People overplay and you say, 'You know, you've already got the job.'"

The producer's influence on a record, and in the studio, will depend on his or her personal approach and the band's musical (and emotional) needs. Some, like Albini, will be minimalists who exist mainly to translate a musician's ideas to tape. Others, like Ramone, use their well-trained instincts to gently and diplomatically nudge artists in certain directions or encourage them to try something new.

CAUTION

Avoiding Bad Notes

Another reason to get along with the producer—and the engineer, for that matter—is you'll spend a great deal of time with this person in a claustrophobic studio space. It won't even have exterior windows. Choose carefully.

Generally, while the engineer concentrates on the little picture, the producer looks at the big picture of molding individual sounds into a cohesive, finished piece. Some producers have little technical studio know-how but terrific "ears" to gauge what's right and wrong about a performance. Others are more nuts-and-bolts, using various computer and recording techniques to improve a sound. Study a producer's resumé so you know which type you have going in.

Can You Produce Your Own Album?

You can definitely produce your own album. In fact, maybe you're the only person in the world who knows how your album is supposed to sound. And if you can find engineers who know what they're doing, you can probably handle the production without being particularly accomplished technically.

Of course, there are excellent reasons not to produce your own album. If your band signs with a major record company, its representatives may try to choose a big-name producer to streamline your sound and help you sell records. (Many producers, such as Swedish teen-pop specialist Max Martin, are chosen because of their proven hit-making ability, which may have more credibility with hit-picking radio-station programmers.) Or if you're enamored of a certain sound you heard on a friend's band's album, you may want to try to hire the same producer.

But if you're determined to do it yourself, one important consideration is your relationship with the engineer. Communication is important, especially if you don't know EQ from reverb. Don't say, for example, "I need it to sound more hot or more cold or more blue or more underwater." Be specific. It often helps to bring records that you like to the studio and play certain instructive bits to the engineer before the session begins. In the end, you may have to learn enough studio basics to communicate using technical terms.

Be Prepared

Studios charge by the hour, so you don't want to waste any time. Don't write your songs in the studio—have them outlined and well-rehearsed by the time you get there. Be aware the engineer and producer may want to record your rhythm section separately, so prepare by holding separate bass-and-drum rehearsals in your home practice space.

It's impossible to plan too much in advance. Should your guitar solos sound a certain way? Plan them out, and bring clear instructions with you to the studio. Do you want to use certain effects, like finger cymbals or cowbell? Bring those instruments with you, and let the studio know where and when you'd like to include them in the songs.

On rare occasions, it is possible to rehearse too much. Some musicians say their studio goal is to be fresh, loose, and spontaneous, and once they reach the point where every band member is locked inflexibly into the song they lose the freedom to stretch out. This balance is a matter of personal preference and collective band style, and it's important to communicate your preferences in advance, during rehearsal.

Some bandleaders like to turn the studio into a challenge for other members. While recording his landmark *Tonight's the Night*, for example, rock singer-songwriter Neil Young purposely didn't bother teaching his sidemen the songs. They struggled initially to keep up, which helped give the album its spontaneous, jittery quality. You need good musicians and a visionary leader to pull off this sort of thing.

Backstage Insights

Try to stay fresh physically in the studio. If you've done several takes of the same song—or the same song snippet—you might feel the tension in your neck, shoulders, and back. At that point, take a break. Stretch. Run around the block. Do jumping-jacks. Then get back to work.

Equipment You'll Encounter

The first thing you'll notice, in almost every studio, is a designated spot for the band to perform and a control room filled with various mixing and recording gadgets. A thick window usually separates these areas, so the control-room crew can talk without worrying the tape will pick them up.

In the band room, the equipment will be mostly familiar—microphones, drums, amplifiers, guitars, and keyboards. You'll probably notice mikes positioned just so next to the drums and various electronic doo-dads hooked up to amps in particular ways.

In the recording room, you may encounter knobs and machines you've never seen before. Here are some of them:

Avoiding Bad Notes

Don't mess with studio equipment until you've talked to the engineer. The professionals know their rooms extremely well, and while you can bring your own equipment to the studio, the existing microphones and other gear have been meticulously positioned for maximum sound quality.

♦ Microphones are already familiar to your band, but the studio will have many brands and styles for different situations. You'll see them set carefully next to drum heads and amps in addition to the usual vocal mikes.

♦ The mixer is the big "sound board" you often see at live music shows. All the recording devices—microphones, amps,

Backstage Insights

Most mixers allow engineers to control the EQ, or equalizing, so the frequencies of high-pitched sounds (treble), low-pitched sounds (bass), and everything in between come out smoothly and compatibly in the recording.

preamps—connect to the mixer so the engineer can make the sound levels consistent. Without using mixers, all the instruments would come out at wildly varying volumes, rendering the recording unlistenable.

◆ A microphone preamplifier is the "middleman" device that allows the mike and the amplifier to communicate seamlessly and enhance the microphone's sound.

◆ Monitors are basically control-room speakers, so the engineer, producer, and band can hear the music as it plays.

◆ Mixers have channels, or slots for input (such as amps and microphones) *and output* (directly to studio monitors or recording devices). Engineers divide the various instruments into channels, putting the low-end bass guitar and bass drum in one channel, say, and high-end guitars and vocals in others.

◆ *Click-tracks,* electronic percussion devices that keep the beat at a certain speed. Although many musicians hate them, they often help bands stay in time.

◆ Effects such as *reverb* (for a deeper, more echoey sound) and *chorus* (fuller, thicker sound) are available via various studio devices (including, sometimes, the mixer).

◆ The mixing board's *faders* are switches that move up and down and control how much signal (essentially volume) the engineer receives from the musician.

◆ A *sequencer* is a high-tech recording machine that allows engineers to quickly and easily manipulate the signals they receive from the musicians' amps and instruments. It uses no tape, just *MIDI.*

Words to Rock By

MIDI, short for Musical Instrument Digital Interface, is a type of computer file enabling musical instruments to talk to each other (and to computers). It was developed in 1983, and is a widely used recording-studio standard today.

Pro Tools and Using Computer Software

We explain Pro Tools, the highly popular computer-based recording equipment, in more depth during Chapter 18. Often, when you record in a professional studio, you'll be thrown into a Pro Tools situation. The engineer and producer will walk you through the high-tech system, but it's worth understanding for future reference.

Thanks to computers, which have made the studio process more accessible and affordable, giant, multi-knob mixing boards and other cumbersome recording devices may be extinct. They still exist, of course, but many engineers use computers as their mixing consoles. The traditional, physical knobs, for controlling EQ, reverb, and so forth, are simply digital images on the screen.

Are computer systems harder to learn than traditional analog recording equipment? Probably not, engineer Macy says, depending on your general comfort level with computers. "It was a bigger learning curve for me, because I came out of an analog generation. Young guys with a little more computer skills come to it a little bit more naturally given video games and computers," he says. "It's not a huge learning curve, but it's definitely a curve. You couldn't just walk right in and fire it up."

In addition to Pro Tools, the most widely known computer-based recording system, producers and engineers choose from Nuendo, which specializes in mixing and other production techniques; Cubase, which is geared more to sequencing and the song-creation process; and Digital Performer, which hooks easily to a laptop and helps home-recording artists "capture" their rough demos for studio polish later.

Typical Costs

Depending where you live, professional recording studios can cost anywhere from $10 an hour to $3,000 a day. The high-end rooms will be prominent places like Southern Tracks, in Atlanta, where Bruce Springsteen, Pearl Jam, Train, and Korn have recorded; Miami-based Criteria Recording Studios, which has produced well-known albums for artists such as Bob Dylan, Dr. Dre, Céline Dion, and Aretha Franklin; and Nirvana producer Butch Vig's Smart Studios, in Madison, Wisconsin.

At least for now, lower-end studios are probably more accommodating for your budget. Be careful, though—$10-an-hour studios often have decrepit equipment and engineers who are either inexperienced or hard to get along with.

Macy, the Denver engineer, is a proponent of tinkering in different venues before plunging into a pay-by-the-hour studio. For example, you might want to hire a local drum technician (ask around for reputable names) to position the microphones for optimum percussion sounds. That way, you'll save time on the drum-*miking* process when you finally enter

Words to Rock By

The shorthand term for setting up microphones next to drums and other acoustic instruments is **miking**. It can be a long, challenging process, but it's crucial to the overall sound.

the studio. Or record yourself using a friend's home studio just to familiarize yourself with the process and fix any major problems that are likely to come up.

A studio, especially an expensive one, can be a stressful place. When the red recording light comes on, it's time to create your album as perfectly as possible, and that can be as much pressure as playing before a crowd for the first time. If you have the money, Macy suggests renting time at a super-cheap "pre-studio" just to nail down technical details, like miking drums and memorizing chord changes. Later, you can enter the more expensive studio—$250 an hour is a solid price level that Macy recommends, although that can be expensive for an independent band—and not have to worry as much about hammering out particularities.

> **Behind the Music**
>
> Studios can actually be cheaper in music-industry capitals New York City, Los Angeles, and Nashville than in other towns. In the big cities, there are countless working musicians, all climbing various rungs of the ladder, and so the demand for studios at every level is extremely high. The studio competition often drives down prices.

Also, before signing on with a studio, do plenty of advance research. Talk to the engineers—are their influences the same as yours? And if not, will they complement each other? You probably won't want to record your bombastic hip-hop-metal album with an engineer whose primary experience is mainstream country-and-western music. "Interview" engineers in advance by asking who else they've worked with and what other projects they've overseen.

Note that in most studios, you'll have to bring your own equipment. The big ones may have a grand piano, and some engineers or producers may loan you their own instruments if they trust you and your stuff just isn't getting the job done. But generally, expect to transport your gear to the studio just as you would transport it to the gig, with the same kinds of load-in and load-out exercises. And remember to budget for the time it takes the engineer to hook up your instruments to studio amps and mixers—because you're paying for that time.

Different Techniques

Every studio has its own unique sound, defined by the ways the walls are arranged and whether the room surfaces are reflective and hard, or soft and sound-absorbent. Many producers and engineers will offer you a variety of situations to take advantage of these physical characteristics. Try different things—move the drums close to the wall and then far away from the wall, and arrange microphones in various places. Remember, though, you're on the clock and every minute costs money.

Should you record each instrument separately, in its own little corner of the studio, or together with the full band? That's another matter of personal preference. Some bands swear by playing live in the studio, spontaneously, as they would before an audience. Other musicians are control freaks who want their individual sounds just so before bringing them to the rest of the band. (This is an excellent way to eliminate annoyances like buzzing amplifiers—although weird "wrong" sounds like the squeaking bass-drum pedal on The Searchers' classic "Needles and Pins" have their charms.)

Behind the Music

Over the last decade or so, recording artists have eliminated the need to perform together at all. Famously, Frank Sinatra's 1994 hit album *Duets* was filled with several big-name singing partners, from U2's Bono to Eydie Gorme, who never once stepped in the studio with the Chairman of the Board. (Critics noticed a certain lack of chemistry on the record.) Technology encourages this trend, which is mostly positive, allowing musicians around the world to connect despite their lack of physical proximity.

If you record separate tracks, you'll have to learn how to perform with headphones. (It may help to try this in rehearsal before showing up in the studio.) Why use headphones? If the rhythm section records its part in a separate session earlier in the day, the guitarist and singer will listen to those parts in headphones while cutting their own. Using headphones may give you much more appreciation for nuances and subtle dynamics. But it also can change the dynamics among band members who are used to playing off each other acoustically and communicating out loud.

This approach can take away some spontaneity—obviously, with a prerecorded rhythm track, all four band members won't be able to speed up or slow down according to each other's unspoken signals and gestures. But to many engineers and producers, recording separate tracks is an efficient way of isolating certain sounds and making them perfect before assembling them into a full-band collage. It may or may not work within your band's collective style. You'll have to try different things.

The Least You Need to Know

- Recording at home can be cheap and convenient, but you might eventually choose the studio's extra space, more sophisticated equipment, and hands-on technical assistance.

- An engineer will probably be on hand for advice, so you won't have to worry about learning how to use complex recording gear while performing.

- As a director oversees a movie, a producer oversees a recording session; this person can be hands-off or "the fifth band member," but either way it's crucial that you get along.

- Engineers usually take instruction from the producer, but they often are the only people in the room who know how to properly work the various studio tools.

- Studio time is expensive, so write the songs and map out your recording plans before you ever go in.

- At least at first, you won't have to worry about setting up mikes or getting the perfect drum sound—that's the engineer's job; but pay attention so you can do it later.

Chapter 21

Do-It-Yourself CDs

In This Chapter

- ◆ Turning your demo into a full-fledged CD
- ◆ Packaging a CD—artwork, liner notes, logos, and the marketing thereof
- ◆ Tracking sales: keeping inventory, using the music industry's SoundScan system
- ◆ Universal price code: what it is, how to use it, and why it's important

Making a record—or compact disc—can be one of the most exciting things a band can do in its career. Performing live is often exhilarating, but there's nothing quite like the feeling of holding in your hands the result of months and months of creative work. Now the main challenge is to sell it. Until you move a little farther up the music-industry ladder, it's not necessary to sell thousands of CDs, although that can be considerably helpful for your budget. Getting CDs into the hands of your fans at shows, and slowly broadening your sales reach, will be the goal immediately after you've printed up copies.

To make a CD, you can expand and rearrange the music on the demo we discussed in Chapter 18. Here, we'll show you how to repackage the demo and sell it to the public. Once you have "product" available, beyond T-shirts and stickers, the band takes another giant leap into music-industry sophistication.

Turning Your Demo Into a CD

Your demo is *not* the compact disc you'll wind up selling to the public. We're talking about two different audiences. Demo recipients—concert promoters, media, record labels, and the like—are in-the-know industry types who have little time and want to be wowed immediately. For them, you'll choose three short songs and try to grab their attention. In short, the demo's purpose is to get attention.

The CD's purpose is to spread the music and communicate your ideas to the public—and, with luck, make a little money. The demo may get you work, which will ultimately pay the rent. The CD may pay for gas and hotel every night, if you're on tour.

The general listening audience takes in music a totally different way than music-industry types, especially if they're already fans of your concerts. On a demo, you probably won't want to include the heavily detailed, 15-minute song about your significant other. On a CD, if the band really enjoys playing that song live, why not include it? The CD should be well played and high quality, but it allows you room to stretch out. It may show a broader range and depth of the band's capabilities—and it's designed for people who actually plan to listen to the whole thing.

Should a CD be produced more professionally—with better sound equipment and a hired, experienced producer—than a demo? In a perfect world, yes. High-end production isn't hugely important for a demo, as the recipients are listening for evidence of raw talent rather than the best recording gear money can buy. Think of the differences this way: A demo is a rough sketch, while a CD is the finished painting.

But despite these distinctions, the demo is the essential core of your finished musical product. If you have no recorded music to speak of, it's intimidating to jump into the studio, or even your usual rehearsal space, and attempt to record an entire CD at once. It's also expensive. But if you've already done a demo, you can build on those three songs—maybe you can rerecord them with longer solos or a few extra verses. Or tweak the production polish a little.

At the least, a demo gives you the recording experience you need to complete a more elaborate CD project. Note that the demo-to-CD progression isn't a requirement—some bands may find themselves with enough material and studio connections to record the entire CD first. Later, to send out the demo, the band can edit the CD down to three songs.

Selling Your CD

To make a full-fledged CD, economics step into the picture. Because you're planning to sell the CD to the public, you may want to estimate costs in advance, determine the selling price, and calculate how many copies you'll have to sell to break even. (Or not break even, as the case may be.) Again, we recommend making the CD as cheaply as you possibly can. (See Chapter 18 for more on recording prices and techniques.)

> ### Behind the Music
>
> Distribution is an important concept in music-industry economics. It basically refers to the "middleman" companies that receive the CDs from the artist or record label and then ship them for a fee to retail outlets. For decades, big-time distributors such as WEA and CEMA have profited greatly from this angle of the business. But with more and more consumers downloading their music directly from the Internet, the future of distribution is in flux.
>
> At this stage, even if you can find a local distributor or want to sign with a smaller national company such as theorchard.com, your band will also probably want to distribute its own CDs. That means setting up a sales table during a gig or selling directly to fans over your website.

Whereas a demo will probably go to a handful of people—maybe 100 at most—the CD is designed to sell in bulk. At the least, you should have enough copies for everybody who attends the gig. Disc Makers offers several options, including a run of 300, in full-color jackets, for $990. Many high-tech companies, including Disc Makers, will also sell you a CD duplication machine in the neighborhood of $1,500—a decent investment if you plan many CDs in the future and don't want to pay $990 every time.

The absolute cheapest you can sell your CD, and still hope to recoup costs, is $5. Under no circumstances do you want to approach $18.98, or whatever the local Tower Records or other retailer charges for the new Madonna CD. "I can buy the new Madonna for *that* price!" is what you'd call a negative reaction, and you never want to alienate your fan base.

"Value-added" is the big buzzword in music-selling circles these days, and it essentially means packaging your CD with an extra tidbit. "Bonus tracks" tacked on at the end of the CD, posters, T-shirts, caps, stickers, or, if you're tech-savvy and well-equipped, live-show DVDS, are all attractive supplements. Check out existing bonus DVDs, from artists such as 50 Cent, Tori Amos, Metallica, and Adema, for ideas in this area.

Which Songs Should You Include?

You already know a demo should contain three songs. For a full CD, think at least 45 minutes of music over 8 or 10 songs—more if you have it.

Backstage Insights _____

EPs, or extended-play singles, were especially popular among rock bands in the 1980s and early 1990s, and underground artists such as R.E.M. (early in its career) and Matthew Sweet made brilliant five- or six-song discs including a few originals, a strange cover, and possibly some live tracks. Today, the music industry isn't quite so receptive. Retail CD outlets, and even smaller mom-and-pop record stores, have little room for EPs and extended singles. They probably won't rack your EP if it competes for limited space against the Avril Lavigne remix disc.

As opposed to a demo, which should knock out the listener after just a few seconds, the CD can unfold at a more leisurely pace. It should be a representative sampling of your band's full range. Include your best material—if you've written original songs, include those. Cover songs are okay, but don't go too overboard; it may be best to include one or two of them (and the more obscure, the better) at the end.

Pace your CD as you would your concert set list. Start off with a fast, attention-getting song, then play a few soulful slower pieces, and then build back up to a crescendo at the end. And maybe employ a "cool-down song" as the last track. But different kinds of bands pace their shows and albums in different ways, so go back to your old classic records to see how the masters did it. In the CD age, when albums are typically 70 minutes or longer, pacing isn't quite as crucial as it was when artists put out 10 short songs.

Backstage Insights _____

If your CD is already filled with 60 minutes of solid original music, but your version of Michael Jackson's "Burn This Disco Out" is too fun to ignore, try the old hidden track trick. Artists from Nirvana to the Counting Crows have included an unlisted song at the very end of the CD that surprises attentive listeners.

Choosing songs for your CD seems like a simple process, but it can be incredibly complicated. Prolific bands complain about it all the time. To name just one example, The Exies, a southern California punk band, wound up with dozens of songs for 2003's *Inertia*. But they wanted to keep the CD short and punchy, so they set a cap of 11 songs. "Dude, you've never seen four guys go back and forth more times over a list of songs than we did," bassist Freddy Herrera told Steve in an interview for *Newsday*.

The usual band-communication rules, as specified in Chapter 6, apply. If you're the leader, don't load up the CD with your own songs simply because they're yours. Don't ignore the drummer's one songwriting contribution. Try to listen to the pool of available songs objectively, and pick the best stuff. Or you can turn a song into a "rare" track for radio stations or your website.

Can We Make a Single?

As of this writing, CD singles, popular throughout the 1980s and 1990s, have almost completely disappeared from the marketplace. But they may be making a comeback. In late summer 2003, singers Ruben Studdard and Clay Aiken, winner and runner-up of the smash television series *American Idol 2*, sold hundreds of thousands of copies of their debut singles. Record labels and retailers paid close attention to these successes, and it's possible the single—a proud concept in pop music since the early days of record players—is on its way to a comeback.

Packaging

As with everything else in the CD-making process, packaging costs can add up quickly. To keep them down, rely on the assistance of a band member (or friend or relative) with basic graphic-design skills or artistic talent. If you do have a little money set aside, consider hiring an outside source, especially if that person has worked on CD covers before. In the old days of long-playing records, artists had plenty of room to turn covers into meticulous works. (Check out Roger Dean's elaborate landscapes for the prog-rock band Yes.) A CD's six-inch square isn't quite the same canvas. Although you can do some creative and imaginative things with the cover artwork, it's not crucial for your first CD.

Other packaging points to consider:

- One of the most distinctive cover images of the CD era is Nirvana's *Nevermind*, with the naked underwater baby chasing a dollar bill on a fishing hook. This is the ultimate simple image; a broad, detailed art concept may be too busy for a potential buyer.

- For the CD booklet, keep in mind staples will cost you extra, especially if you're printing thousands of units. A simple fold will save money.

- Black-and-white is cheaper than color printing.

- Keep the liner notes short. Limp Bizkit may need pages upon pages of thank yous, but your gratitude can be limited to a few lines for friends and family.

For various personal and legal reasons, your liner notes will have to be more elaborate on the CD than they were on the demo. For legal reasons, you need to include the name of the songwriter, copyright, and publishing information; and if you used a producer or studio engineer, it's professional courtesy (and sometimes a contractual necessity) to give that person proper credit—after all, you might want to hire the same producer for future CDs. Study existing CDs to see how and where experienced artists position this information. But be creative, too.

Other important information for liner notes:

♦ Song titles, spelled correctly, and properly numbered.

♦ Length of song (optional, but especially handy for fans in the CD era), in minutes and seconds.

♦ Website and contact information (a post-office box or manager's business address if you don't want people to know where you live).

♦ Name of the studio where you recorded the CD (if it's in your rehearsal basement, make up a name, like "Flooded Basement Studios," just to look more professional).

♦ Band members' names, plus guest musicians and (in same cases) managers and engineers.

♦ Band logo, stamped on the cover, and at least one or two times in the liner notes or on the back.

Marketing Basics

"Marketing" is a corporate concept with many facets—selling, packaging, promoting, and distributing items from a creator to a buyer. It all comes down to finding creative ways to make a sales item more attractive to consumers.

With your CD, one basic marketing technique involves getting a good position in a record-store rack. (Or on an online package or banner ad, if you're talking about selling through amazon.com or CDBaby.com.) The most straightforward method involves approaching a small record store and asking it to stock the CD; if you're popular, or if the store is inclined to support local music, this may just work. Or contact a small, independent distributor and use the middleman's connections for racking.

Another facet of marketing is advertising. Just as you can advertise an upcoming gig in the local newspaper or alt-weekly, so, too, can you advertise a CD release. (Many bands will play special "CD release parties" and place ads for both things at once.) Often a local record store will split the costs with you for a co-op ad—it's in the store's interest to sell your CD, too. Creativity often helps: Consider printing a $1 coupon in the ad.

Promotional items can be handy. You're already familiar with T-shirts and stickers, but many bands print up matchboxes, ear plugs, or other off-kilter items. Mark once managed two bands, Leftover Salmon and the Ugly Americans, who weren't exactly known for their fashion sense. He paid almost nothing for 500 combs marked "Good Grooming Pays: Ugly Americans." This sarcastic joke worked amazingly well, as people lunged for them when the bands tossed combs from the stage.

Promotional events are also effective. And you may be able to work with radio stations or record stores for special live events at which you can sell many CDs. Many big-time radio stations have regular local-music programs; contact that particular DJ about placing your music there.

> ### Behind the Music
>
> There's an art to promotional campaigns. The rock band KISS is particularly brilliant at this, creating the concept of a KISS Army in the 1970s, filled with people wearing elaborate makeup and large, black platform boots. Naturally, this army wanted to buy stuff—even today, the band sells KISS Koffins, action figures, comic books, and of course, makeup.

Now that you have a CD to sell, when printing fliers, include an inset picture of the CD cover and the words "on sale now"—along with your website. (We can't stress that enough: Include your website address *everywhere*.) Oh, and don't forget to contact the media.

Selling on Your Web Page

Check out Chapter 16 for more information on selling CDs online, linking to e-retail outlets and setting up a virtual store.

But also use the Internet for marketing purposes: Post lots of banner ads on every page at your website. Go to newsgroups or other bands' bulletin boards and post a note about your new CD.

Your most receptive online audience, however, may already be signed up on your mailing list. Using a computer database, send an e-mail with details on the CD release to everyone on your list.

Setting Up Tables at Concerts

Your primary audience for CD sales, at least at first, will be the fans who show up at gigs. They're already predisposed to your music, and there's no self-promotional shame in announcing, from the stage, "CDs are available in the lobby!" Bands do it all the time—and don't forget to sneak in the title and maybe say how great it is.

Never assume the venue will provide a sales table for you. (The small club manager will probably allow you to sell CDs, but the venue typically makes no money off this particular type of merchandise, so you may encounter little enthusiasm for sales help.) When you scout the venue, as we suggest in Chapter 12, ask the club manager whether you can sell CDs and what table facilities are available. If you're playing a wedding, bar mitzvah, or other private function, you may irritate the planners by selling personal merchandise without advance notice. Ask first. Many venues will take a percentage of your merchandise sales.

Finally, try to realistically estimate how many potential CD buyers will show up at the gig. You don't want to get caught with just 20 CDs at your merchandise table when hundreds of interested customers have bought tickets for the show. After you sell merchandise a few times at concerts, you'll develop a routine—and a formula—for this sort of thing. Until then, find out the venue's crowd capacity in advance of the show, and estimate what percentage of the crowd might consider buying CDs.

See Chapter 12 for more information on selling your CDs and with other merchandise.

Backstage Insights

Once you've paid big money to produce the CDs, think twice about giving them away for free. For business and networking purposes, you'll want to give away a certain number—to club owners, radio stations, record stores, and media. But most friends and family should know they're stuck for full price. If you start giving free copies to some people, everyone will want them. Avoid that situation.

How Do You Know If It Sells?

Keep a good inventory. There's no substitute for the knowledge that you had a box of 1,000 CDs, you gave away 200 to radio and media outlets for promotional purposes, and you, therefore, have 800 left to sell.

SoundScan

SoundScan, unveiled in 1991, is a system record labels and retail stores use to track sales numbers. Before SoundScan, the process was slipshod and disorganized, so some stores reported accurate numbers and others were inaccurate or, in many cases, not counted at all. This system was open to manipulation and wreaked havoc for decades on the influential *Billboard* charts, which use sales figures to determine hit singles and platinum albums.

In effect, SoundScan uses electronic technology to count every unit sold, as accurately as possible. (Even today, certain stores don't participate in SoundScan, and so some critics wonder just how accurate the numbers really are.) Now it works more like the grocery store: Whenever you buy a CD at a record store, the cashier scans the bar code on the CD and presto. That's one more unit sold.

> ### Behind the Music
>
> When it was first introduced, SoundScan had shocking effects. Suddenly, country-music artists, who had traditionally been undercounted, became gigantic stars—Garth Brooks, Reba McEntire, Clint Black, and others topped the pop charts for the first times in their careers.

For your purposes, participating in the SoundScan system is relatively cheap and gives you credibility with retail stores and, perhaps, record labels. Whenever your CD is sold at a store, it will get officially counted.

The formal name of the "bar code" that SoundScan uses is the *universal price code*, or UPC. (On other products, you've undoubtedly seen this black-and-white symbol with thin, vertical stripes and tiny numbers.) You can pay various entities to get the code—the Colorado Music Association, for example, includes it free with an annual band membership. Or you can buy one outright for $400. You can also contact SoundScan (home.soundscan.com or 914-684-5525) for more details.

Once you have a copy of the UPC design, print it onto the master artwork for your CD. (It should appear, as inconspicuously as possible, on the bottom left or right of the back cover.) The UPC design gives you the sheen of professionalism, but more importantly, stores might not stock your CD if you don't have the code. You should consider participating in SoundScan even if your band sells CDs exclusively at gigs. It offers a "venue sales account" for bands. All you need to do is submit a form, signed by the venue, showing that you sold a certain number of CDs at a certain date and place. The data must be reported by the following Monday.

This may seem like a lot of work just to officially prove you've sold 10 CDs at a gig. But in the bigger picture, say you've made contact with a record label's A&R department. Say the A&R scout vaguely remembers your name from the demo you sent. Say she calls up the label's SoundScan report on her computer screen and sees, at the bottom, "Fabulous Dogs: 10 copies." That may not seem like much, but it may refresh her memory—and show that you're selling CDs professionally.

The Least You Need to Know

- A CD should be longer than a demo and more accurately reflect what the band does on stage.

- Charge roughly $5 to $10 for the homemade CD you sell at gigs, local record stores, and on your website. Your goal at this point is to circulate as much music as possible—while still breaking even.

- Consider marketing the CD with newspaper ads, fliers, or creative promotional items.

- Once the CD is ready for sale, participate in SoundScan, the music industry's official sales-counting system. Also, make sure your artwork includes a bar code.

Part 6

Taking Your Band to the Next Level

Now what? You've built a large touring base, fans have come to recognize your songs, the media have given you publicity, and you may have even scored a spin or two on local radio. The band is convinced it's time to become, if not gigantic superstars, then a little bigger in the public eye.

That means more aggressive networking. Remember the press kits and demos you sent to local media and clubs? Polish them, add more credentials, and send them to record-label executives. Talk to everyone you know, especially other bands, about finding connections in the music industry. And sign up for showcases such as South by Southwest.

If you're lucky enough to draw interest from a major label—or an independent, which can be at least as good—proceed carefully. Hire a lawyer before signing anything. And surround yourself with knowledgeable people. It's one thing to get suckered out of a gig fee; it's quite another to lose creative control on your record. And remember, if the band doesn't work out, your experience may help you get a desk job in the music industry!

Chapter 22

The Record Deal

In This Chapter

- ◆ When should you aim for a big-time record deal?
- ◆ "The Big Five" record labels
- ◆ Going independent, and running your own label
- ◆ A&R, product managers, legal affairs, publicity, and other label departments you should know about
- ◆ How to navigate (and not get bamboozled by) a record contract
- ◆ When (if ever) will you make money?

Signing a record deal has always been a romantic concept in pop music. For years, the only way to expose your music to a large national audience was to hook up with one of the many big-time record companies. But during the 1990s, the music business underwent an intense period of consolidation, leaving five gigantic labels, all obsessed with the bottom line. You may be talented and lucky enough to hook up with one of them—but it isn't necessary. To sell 15 million copies of your record and get on the cover of *People* magazine, you'll definitely need a major record label. Otherwise, doing everything yourself works just fine.

When to Pursue One

Go for the big-label deal when you're ready. When will that be? Your crowds will tell you. If you've grown to the point where you're attracting bigger and bigger audiences and selling more and more discs, you may be ready. If local and perhaps even national media have commissioned stories about the band, you may be ready to take the next business step.

Usually the process from the band-formation to the record-label stage lasts two to five years—with exceptions, of course. The Clarks, a straightforward rock band from Pittsburgh, toured heavily for almost 15 years before signing with a small national label. Conversely, San Francisco band Third Eye Blind took just over a year to land a deal with big-time Elektra Records, and then a few additional months to earn a smash single, "Semi-Charmed Life."

Without one of the following bases, you'll have to be extremely lucky, or have extremely good connections, to get any label attention at all:

- **Touring.** If you do it properly, you can almost never go wrong with building a touring base. If fans pack your shows in several different cities, including your home base, you'll bring clout to any record-label negotiation. You'll also have the power to walk away from any potential deal and simply continue your successful touring career.

- **Press.** Have you heard the term "critical darling"? Before they even get to the touring or record-label stage, many bands are good enough to generate positive reviews in newspapers, alt-weeklies, and magazines. Such "buzz" (see Chapter 14) can catch an A&R rep's attention.

- **Radio.** This is the hardest of the three bases to build. Unless you have a big-time record deal, many radio stations won't even bother to listen to your demo. But luck, connections, catchy singles, a strong fan base, and marketing campaigns occasionally pay off, and if you've landed on at least one major station you'll almost certainly get some sort of label attention.

The Record Labels

In years past, big, progressive labels such as Warner Bros. and A&M took chances on "developing artists," enduring slow-selling early albums to achieve big success later on. Among the beneficiaries of this system have been Neil Young, Blues Traveler, Tool, Metallica, and Bruce Springsteen.

Backstage Insights _____

Sending your demo to the local corporate-owned station is unlikely to lead to air-play. However, pay attention to smaller, more free-form community and college sta-tions. KGNU-FM in Boulder, Colorado, for example, is open to all kinds of sounds, and WBEZ-FM in Chicago has jazz, classical, and folk programs. In addition, many stations have local music programs that accept solicitations and demos.

Whenever you're touring through a town, contact the college, independent, or commu-nity station in advance. In addition to playing your record, they may invite you to the station to do an impromptu live performance and interview.

Today, a major label isn't likely to sign you unless you have a pretty good shot of making money with the first album. "The bean counters won the war," Mark says.

Why the change? In the mid-1990s, for various reasons, labels went through an intense period of consolidation. In part this was because giant corporations decided CD sales were big money and started buying up labels of all sizes, from PolyGram to A&M to Def Jam. Many layoffs followed, as chief executive officers began to pay far more attention to the bottom line than to the creative development of their artists.

Which isn't to say record labels have ever been staffed completely with laid-back, "art-first," altruistic types. The music industry, from Frank Sinatra to Elvis Presley to The Donnas, has always existed to make money. No matter how supportive your A&R rep, you won't last long unless you have a chance of making commercial music. It's important to keep this in mind if you're fortunate enough to get to the fine print of label contracts.

"The Big Five": EMI, Sony, Warner, BMG, Universal

Years ago, it was difficult to count all the important record labels. On the big side, you had Columbia and Capitol, which signed Bob Dylan, Johnny Cash, and Bruce Springsteen; and The Beatles and The Beach Boys, respectively. On the smaller side, you had Motown, which became famous in the 1960s for breaking artists from The Supremes to Marvin Gaye; Stax, an important Memphis soul label; and Elektra, which took chances on important artists from Tom Rush to The Doors to Metallica.

From the 1950s through the 1980s, there was a certain romance to record labels. Music consumers immediately recognized the distinctive yellow-sun label spinning at the center of Elvis Presley's singles. If something came out on Stax Records in the 1960s, soul-music fans took it seriously; same with Vanguard Records for folk and, later, England's Stiff Records for punk and new wave.

In recent years, many of these small, important labels have folded or sold out to the big labels. Motown, for example, is part of Universal, regularly breaking middle-of-the-road R&B artists like Brian McKnight. Atlantic, once a legendary soul label that took off with Ray Charles and Aretha Franklin, is now the home of Matchbox Twenty and Brandy.

Here's a brief breakdown of the "Big Five" and who owns what (although the list changes constantly):

- The **EMI Group's** main holding is **Capitol,** whose catalog of Beatles and Beach Boys recordings is one of the richest in the business. The label also owns **Virgin** and **Blue Note Records** and represents Radiohead, Norah Jones, and the Foo Fighters.

- **Sony Music Entertainment** is one of the oldest and best-established labels; its **Columbia Records** imprint began in the early twentieth century with crooner stars such as Russ Columbo. (Columbia's "race records," featuring the legendary Robert Johnson and Mississippi Fred McDowell, among others, have ultimately become better known and more influential.) Columbia scout John Hammond signed Benny Goodman, Aretha Franklin, Bruce Springsteen, Bob Dylan, and Miles Davis. Today, the label's big "holdings" include Michael Jackson.

- **Warner Bros. Records** was, for years, a haven for off-kilter but groundbreaking artists such as Neil Young and R.E.M. Like every other label, Warner streamlined in the 1990s; its **Atlantic** imprint has Kid Rock and Tori Amos.

- Owned by the German media conglomerate Bertelsmann, **BMG Entertainment** spent the 1980s and 1990s breaking interesting acts including hip-hop band Boogie Down Productions. It exploded in the late 1990s, signing teen-pop sensations Britney Spears and the Backstreet Boys. Today, BMG also owns **RCA Records,** home of the Dave Matthews Band and Elvis Presley's profitable catalog.

- More than any label in the 1990s and early twenty-first century, **Universal Music Group** underwent serious consolidation. First, Canadian drinks-and-spirits company Seagram bought **PolyGram Records** and the rest of Universal's movie and music holdings; then, French media conglomerate Vivendi bought the whole thing and repackaged the company as Universal. It owns **Mercury, MCA, Interscope, Geffen, Def Jam, Island,** and other longtime homes of U2, Limp Bizkit, Marilyn Manson, Stevie Wonder, and Jimi Hendrix's catalog. As of this writing, Vivendi Universal was putting its U.S. entertainment assets up for sale to the highest bidder.

Independents

Indies, or independents, is music-industry shorthand for grassroots record labels that are not part of the giant conglomerate network. In pop-music mythology, they're usually owned by self-built, entrepreneurial types.

The "indie spirit" is rooted in rock 'n' roll history. From the very beginning, Chicago's Chess Records, Memphis's Sun, Detroit's Motown, New York's Def Jam, London's Stiff, Seattle's Sub Pop, and even the Frank Sinatra–owned Reprise sent people out on the streets to find exciting new talent. In many cases, these labels signed artists that the larger companies had ignored completely.

Independent labels have had several major renaissances. They became part of the "do-it-yourself" movement in the mid-1970s, when scruffy punk rockers used indie deals to get attention they would have never received via major labels. This led to an "indie rock" sound, fashion, attitude, and philosophy that still exists today with Matador Records, for example, and the respected indie-rock trio Yo La Tengo.

Independent labels remain easier to crack than major labels. Indie A&R scouts, by and large, are more likely than their big-label counterparts to check out unknown talent. Also, indie labels tend to specialize in particular genres of music, so if your style is blues, country, jazz, or hip-hop, try approaching small labels that specialize in your music first.

Chicago's Alligator Records, for example, focuses exclusively on blues; Bloodshot, also in Chicago, signs alternative-country bands (in the style of Wilco and Ryan Adams); Not Lame, in Fort Collins, Colorado, has a power-pop niche; and while many important hip-hop labels have been gobbled up by the majors, some, such as rap star Master P's No Limit, operate mostly outside the major-label system.

Although they may not be able to give you the multimillion-dollar advances or land your video immediately on MTV, independent labels are often prestigious and receptive.

Creating Your Own Record Label

Before they venture out into the murky world of big-name record labels, many bands decide to release their own music on their own budgets. The simplest method is to create a debut CD (see Chapter 21), think up a good record-company name, and print it (along with website and contact information) in the rear-panel liner notes.

The next step is to form an actual business. We won't get into the particulars here of creating a legal partnership or Limited Liability Company, but it's a pretty simple process you can learn about by contacting the local secretary of state's office. And forming a business may not even be necessary, in most cases, unless you have particular accounting or health-insurance needs. An attorney may be helpful for certain tricky company-forming issues and, especially, if one of your client bands or CD-buying customers decides for whatever reason to sue you.

You will, however, need some infrastructure to record, release, and distribute music. And therein lies some hard work—and maybe a financial investment.

Your label will probably begin its career by putting out your band's CDs. To record, use your own rehearsal space or buy studio time, as we've discussed in previous chapters.

The distribution process is more complicated. The easiest way to put out a large number of records—say 1,000 or more, at first—is to hook up with an established distribution company such as theorchard.com. These companies often have excellent connections and can get your CD into a master database—that way, any clerk in the world can access your disc if somebody asks for it.

On a regional level, it's fairly easy to distribute CDs yourself—literally sell them directly to retail outlets and individual consumers out of the trunk of your car. It's far more complicated and costly to self-distribute CDs on a national level. To do so, you'll probably need the help of a record label or large-scale distribution company.

And you'll need the capabilities to copy and print a large number of CDs at once. Many computers and CD-burning machines will help with this process, but you may have to approach a company such as Disc Makers (discmakers.com). See Chapter 21 for more on this service.

Deciding whether to stretch the label beyond your own band's recordings depends on your interests, time, and resources. Once you bring another artist into the mix, everything becomes more complicated. You may need to make new studio arrangements (not everybody will be satisfied with your band's distinctive drum sound). You'll have to negotiate financially with the other band. And you'll have to deal with clients and customers regarding music and products that don't involve you as much creatively.

When should you expand to another artist? If you've put out a few CDs and secured a distribution deal, and you've sold 5,000 to 7,000 copies of each release, that's probably the time. Many distributors are more anxious to work with labels with their own "catalog"—which is to say, more than one CD by more than one band on the label. Just take care not to embark on this venture at the expense of your own projects. Your own band remains the bottom line.

Approaching the Record Label

Your contact at any record label, big or small, is the *A&R* department. It's filled with scouts hunting for undiscovered talents—which means, maybe, you. Don't wait for a scout to show up at your gig unannounced, though, the way baseball scouts are said to show up secretly at a high school game. In this business, you have to send demos out yourself.

How do you find the right A&R contact? Many musicians' directories carry names and contact information for major-label employees—the Music Registry (musicregistry. com) and The Musician's Atlas (musiciansatlas.com), for example, are regularly updated, and include e-mail addresses. Still, double-check the information before firing off a package, e-mail, or phone call.

> **Words to Rock By**
>
> **A&R** stands for "artists and repertoire." Although today's A&R department employees are basically talent scouts, looking for talented musicians to make profitable hit records, they used to do something completely different. In the 1950s and 1960s, before most artists wrote their own songs, A&R executives linked talented singers with other people's songs and big-time arrangers, and generally ran the studio sessions (as producers do today).

"Cold-calling" an A&R department is hardly ever successful, but it can't hurt to try. More effective is finding a personal connection. Do you have a friend who does local promotion for the label? Ask this person to sneak in an enthusiastic reference to your demo if he ever does an errand for the A&R person. Or, as we mentioned in Chapter 19, contact an entertainment attorney or someone else who has experience doing business with this particular label.

No matter what, don't get discouraged. If being in a band, playing music, and writing songs are absolutely what you have to do, you'll be okay, as long as you develop an extra-thick skin and learn to deal with rejection. The more you try to gain access to the big-time music business, the more you'll encounter short attention spans, gruffness, lack of tact, and perhaps downright crude behavior. Don't let it dissuade you from concentrating on your own music.

And that's not to say there aren't nice people in the music business. There are—and you can find them. When making the calls, befriend the secretaries and assistants over the phone. Those assistants may move up and run the label someday.

Do these connections seem too lofty and out of reach? The first time around—and probably the second or third—you'll probably wind up disappointed. Few musicians connect with big-time record labels on their first attempts. But as you go, it's possible somebody at the company will remember your name, which could pay off months or years from now.

Small record labels can be just as frustrating as the big ones. But check your local phone book for local labels. Just as colleges are more likely to admit in-state than out-of-state students, small record labels are often pleased to find nearby talent. Be professional, as usual, when dealing with them, but rather than following up by mail or phone, try to set up a personal appointment

It may be that you're just not ready for record-label attention at this point, but don't let that discourage you. Plenty of bands have stayed "independent" years into their success, and one could say they've done even better without submitting to the politics and contracts of major labels. The Dave Matthews Band sold CDs via its own record label for years. When it came time to sign with RCA Records, the band already had a sales base.

Behind the Music

No connections, you say? Look up the local music association—the Colorado Music Association, for example, is at coloradomusic.org, and Mark's website bandguru.com lists dozens of others on its links page. Although some of these groups focus on classical musicians, others may be valuable for resources and networking. If you want to pitch your demo to a record label and need a connection, perhaps a more experienced friend on the association board can help drop your name.

Players at the Record Company

Repeat this mantra: Record companies exist to make money. Record companies exist to make money. Record companies …

Some labels tend to be more "artist-oriented" and others want immediate hits, but they all exist to, yes, make money. Still, your relationship with the label comes down to the people you work with. The person at the top sets the company's tone, so pay attention to press reports and scuttlebutt about how that person operates. Lower down the food chain, if you find a receptive person, stick to him or her as long as you can.

A&R

We discuss the A&R representative's role in signing your band in the previous section, "Approaching the Record Label." But you should also know, once you've signed with the label, the A&R person becomes your creative liaison to the company. Whenever you need to request money or financial statements, or ask permission to make a video, you'll almost certainly check with the A&R contact. Don't get too codependent, though: Frequently an artist develops a warm relationship with the A&R rep, who for whatever reason winds up leaving the company. Without a liaison, you can often become stranded—and may need to fall back, again, on your touring, press, or radio bases.

> **Behind the Music**
>
> Not all music-fiction books center on famous rock bands. Before he became a VH1 senior vice president, Bill Flanagan penned *A&R* (Random House, 2000), a dark novel about a fictitious record-label A&R person who can't avoid bamboozling an up-and-coming band he works with. None of it is true, but some of the inside dirt is instructive.

Product Manager

Once you have a record deal, the label will immediately assign you to a product manager. This person has the final financial word over your transactions as they relate to the label. He or she will also be your point person for daily tasks, projects, and scheduling. In a perfect world, the product manager will know everything about the band and be able to make educated decisions in your best interests. But it isn't a perfect world, and if the product manager loses interest, you'll have to be assertive to get what you want.

Legal Affairs

Once you and the label get serious about signing a deal, this department will arrange your contracts. At that point, you must have an attorney; the label, especially a big one, may not even deal with you otherwise. All contracts and negotiations go through legal affairs. From the beginning, view these discussions with a very jaundiced eye. As many musicians have learned, you can't trust these lawyers to have your best interests in mind.

Promotions/Radio

The promotions department's main job is to get your record on the radio. Sometimes this just involves smart, persistent marketing and salesmanship. Other times it involves paying an "independent promoter" large sums of money to buy a song's way onto the radio. This concept is known as *payola*, a controversial, long-standing, and complex music-industry issue.

In the 1950s, payola was a huge scandal—the U.S. government, likening it to black-mail, began a high-profile round of subpoenas, investigated the practice, and made an example of people like the legendary early rock DJ Alan Freed.

More recently, as the government has relaxed restrictions on radio stations around the country, the trend of "independent promotion" has seeped back into the business. According to *The Denver Post*, as of 2003, middleman radio promoters paid $100 million a year to push music from the record labels. However, some large radio companies, including Clear Channel, have said they plan to stop the practice.

What does the payola controversy mean to your band? Just that there are forces far beyond your control influencing whether your song lands on the radio. Also, if you do get a hit, you may want to remember "how milk is made" so you don't have any illusions if it comes to abruptly quitting the label and pitching your own music to a radio station.

The independent-promotion practice, we should point out, is perfectly legal. Plenty of honest people work in the music business, and you may have a long career in their care. But it's important to know about the inner music-business machinations and how they affect you.

Publicity

We taught you in Chapter 14 how to do your own publicity, or "selling" your band to media outlets for exposure. Big record labels have fully staffed publicity departments with serious resources.

Record-label publicists have many tools—free CDs, online and snail-mail campaigns, experienced press-release and bio writers—at their disposal to help "break" your band. Work closely with these professionals. The good ones will understand your music immediately and help tinker with your image. (You think Madonna and David Bowie invented all those bizarre pop-culture personas by themselves?) They will also have excellent media connections and might help score stories about your band in prominent magazines and perhaps on TV.

Distribution and Why You Need It

Yes, you can avoid the record label entirely, sign up with a distribution company, and push your CDs directly to the record stores. But major record-label distributors, such as CEMA and WEA, and smaller ones like Koch and Navarre, have more muscle than you can possibly generate on your own.

Ever wonder why Wal-Mart, to name one example, displays a particular CD on a rack at the front of the store while other CDs are buried in the racks? It's because of money. You can pay a certain amount of money for *point-of-purchase displays*, or more prominent placement of your product, at retail stores big and small. (Grocery stores do it, too.) Can your band afford this? It depends on your budget. Is it worth it? Probably not. Unless you have a major record label funding your promotional budget, it's probably best to stick with smaller marketing devices such as fliers and websites.

The bottom line in distribution is the ability to get mass copies of your record into consumers' hands as quickly as possible. You can do this yourself, to an extent—artists such as folk singer Ani DiFranco and punk band Fugazi have made a solid living at it for years. But to really sell big numbers—in the millions, say—you need record-label distribution power.

The Record Contract

Say you sell out concerts around the country, radio plays your song, and major media picks up on the story—and a record-label A&R person "discovers" your music. Suddenly the band finds itself, with lawyer in tow, staring at a "standard" contract full of legalese and tiny print. (Yes, you need a contract; if a small label wants to sign you without one, insist on it. Having one is in your interest in addition to the company's.) Now what?

Standard Contracts

In truth, there's no such thing as a standard contract, although the company's lawyers may describe it that way to get you to sign quickly. Contracts range from simple to complex, from 6 to 600 pages, and it's important to read every word.

What to Look For

Every recording deal contains a few basic premises. You'll be able to negotiate the terms of some of them. Others, such as the split of profits between the label and the band, will depend on how much leverage (which is to say, star power) you have. Here are some premises for every deal:

- **Term.** How long will you be signed? One or six CDs? One year? Eight years? Life?

◆ **Exclusivity.** At what point, if ever, will you have the right to go to another label?

◆ **Royalties.** The bottom line. You'll be doing pretty well if you can get a 12-14 percent rate, or 12¢ to 14¢ on every dollar the label makes off a sold CD. Pay close attention to this part of the contract: Sometimes the company will try to "discount" your rate on sales through record clubs or promotional campaigns.

◆ **Production budget.** How much will the label pay to make your record—or, in some cases, video? A *budget* means you'll get a fixed amount of money, but if you run over that amount, the excess comes out of your expenses. (Sometimes that happens without your knowledge, and you have to pay it back later.) A *fund* means it's your money, and if the record costs less to make than originally predicted, you keep the extra money. A fund arrangement is generally better than a budget.

◆ **Creative control.** Will you make *all* the decisions—songs, sound, producer, artwork—about your record? It's hard to get this, at least 100 percent, as a new artist.

◆ **Ownership of masters.** Who owns the physical recording? In 10 years, when all your contacts have left the label and nobody wants to push your old record, are you out of luck? Do rights to the masters ever revert back to you?

◆ **Commitment to release (and promote) the CD.** The label makes a commitment to *record* your CD, not necessarily to release, distribute, sell, or promote it via radio and other media. Obviously, you'll want to put language in the contract ensuring the CD will make it to record stores after you've worked so hard on it. But again, this point will have to be negotiated with the label.

◆ **Publishing.** The label may try to give you a publishing deal—which is to say, paying royalties for the songwriter in your band—through its own subsidiary. This may or may not be a good thing, depending on the terms. (See Chapter 24 for more information on publishing and royalties.)

◆ **Video rights.** Who pays for the video? Who owns it?

Who Should Look It Over Before You Sign?

Certainly the band members should go through the contract. But always, always, always hire a competent attorney who specializes in music or entertainment law. Your family friend who specializes in real-estate law will be almost no help here. The web has some resources for this—FindLaw, at lawyers.findlaw.com, searches for attorneys by category—but it's more reliable to contact other bands or managers at your level for first-person recommendations.

The Fine Print

Here's why many musicians avoid big record labels entirely: No matter how well you scrutinize the contract, your band (if it's young and relatively unknown) has no power. In the end, you'll probably have to submit to most things the label demands. This may mean surrendering creative control of your own album, or going into massive debt if your first album or two don't sell enough copies. So enter a deal with your eyes open, and be prepared for disappointment and negotiation.

Why an "Advance" Isn't an Advance

Heavy-metal band Anthrax, in 1992, signed a new contract with big label Elektra Records for more than $10 million, according to music-industry magazines. But the band didn't get rich off the deal. It was a five-album commitment, and as with most major-label contracts, Anthrax had to take all of its recording expenses out of the $10 million. After renting studio time, hiring big-name producers, and making videos, there wasn't much left for the four members to divide.

Two albums into the Elektra deal, Anthrax left the label. After selling 7 million records in the 1980s and early 1990s, the band downsized from small arenas to small theaters. Its albums since 1993 haven't even gone gold (500,000 sales).

The lesson here is to be wary of the "big money" from record labels. If you're not careful, as great bands from The Replacements to The Fluid discovered before breaking up, your big break may turn out to be the beginning of the end. Once you sign a label deal, you have to sell a certain number of records just to break even; if that doesn't happen, you may wind up in crippling debt to the label.

> **Behind the Music**
>
> Most major-label bands don't make any money unless they've sold lots of records—usually at least 500,000, or gold.

Another key lesson: Keep costs down. If the label pressures you to go into a fancy Hollywood studio (far from home) with a super-hip producer, remember who's paying (you!). It may be better to stay near home, work with your usual producer in his affordable studio, and make a great cost-conscious CD.

Record Label as Not-Very-Benevolent Bank

The record label is not your pal. At best, it will offer no-interest loans. It may be exciting at first to spend tons of money on the label's expense account. But everything you spend will be meticulously tallied by the label's legal affairs and accounting departments. You *will* get the bill for it later. And if you can't pay, you'll be in debt to the label.

Behind the Music

If you do wind up in debt trouble with the label, an "out" is available. You can file for bankruptcy, or legally declare that you have no money, then start all over again from scratch. The R&B trio TLC did this in the mid-1990s, with a price: It took five years for the band to release a new album. After that, they put out the *Fanmail* CD, which sold more than 6 million copies. Filing for bankruptcy is a depressing, difficult, time-consuming, but sometimes effective option.

When You (Might) Make Money

Again, the less you spend, the better off you'll be. Your band might be in the "big time," working with a major record label, playing large concert venues, and winding up in glossy magazines or on MTV, but all the do-it-yourself and cost-saving techniques we've described so far in this book remain effective. Be smart on what you spend—and stay on top of costs so you don't sink into endless label debt.

The Least You Need to Know

- In some cases, after two to five years as a band, you may be ready to sign with a (big or small) record label.

- Don't even think about a big label until you've developed a "base" through touring, radio, or the press.

- The "Big Five" labels are the hardest to crack but have the most distribution and promotion resources to boost your career. As with any "deal," hire a lawyer to go over any contracts.

- If you're lucky enough to get a big advance from a record label, remember it may not cover all the band's expenses—renting a studio, making a video, and so forth. Keep costs down so you don't wind up in debt.

Chapter 23

Video Saved the Radio Star

In This Chapter

- ◆ Can a video make your band reach a wider audience?

- ◆ Equipment you'll need to make your own video

- ◆ The art of music-video direction

- ◆ Using a video as part of your press kit

- ◆ How to hit the big time—MTV, VH1, and CMT—and why it isn't nearly as easy as it looks

Before MTV, music and video joined together only on the occasional *Ed Sullivan* broadcast, *American Bandstand*, *Soul Train*, or Sonny & Cher variety-show episode. When the music-video channel made its debut in 1981, it turned music into a more visual medium and required, forever after, that all pop musicians at least consider how their ideas play out before people's eyes. For the past two decades, regular rotation on MTV has translated into big sales, and so bands, managers, and record labels have aggressively created and marketed videos. But in recent years, two developments have changed the game: MTV has gradually downplayed music videos in favor of shows like *The Real World*, and technology has allowed artists to make cheap, professional videos on their own. New video outlets have also popped up on the web, so if you do take the plunge and make a video, you may have a decent shot at some airplay.

How a Video Can Help Your Career

Like the demo and press kit, a video is an attention-getting device that may lure a club booker, radio programmer, manager, booking agent, media outlet, or record label to your music. It's effective as a "second step" once you've mailed out the original package and the recipient expresses interest. For practical reasons, this person may not be able to catch your live show—so a video can be the next best thing.

If your band lands a local or national television story (network or public-access cable), the video can also be used as *B-roll*. This is preprepared, edited footage you provide to supplement whatever new interviews and performance video the producer chooses to flesh out the feature.

"It's really necessary to have some video of the band," says Michael Kudreiko, a freelance cameraman and member of the Detroit rock band Robb Roy, which has produced its own music videos. "It shows that you're more than just a bar band."

The video is also a ticket to many new, and possibly lucrative, exposure outlets. Although it's extremely difficult to land airplay on MTV, VH1, CMT, or the other big national cable outlets, there are plenty of opportunities via the web and local cable channels.

Making Your Own Video

As we've mentioned, a video is an excellent business tool that can help your band get exposure. But it's also a great canvas for artists who are talented in more areas than making music or writing songs. Somebody in the band may turn out to have graphic-arts skills (or even experience); somebody else may have technical knowledge of shooting video and editing it with computer software. Take advantage of these extracurricular interests.

Making a video can be great fun, whether you simply turn on the camera to shoot a live concert or concoct a concept involving a story line, animation, or special effects. It's hard work to make a good video, though, and you might choose to spend money on professional assistance with the conception, shooting, and editing processes.

Cameras, Equipment, and Costs

Because of the Mini DV Camcorder, or handheld digital-video camera, the process of recording professional footage has become far easier and more affordable in the last few years. In the old days, to shoot a professional-quality video, you needed huge television cameras, producers, camera people, stagehands, and perhaps a crane. Today, requisite equipment is a Panasonic PV-DV202 (roughly $370), a Canon GL1 Mini DV Camcorder ($1,750), a Sony DSR-PD150 ($2,500), or one of many similar products available at most electronics stores. The more you spend, the more features and professional-quality video you'll end up with, but cheaper Mini DVs may suit your needs.

The other thing you'll need is editing software, and for that, consider a Macintosh computer and the iMovie software that comes bundled with it. Reading the manuals for your Mini DV and software should give plenty of instruction—it's as simple as hooking up the camera to the computer with a FireWire cable, booting up the software, and clicking on "import." Once your video pops into the computer, you can manipulate it with iMovie.

> **Behind the Music**
>
> iMovie software comes bundled with new Macintosh computers and is fairly easy to use. PC users will have to buy their software separately, but they have several video-editing options. The choices range from EZDV TV (about $200) to DVStorm2 ($1,000). We recommend plugging "video editing software" into a consumer-review site like ZDNet (zdnet.com) for more detailed information.

Can you make a professional music video with such low-cost equipment? It depends. MTV these days generally demands a high level of production and costly effects. But for almost any other purpose, Robb Roy's Michael Kudreiko says, "As long as you have the interest in learning how to do it, and are familiar with a lot of music videos, you can do a decent job." Kudreiko says the White Stripes, a well-known garage-rock duo from Detroit, shot their first two videos in one afternoon using, yes, a Mini DV Camcorder.

Ultimately, the type of equipment you use isn't as important as your enthusiasm, imagination, and talent. The White Stripes' 2002 breakthrough video, for "Fell in Love with a Girl," was an elaborate animated Lego-sculpture portrayal of the band. With time and energy on your side, you can easily shoot this kind of concept video on affordable gear.

However, if none of this do-it-yourself video stuff sounds like fun to the band, take the money you would have invested on equipment and spend it on a professional production team. Michael Yarmy, of the Royal Oak, Michigan, video-production company Dark Spark Media, says professionally made videos can cost in the neighborhood of $3,000—cheaper than the cost of the camcorder and editing software.

"People say all the time: 'How much does a video cost?' And I say how much does a car cost?" Yarmy says. "Do you want to get from point A to point B or do you want a Cadillac?" For most major projects, Yarmy points out, you'll need to hire a producer, director, and cameraperson, who will supply the equipment and expertise.

Film, Videotape, or Digital?

The Mini-DV-and-computer-editing process we've described is probably the cheapest and easiest for your needs. Plus, it allows you to record digital-to-digital, which means you won't need to deal with physical bits of film reel at all. The camera records digitally, the software edits digitally, the final product is digital and everything's compatible.

That's not to say you shouldn't tinker with other media, such as old-fashioned VHS videotape or a specialized movie format like Hi-8 or Super 8. For more information on these film styles, check out the SimplyDV website (www.simplydv.co.uk) or a do-it-yourself video book such as *Digital Filmmaking 101: An Essential Guide to Producing Low Budget Movies* (Michael Wiese Productions, 2001), by Dale Newton and John Gaspard.

"Sync" and Staying in It

With the music video age came the lip-syncing age. (There was lip-syncing in the old days, too, but never quite as prominent as on MTV.) As you may have noticed from watching, almost no musicians actually sing while creating a video. They just move their lips to prerecorded music. (Many pop stars, such as Britney Spears, are known to lip-sync in concert. Grammy-winning duo Milli Vanilli took the concept a little too far, lip-syncing to *other* singers' voices; this indiscretion wrecked the band's career.)

Backstage Insights

MTV's first-ever non-lip-synced video was Pearl Jam's "Alive," released in August 1991.

Unless you're recording the band in a live setting, with live audio, your video-making process will probably involve lip-syncing, too. Because films require many "takes," it's almost impossible to perform an adequate version of a song while recording a proper video. One secret to effective lip-syncing: Don't try to mouth the words. Sing them, just as you normally would. You may feel like you're singing in the shower, but because you're actually singing, you can't help but come across more realistic.

Using Storyboards

"Storyboarding" is the process of sketching a rough draft of the film or video you plan to make. (And some art stores sell special "storyboarding pads.") Think of your video as an animated cartoon: Draw everything out in advance, scene by scene, and then attempt to reproduce these ideas on film. When you storyboard, you start thinking in terms of scenes, which may well save you time and money as the shoot goes on.

"It doesn't necessarily have to be storyboarding," says Michael Yarmy of Dark Spark Media. "What's the best way you communicate? If you can draw, draw it out. If you're a better writer, write it out." The idea is to have a working blueprint, so everybody knows what to do next—and your fellow musicians have something concrete to edit and tinker with as a group.

Basic Styles

"Be true to the music," Mark says. A great video reflects the band's musical and personal style. If you're a punk band that frowns upon wearing anything other than torn T-shirts and smelly Converse sneakers on stage, you probably don't want a big-production video featuring high-kicking Rockettes. Conversely, if you're a stately diva who models elaborate ballroom gowns during concerts, you'll want to pass on the director with the skateboarding concept.

> **Backstage Insights**
>
> People talk all the time about how MTV has changed the music industry. But the channel's greatest impact may have been on the advertising industry. Although critics mocked MTV's quick-cut, richly colored style at first, almost every television commercial these days acknowledges music videos' influence. Many prominent video directors have gone on to success in the advertising industry.

You are limited only by your imagination when choosing a video style. But you should be aware of a few basic prototypes of successful videos that have appeared on MTV over the years:

- **The story video.** The story doesn't have to be coherent (see Guns N' Roses' classic "November Rain"), but it should have some semblance of plot, characters, conflict, and resolution. Ultimately the point of the song should match the point of the video, but this isn't always the case.

- **The surrealistic video.** Rocker Tom Petty became a video star in the 1980s because he participated in Alice-in-Wonderland dreamscapes for "Don't Come Around Here No More" and others. For these, you'll need elaborate, colorful costumes and interesting background sets.

- **The animated video.** From a-ha's classic "Take On Me" to The White Stripes' all-Lego "Fell in Love with a Girl," animation has had a prominent role in video hits. But they're much more laborious and potentially more expensive than they look, as you have to render every image in every frame individually.

- **The message video.** Clarity isn't a requirement here, as Nirvana's ground-breaking anarchist-cheerleader "Smells Like Teen Spirit" video proved in the early 1990s. Pick a political or social statement and roughly try to relay it through an image or a brief story.

- **The "babes" video.** It may be pandering to an audience's baser instincts, but a reliable way to catch male viewers' eyes involves hiring really, really attractive and well-endowed women (and, in fewer cases, men) and placing them prominently in the video. Beyond this, you may have to do very little creative work at all.

Video Directing 101

The video director—which could be you or a hired professional—is the person who "equates your vision to film," in the words of Dark Spark Media's Michael Yarmy.

The director's role is loosely the same as that of a producer in the studio. A good director will know what equipment you'll need, from photography to editing, and how it all works. He or she will also have strong creative ideas and good listening skills in order to implement what the band wants to do. A superb director will become more assertive if the artist isn't sure of his or her direction, and step back into "suggestion mode" if the artist has a strong vision and assertive personality.

"The director is responsible for the overall look and texture—he suggests 'this should be done in black and flames,' or 'this should be done on a rooftop, because the song is about the sky' or whatever. He decides where the camera's going to go," Yarmy says. "It's important that you get along with the director. He's the guy who will make you look good."

In addition to a director, most high-level music-video projects require a producer and a director of photography. The producer is the project manager, who coordinates the business and logistical aspects of the video—hiring and firing people, coordinating locations, dealing with legal issues, perhaps finding the right director for your idea. The director of photography is essentially the cameraperson, who's responsible for lighting, photography, and working with the director on choosing lenses and where to put the cameras.

Note that these specialists aren't required to make a music video. For a low-budget video, shot on a Mini DV Camcorder and edited on personal-computer software, members of the band may have to assume all three of these duties. Or you might want to hire a director who can take care of it all.

Do You Need Acting Lessons?

Please, no! Acting has almost no place in a rock video—unless, of course, you're an actor hired to play a particular role, like Christopher Walken in Fatboy Slim's happy-dancing "Weapon of Choice" video. If you try to act, you'll look like you're trying to act, and will come across forced at best and silly at worst.

On the other hand, music videos are often a jumping-off point for acting careers. Alicia Silverstone got her start, for example, as the "It Girl" in Aerosmith's "Cryin'" video. And music stars LL Cool J, Queen Latifah, P. Diddy, Randy Travis, Ice Cube, Reba McEntire, Lyle Lovett, and many others graduated from videos to movie and television acting careers. So if you're in a band and aspire someday to perform in movies, this is one possible way of doing it.

How to Use a Video

As we discussed earlier in this chapter, a video can be a vital part of your press kit (or electronic press kit). It can also expose people to your live performances if they're not in a position to attend one in person. And you can get public exposure through local cable channels, college television programs, and posting streaming video online. You may even get lucky and score major video airplay someday.

"In most major markets there's going to be one knucklehead who doesn't have enough abuse in his life and wants to do a local cable video show," says Michael Kudreiko of Robb Roy. Needless to say, these are opportunities for your band—and you should send demos, press kits, and videos to such "knuckleheads" when you tour through their hometowns.

Until then, here are some outlets to which you should most definitely send your video:

  ◆ **Local cable channels.** From the Bay Area's California Music Channel (cmctv. com) to the homemade Chicago variety show *Chic-A-Go-Go!* (roctober.com/ chicagogo/), local cable access offers your band many video-exposure opportunities. Producers of these shows often air local talent, and viewers may be more influential than you think.

- **Muzak.** The company once known for its canned, easy-listening broadcasts in supermarkets and restaurants has been expanding into more sophisticated markets for the past two decades. Today, one of its services involves distributing VHS music footage to bars and health clubs—it's possible to land your video on this widely distributed service. Check out muzak.com for more information.

- **Online video channels.** The Canadian MuchMusic.com and the record-label-owned Launch.com broadcast a large number of diverse videos that never seem to land on MTV or VH1.

- **Video contests.** Check out garageband.com and broadjam.com for information about entering your video in national contests. (Or the opportunity to land on an online top 10 list.) If your video is more of a short film than basic concert footage, consider submitting it as a creative entry to atomfilms.com, which posts interesting videos in many forms.

- **Record labels, radio stations, concert promoters, media outlets, and television advertisers.** Bundle your video, on DVD or videotape, with your press kit and send it as part of the band's "calling card" to important recipients. (See Chapter 14 for advice on mailing and following up.) You can also e-mail a video as a digital attachment, but check first with the recipient; large video files can lock up computers.

The Big Time

The pecking order of exposure outlets generally goes like this:

High-profile national video channels

Television networks

Local television stations

Radio stations

Magazines

Newspapers

Alt-weeklies

As your band generates more and more sold-out shows, and sells more and more records, you may find yourself moving up the list, beginning with stories in the local papers and eventually hitting a radio playlist.

National music-video outlets are the top rung of this ladder. Don't even count on that level of exposure at first, but you can dream. If you're interested in someday having a video hit, study the types of things that get on the air, and try to figure out where you can sneak in—maybe as background music for a scene on MTV's *Undressed?*

And if MTV and VH1 won't take you, remember there are all sorts of television opportunities. Pilots are being filmed all the time, and need theme songs, background music, and even little recorded instrumentals for scene changes.

Backstage Insights

Many bands gain exposure through television-show music. Big TV hits usually choose from a pool of established artists, but there are opportunities for younger bands on edgy, experimental shows such as HBO's *The Sopranos.*

The Rembrandts, a pop duo, were going nowhere when they landed "I'll Be There for You" on a questionable television pilot called *Friends.* Once that sitcom took off, the band sold more than 1,000,000 copies of 1995's *LP.*

MTV, CMT, and VH1

MTV will make you a star. The channel reaches millions of viewers and is so influential that artists placed in regular rotation automatically start to sell hundreds of thousands of records. Almost single-handedly over the years, MTV has turned relatively unknown artists such as A Flock of Seagulls, Bon Jovi, Madonna, Nirvana, Weezer, the Spice Girls, and Britney Spears into major rock superstars (albeit, in some cases, briefly).

When it started in 1981, MTV was a strange pop-cultural venture that few in the music industry took seriously. Its debut video, famously, was The Buggles' "Video Killed the Radio Star" and mid-level 1980s stars such as Phil Collins, the J. Geils Band, Dire Straits, and Devo were among the first to get airplay.

The channel quickly became a star-maker, solidifying the multiplatinum careers of pop stars Michael Jackson, Madonna, Peter Gabriel, Prince, and Bruce Springsteen. As the channel has grown, it has somehow still managed to attract massive audiences. The channel's *120 Minutes* show anticipated grunge in the early 1990s, and its *Total Request Live* countdown helped create teen-pop stars Britney Spears, *NSYNC, and the Backstreet Boys beginning in the late 1990s.

These days, it's almost impossible to get on MTV. For one thing, the channels accept submissions almost exclusively from artists signed to major record labels. For another, MTV plays few actual music videos these days, given the popularity of nonmusic

---

> **Behind the Music**
>
> MTV's lesser-known spin-off channel, MTV2, focuses on actual music videos as opposed to prepackaged variety shows. It also airs videos by new and developing artists as opposed to the big stars—The Strokes and Nelly Furtado are among the musicians who started on MTV2 and "graduated" to the bigger channel. The competition is stiff, but it might be worth trying.

shows like *The Real World, Dismissed, Jackass,* and various professional wrestling displays.

It's nearly as difficult to land a video on other major video channels VH1 and CMT, or Country Music Television. (Black Entertainment Television, or BET, also plays videos regularly, as do Oxygen and other specialty channels.) To appear on these channels, at the very least, you'll need a significant amount of popularity, and you'll probably need the power of a label or big-time manager.

For years, every artist had to make a video if he or she hoped to sell millions of records. Since the late 1990s, though, as MTV and VH1 have stopped playing videos per se, many artists have given up trying.

Some use commercials as a promotional venue instead—although many rock artists, including John Mellencamp and Tom Waits, refuse to sell their songs to commercials, Sting effectively forewent MTV and the radio to appear on lucrative Jaguar car commercials in the late 1990s. Electronic artist Moby went even further, signing advertising deals for the use of each song on his 1999 album *Play.*

Smaller artists have effectively used online video services such as Launch.com or Garageband.com.

When the Record Company Pays

Once you've signed with a major record label, the standard video-making deal is for the label to pay half and the band to pay half. (Smaller labels, obviously, don't have this kind of money—or the clout to get your video on MTV.)

Your contract should stipulate that videos are separate from any recording and promotional costs you incur for making a record. Otherwise, you'll run into a problem: The label might take video expenses out of your advance payment. If that happens, especially for an expensive video, you'll wind up with much less money than you expected. You may even end up owing the record label significant amounts of cash.

Well-Known Directors and Their Styles

In the early years of MTV, directors focused exclusively on the music-video medium. The style was unique, fast-paced, and busy, with strange new images such as the

J. Geils Band's drummer pounding his sticks into a snare-sized container of milk and Phil Collins air-playing several different instruments against a pure white background.

A few directors emerged as stars of this early, herky-jerky style: Ex-10cc members Kevin Godley and Lol Creme were best known for their own hit video, "Cry," but worked with The Police, Yes, and Ultravox. (Later, they did videos for "Theme from 'Mission: Impossible'" and Eric Clapton's "Tears In Heaven.") Their cinematic style often zoomed in on people's faces for dramatic impact.

Steven R. Johnson, who directed Talking Heads' "Road to Nowhere" and Peter Gabriel's "Sledgehammer," among others, was a pioneer of animation. His claylike characters morphed in and out of strange configurations.

Over the years, video directors have come to represent an imaginative, creative wing of the film industry. Before directing "Blow," the late Ted Demme directed several mid-1990s videos, including (with his brother, Jonathan) Bruce Springsteen's "Streets of Philadelphia." After becoming a star director for Billy Idol, Rolling Stones, and other videos, Julien Temple directed the films *Earth Girls Are Easy*, with Jeff Goldblum and Geena Davis, and *Absolute Beginners*.

There are tons of examples of video directors who've graduated to the big-time movie business. Perhaps the best known and most successful is Spike Jonze, whose skewed, herky-jerky vision of the world turned alternative-rockers Weezer ("Buddy Holly"), Björk ("It's Oh So Quiet"), and R.E.M. ("Crush with Eyeliner") into major video stars. Jonze went on to direct the similarly offbeat movies *Being John Malkovitch* and *Adaptation*, and star in *Three Kings*.

Before directing your own video, whether you're interested in landing on MTV or not, try watching music videos. MTV2 is probably the best place to start, in addition to many local cable-access video channels. Plus, there are plenty of artist DVDs, some of which come bundled with the CDs, that can give you a sense of the basics. Also, *You Stand There: Making Music Video* (Random House Trade Paperbacks, 1997), by David Jr. Kleiler and Robert Moses, and *Thirty Frames Per Second: The Visionary Art of the Music Video* (Harry N. Abrams, 2000), by Steven Reiss, Neil Feineman, and Jeff Ayeroff, give insight about videos as an art form.

The Least You Need to Know

- Videos aren't crucial to the band's survival, but they can push the band into new outlets for exposure.

- You can make your own video using just a Mini DV Camcorder and a computer with editing software. Or you can hire a professional director. In either case it's important to approach the project with creativity and imagination.

◆ Once you're finished, send the video to online contests, local cable channels, Muzak (the company), and, yes, MTV, VH1, and CMT. Package the video with your demo and press kit and send it out to the usual recipients.

◆ Can you get on MTV? Probably not. But if smash videos interest you, consider MTV airplay a goal and try to work your way up to it. Study styles and directors.

◆ Many well-known video directors, from Julien Temple to Spike Jonze, have graduated to movie-industry success. Learning to direct, shoot, and edit a video may take you places you never considered.

Chapter 24

Creating a Hit

In This Chapter

- ◆ Pop music's cozy relationship with "the hit"
- ◆ Radio, regional, and video hits.
- ◆ Key elements of almost all hits
- ◆ Promoting your next hit
- ◆ One-hit wonders

A hit record starts with a song—if you don't have that, you have nothing. As with a movie, book, or play, the centerpiece of any hit is quality writing. Pay attention to hits on the radio and MTV. What common characteristics do they have? You probably don't want to copy exactly what you've heard, but be aware of what constitutes a hit in any given period of time.

Technically, a "hit" is something that a large number of music fans have bought or listened to on the radio. They're listed on pop charts and in trade magazines. Still, you may spend a career, like the great singer-songwriter Richard Thompson, never having a hit to speak of. Or you may rack up tons of hits early. Either way, it's worth knowing how they work and what goes into them.

What's a Hit?

Like "pop music," "hit" has a particular definition but has come to represent many different things. If your single, CD, video, or DVD sells a large number of copies to consumers—at least 500,000, in order to go gold—it's a hit. Once you have a hit, your band almost automatically begins to get famous and, depending on the record deal, rich.

But there are many other interpretations of "hit." If your band's single gets played regularly on the radio, regionally or nationally, it's a radio hit. If MTV puts your video into its "Buzz Bin," you have a video hit. If you perform a concert at a college, and the next day everybody at the show goes to a record store and buys your CD, you have a regional hit. These events can lead directly to massive national sales, but not always.

A "hit" has an aesthetic definition as well, and it's open to wide interpretation. Some would say a pop hit has a certain kind of sound—shiny, polished, heavily produced in a recording studio, like Britney Spears's "Oops I Did It Again" or Madonna's "Borderline." But less-traditional-sounding hits, like Nirvana's raw, incomprehensible grunge classic "Smells Like Teen Spirit" or Norah Jones's light, jazzy sing-along "Don't Know Why," prove hits are as diverse as the artists who make them.

Sometimes hits shoot up the pop charts or receive massive radio play as soon as they're released. Other times, they build slowly, as in the case of Jones, who put out her debut CD in early 2002 and didn't reach the Top Ten until after Christmas that same year. Hits have one primary musical characteristic in common: They're catchy. They have short, repetitive "hooks," like a snappy guitar riff or a rhyming chorus, that grab listeners and make them want to hear more. Usually the lyrics deal with universal themes, notably love and heartbreak, as opposed to weird esoteric concepts. But there are exceptions to almost every rule you can cook up.

The biggest hit singles in music history, according to the Recording Industry Association of America as of late 2002, by number of units sold:

- Elton John, "Candle in the Wind '97," 33 million

- Bing Crosby, "White Christmas," 31 million

- Bill Haley and His Comets, "Rock Around the Clock," 25 million

- The Beatles, "I Want to Hold Your Hand," 13 million

- The Beatles, "Hey Jude," 10 million

- Elvis Presley, "It's Now or Never," 10 million

- Whitney Houston, "I Will Always Love You," 9 million

- Elvis Presley, "Hound Dog," 9 million

- Paul Anka, "Diana," 9 million

- Bryan Adams, "(Every Thing I Do) I Do It for You," 8 million

Gold and Platinum Records

The Recording Industry Association of America, which is the trade group for the "Big Five" record labels plus many smaller companies, is in charge of certifying singles and albums that have sold a certain number of copies. Sales of 500,000 means a *gold record*, while sales of 1 million means *platinum*. These are holy trophies in the music industry—once you've attained this level, more often than not, your band is commercially successful, financially solvent, and reasonably famous.

The biggest albums in music history, according to the Recording Industry Association of America as of late 2002, by number of units sold:

- Eagles, *Their Greatest Hits 1971–1975*, 28 million

- Michael Jackson, *Thriller*, 26 million

- Pink Floyd, *The Wall*, 23 million

- Led Zeppelin, *Led Zeppelin IV*, 22 million

- Billy Joel, *Greatest Hits Volume I & Volume II*, 21 million

- Fleetwood Mac, *Rumours*, 19 million

- AC/DC, *Back in Black*, 19 million

- The Beatles, *The Beatles*, 19 million

- Shania Twain, *Come On Over*, 19 million

- Whitney Houston, *The Bodyguard* soundtrack, 17 million

Billboard and Other Charts

Somebody has to tally up the record-sales numbers and determine what singles and albums get to be hits. For decades, that somebody has been *Billboard* magazine, which compiles the weekly master list of top albums and "hot singles." The magazine also contains specialty charts on country, R&B, jazz, and "developing artists." Study these

---

charts—you may just have the ability to place a song on one of them, then use the notoriety in your press kit.

A subscription to *Billboard* is can be pricey, but billboard.com posts free truncated versions of most of the charts every week. (Also check out riaa.com's "Gold and Platinum" link for lists of historic best-sellers.)

In addition to *Billboard*, many other publications compile specialty charts. *Radio & Records* magazine (radioandrecords.com) prints radio-airplay charts, including country, Christian, Latin, and rock. The *College Music Journal*, or CMJ, also focuses heavily on radio, but from a college-rock perspective. What sells outside the United States, especially England and Canada, may also be relevant to your band.

You can find a music chart for almost anything: Check out lanet.lv/misc/charts for obsessive information on the topic.

Keep in mind that while the people who compile chart information are obsessed with hair-splitting categories—is Wilco "alternative-country" or "indie-rock"?—your band doesn't have to be. Sometimes the broad categories won't fit your musical style. Be true to the music; if you attempt to tailor a song to a particular radio playlist, you may wind up creating product that doesn't please anybody. Find songs in your repertoire that may already work in a given radio format.

Airplay

Radio is a hugely important tool for mass exposure—by and large, without a certain amount of radio play, a band can't make the leap from midlevel concert popularity to big record sales. This has always been the case in pop music: Landing songs on the radio helped bluesman Sonny Boy Williamson in the 1930s, Elvis Presley in the 1950s, The Beatles in the 1960s, and the Backstreet Boys in the 1990s.

What's different today is that radio *formats*, although there are a lot of them, are far more restrictive and regimented than they were in years past. It's extremely unlikely that a relatively inexperienced band, especially one without the big-time promotion of a major record label, will land on a prominent radio station. So you have to improvise, beginning with college radio and smaller community stations, and work your way up.

Words to Rock By _____

A **format** is the narrowly defined type of music a radio station plays, all the time. Today, there are more formats than ever, all in hair-splitting categories: AC (adult-contemporary, or lite rock), Hot AC (a slightly sexier and faster-paced version of AC), Album Rock (meat-and-potatoes rock by groups such as Metallica and Limp Bizkit), Classic Rock (hits from the 1960s and 1970s), Oldies (rock hits from the 1950s and some 1960s), and … you get the idea.

If you're interested in getting on the radio, study the formats in your area. If you're a jazz combo, does the smooth-jazz station ever play local groups? If you're a funky pop band, can you perform a promotional event sponsored by the local Hot AC station? Working with radio stations may lead to airplay in the future.

Once you get on the air, you may get enough "spins" to qualify for one of the many prestigious radio charts. A little promotional ingenuity can parlay a No. 15 showing on the *College Music Journal*'s Loud Rock Top 20, say, or *Radio & Records*'s country-radio chart into even bigger hits.

The easiest way to push your music to radio stations is to let your record company's promotions department handle everything. Of course, not all bands have those kinds of connections, so fall back on the standard procedures: Sending demos to programmers, following up, staying in touch, and making connections.

Regional Hits

Until recently, regional hits could be a relatively easy way to jump onto radio play-lists. Perhaps the most famous example of this was Elvis Presley, whose record-label chief took his new version of Arthur "Big Boy" Crudup's "That's All Right" to Memphis DJ Dewey Phillips in 1954. Phillips immediately decided to spin the song—over and over and over. It became a huge hit in Memphis, then the South, and then the United States.

This rarely happens today. A small record-label owner couldn't possibly walk over to a DJ at a major radio station and get something played based on its merits. There are well-paid independent record promoters for that. There are also station focus groups, listener polls, and reams of research that determine which songs get on the air.

Sadly, the era of regional hits is just about over. That's not to say you can't shoehorn one of your band's songs onto a prominent local-music program, or play a live promotional show in the hallway of a community station. But if you want a really big hit, quickly, one of the few ways to do it these days is to sign with a big record label first. Only their promotion departments have the clout to help you sell 15 million copies and get on the cover of *People*.

Musical Elements of a Hit

As we mentioned earlier, hits almost always have catchy choruses, distinctive, repetitive "hooks," and usually something extra, like a good story in the lyric or a beautiful vocal performance or guitar solo.

But hits also have a certain indefinable mojo that catch the right ears at the right time. Two Spanish flamenco artists, Rafael Ruiz and Romero Monge, put out music for 30 years before their lightly pulsating little ditty "Macarena" became a hit in 1996. Suddenly, everybody wanted to dance to the Los del Rio song, and it became a massive, out-of-nowhere smash.

Hits often beget crazes, often because they go with a popular, easy, distinctive dance step. Chubby Checker's "The Twist," in the 1950s, spawned a cottage industry of imitators. An early R&B theme was "Work with Me, Annie" songs, while an early hip-hop theme involved a down-the-block siren named Roxanne. Disco was one massive craze in the mid-1970s, culminating in the *Saturday Night Fever* movie and soundtrack. Other crazes have included the mambo, the achy breaky heart, the surfing bird, and the hustle.

Writing Catchy Choruses

Pay attention to hit songs you like, whether they're on MTV or the radio. Analyze them. What do you like about them? Is it something about the bridge that takes it into the chorus? What makes the chorus catchy? Try to apply those observations to your own material.

You don't have to have a hit—ever. And if you try too hard to make one, you could easily fail. The "formula" for making a hit is elusive, and countless songwriters are holed up in Nashville offices as you read this desperately trying to come up with one. Sometimes the harder you try, the less likely it is to happen. On the other hand, if your band plunges enthusiastically into the music you all love, hits can happen spontaneously, unexpectedly.

Having said that, knowing the rudiments of successful pop melodies and dynamics can never hurt a band. Nirvana was one of the loudest and most punishing rock bands ever to have a hit—"Smells Like Teen Spirit," among others—but singer Kurt Cobain learned his melodic instincts from 1970s Kiss and Blue Öyster Cult records. The

Beatles' Paul McCartney and the original Sex Pistols bass player, Glen Matlock, despite their revolutionary material, had great ears for hit-making.

It's up to you whether you write the lyrics or the music first. Some songwriters think up melodies in their head, or tinker with them on a guitar or keyboard, and then wedge in words later. Some songwriters do the opposite. Also, it might turn out that one member of the band is handy with the melodies, while another proves to be an accomplished lyricist. Be willing to share the songwriting process with a friendly collaborator.

> **Backstage Insights**
>
> As with fiction, write what you know. Attempting to write about wandering the dark streets of London when you've never traveled beyond Poughkeepsie can be a frustrating experience. (On the other hand, maybe you have a gifted imagination—and if so, go with it.) Don't worry at first about clichés or proper rhymes, just spew everything in your head onto paper and polish it after you're finished.

The Hook

The hook is the one intrinsic element in every song that makes a hit. It may be a chorus, verse, guitar riff, sound effect, or something indefinable. It "hooks" you in like a lure on a fishing line.

Examples of notable hooks in pop hits:

- Singer Roger Daltrey's stuttered choruses in The Who's 1965 classic "My Generation."

- Otis Redding's whistling in his posthumous 1968 soul ballad "(Sittin' on) The Dock of the Bay."

- Donna Summer's sexual moaning in 1975's 17-minute disco smash "Love to Love You Baby."

- The persistent cowbell in Blue Öyster Cult's 1976 single "(Don't Fear) the Reaper." (Christopher Walken's "more cowbell!" line in a *Saturday Night Live* studio parody, years later, reinforced the gimmick's importance.)

- The deep railroad-engine guitar chords anchoring Metallica's 1991 anthem "Enter Sandman."

- The scratched "voopah-voopah-voopah-voop … Slim Shady!" sound effects in between verses of Eminem's 1999 hip-hop breakthrough "My Name Is."

- The exaggerated Asian rhythms in Missy Elliott's 2001 rap hit "Get Ur Freak On."

Polish: Studio Production Techniques

After you've recorded tracks in your home studio, as we discuss in Chapter 18, consider taking them to a professional recording studio for sweetening. Some musicians frown on this practice—they say it allows others to "dumb down" their artistic work—but smoothing rough edges and adding certain distinctive sounds can lead to hits.

To use Nirvana as an example again, the Seattle grunge trio made a late-1980s record that was so loud and raw it never had a chance of catching on with the mass record-buying public. Later, they hooked up with Wisconsin studio veteran Butch Vig, who pumped up the guitar volume, excised some of the mistakes and false starts, and turned *Nevermind* into a surprisingly polished hard-rock masterpiece.

When submitting to this process, it's important to remain involved creatively. The last thing you'll want to do is drop off your tapes and deputize a studio wizard to do what he or she wants. You'll inevitably wind up with a finished product that's frustratingly far from what you envisioned. Work with the producer to add effects and *overdubs*, consider adding keyboard bits or even strings. Mixing time in the studio isn't usually as expensive as regular recording time, depending on what you decide to do.

> **Words to Rock By**
>
> **Overdub** is a recording-studio term for adding new sounds onto the tape after the band has completed its basic tracks. Such sounds can be elaborate—John Entwistle re-recorded many of his bass parts on the Who's *Quadrophenia* for the film soundtrack, released a few years after the album—or more minimal "touch-ups."

Sing About Rudolph at Christmas: Timing, Timing, Timing

When you're planning to release a single, at least on the large scale, keep in mind what time of year it is. *Summer singles* are a hallowed tradition in pop music, as songs from the Jan and Dean's "Surf City" to DJ Jazzy Jeff and the Fresh Prince's "Summertime" to Nelly's "Hot In Here" have had just the right spark for beach parties and convertibles.

If your song contains anything resembling a seasonal theme, put it out in that season. Alice Cooper released his signature "School's Out" in May. Current events, too, turned Staff Sgt. Barry Adler's "Ballad of the Green Berets" into a hit during the Vietnam Era and Alan Jackson's tear-jerker "Where Were You (When the World Stopped Turning)" into a hit immediately after September 11.

The December holiday season, after decades of festive smashes by Bing Crosby, Frank Sinatra, Phil Spector, Mariah Carey, and Christina Aguilera, remains a big deal. Every year, bushels of artists release Christmas albums (and, more rarely despite comedian Adam Sandler, Hanukkah or Kwanzaa albums). This time of year also gives you niche opportunities, as many radio programmers and media writers are looking for quirky alternatives to the flood of "White Christmas" retreads. (James Brown's "Santa Claus Go Straight to the Ghetto" is one of literally thousands of examples, in every genre.)

Study the annual rhythm of CD-release schedules, too. If you want a decent shot of landing a hit, by all means, don't put it out in the late fall, because that's when the Paul Simon box set and Justin Timberlake DVD go on the holiday-shopping market. It'll be tough to compete with them. On the other hand, almost nothing mainstream comes out in January or early February, so you might be able to take advantage of music critics desperately searching for something to write about or radio programmers craving something new to play.

Promotion 101

When people in the music business talk about promotion, it's usually in reference to getting a song on the radio. We've already explained that there are many ways to do this—often, these days, record labels pay independent promoters to encourage their radio-station contacts to play a new song. (There are video promoters, too.)

Short of relying on a record label's power and connections, though, you can push your own singles to radio stations. It's the usual formula: sending out a demo and press kit, following up and being persistent without being a pest. You can also stage promotional events, like in-store performances at local radio stations, or performing for a popular political candidate or respected charity. In such cases, newspapers and radio stations may not be able to resist giving you some coverage.

Regional Hits Through Touring

In the old days, before large corporations bought up most of the radio stations and drastically reduced the playlists, you could tour through a city and have an excellent chance of snagging airplay on the local stations. These days, as we've mentioned, that's extremely difficult—radio programmers are chained to formulas and focus groups.

Nonetheless, you can try to generate some semblance of a "regional hit" without airplay. On stage, for example, you might have a song that nails the crowd every time. (And if you're lucky enough to have such a song, don't get tired of playing it—do it over and over and be happy with its crowd-pleasing results.)

Although "live hits" aren't hits according to the traditional definition, it means a lot to have a song or songs that fans associate with your band. You can print the song title in big letters on fliers and upcoming-show advertisements. And given the right promotion and plenty of word of mouth, local radio stations may not be able to ignore the song forever.

Getting Your Song Into the Movies, Television, and Commercials

In order to land in these lucrative markets, you'll almost certainly need a representative who specializes in placing songs in film and television. Most will want a negotiable percentage of the profits—and you'll owe most of them nothing until they place a song. But a good way to circumvent this expensive procedure is to hook up with a friend who's doing an independent film or a class-project video. Maybe you could provide the soundtrack—it'll give you valuable experience and you may wind up with a demo for which somebody else pays. Big-movie soundtracks are surefire hit formulas these days, but occasionally smaller movies (like *The Blair Witch Project*) become out-of-nowhere hits.

Breaking into these markets is often a fluke. Somebody at an ad agency may have happened to attend one of your shows and want to use your song. (And you can make friends with film and television music supervisors and at ad agencies to help such "flukes" occur more often.)

Backstage Insights

The Hollywood Reporter, among other publications, lists television shows and movies "in production"—plus producers' needs for the project. For example, the television series *Smallville* may want a song for a particular scene, and you can sometimes find a "help wanted"–style ad for that in the publication. Also check online and the Hollywood trades for subscription services that will alert you, perhaps by e-mail, for upcoming opportunities.

Another potential opportunity is marketing your music to sporting events or venues. The Baha Men, who sang "Who Let the Dogs Out," hooked up with a major sports-marketing company and helped turn their innocuous, upbeat pop song into a smash hit compiled on seemingly every sports CD. Usually sports-arena marketers pick these songs individually—Gary Glitter's "Rock and Roll (Part 2)" grew organically into a fist-pumping anthem—but you can try to push the process.

Publishing Companies

When signing with a record label, artists will also often negotiate *publishing deals*. Sometimes this will be with an affiliated company—for example, Sony Music's label, Columbia, might sign a recording artist to a contract with Sony/ATV Music Publishing. But often the contracts will be with separate companies.

> ### Words to Rock By
>
> If you write a song, you automatically hold its **publishing rights.** Not only that, but every time the song makes money, on a CD, via radio play, or in a movie or television program, you're owed a certain amount of money in royalties.
>
> The royalty rate changes every year—these days, it's about 8¢ per song per CD sold. So if an artist records one of your songs and sells 500,000 copies, you get $40,000.

But you can sign a publishing deal long before you hook up with a record company. A music-publishing company's function is to copyright musical compositions in the United States and look out for protections in foreign countries—and make sure the writers receive the appropriate royalty payments. Publishing companies also try to license writers' songs for use in TV shows, movies, plays, and on other artists' albums.

There are many music-publishing companies, ranging from Sony/ATV, which owns the rights to The Beatles and Hank Williams Sr. songs, among many others, to Bug Music, which represents literally hundreds of well-known and obscure artists.

Even if you don't sign with a well-known music publisher, you have the right to royalty payments for your songs. Three *performance-rights societies*—ASCAP, BMI, and SESAC—are responsible for collecting songwriters' payments. The first thing you should do, after completing your first original song, is file a copyright form with the U.S. Library of Congress (see www.loc.gov/copyright). If your song winds up on a record, your own or somebody else's, check out the rights societies' web pages and sign up. You never know when somebody will cover (or try to steal) one of your songs rather than paying you royalty payments.

Copyrighting a song is relatively cheap—$30 per musical work as of this writing, according to the U.S. Copyright Office. Joining ASCAP and other performance-rights societies is free; check the society website or contact a membership representative by phone for more information.

Signing with a publishing company won't necessarily lead to a major record deal, or even stardom of any kind. But it's certainly an excellent way to get exposure, especially if you write a really great song.

A Note on One-Hit Wonders

A one-hit wonder is a pop artist who has had exactly—you guessed it—one hit. One-hit wonders tend to be famous for breezy, catchy, fun singles such as The Knack's "My Sharona," The Vapors' "Turning Japanese," and Right Said Fred's "I'm Too Sexy."

But one-hit wonders sometimes transform into tragic characters. Rapper Vanilla Ice, for example, scored a gigantic early 1990s hit with "Ice Ice Baby," then failed to appear on the major pop charts ever again. He became a bitter, somewhat desperate figure (at least in public) who destroyed his own video with a baseball bat on MTV.

Notable one-hit wonders in pop-music history:

- ? & the Mysterians, "96 Tears," 1966
- The Weather Girls, "It's Raining Men," 1983
- Billy Ray Cyrus, "Achy Breaky Heart," 1993
- Los del Rio, "Macarena," 1996
- Vicki Sue Robinson, "Turn the Beat Around," 1976
- Sir Mix-A-Lot, "Baby Got Back," 1992

Don't take the prospect of one-hit wonderdom too seriously. Your band's goal may be to have a long career, but there are musicians who have based long careers on one hit. Billy Ray Cyrus continues to fill up state-fair stages across the country based almost exclusively on the popularity of "Achy Breaky Heart."

The Least You Need to Know

- Technically, a hit means you've sold at least 500,000 (gold) or 1,000,000 (platinum) copies of a single or album.
- *Billboard* magazine compiles the best-known singles and albums charts; specialty charts are also in *Radio & Records* and the *College Music Journal*, among others.
- Hits don't have to be any one thing, but they almost always have a memorable chorus and some kind of "hook," or catchy little bit that sticks in your head.
- Whenever you write a song, copyright it through the U.S. Copyright Office.

Chapter 25

Climbing to the Next Level

In This Chapter

- ◆ Expanding your base to the big time
- ◆ Graduating to bigger concert venues
- ◆ Getting the most out of your record label
- ◆ Using band experience to work in the music business

By now you've bought the van, trudged through the small local clubs, sold a lot of compact discs, and built up your audience from a few dozen to a few hundred people per show. The entire band believes—musically, economically, emotionally—it's time to become stars. So what's next?

Take a giant step up the ladder of success and fame. From now on, you'll do almost everything exactly as you always did it, only on a bigger level. Your stages may increase in physical size. You may have to hire a business manager in addition to your personal manager. Rather than negotiating with small club owners, you may deal with big-time concert promoters. And if you're lucky, a little money may come in and people may recognize you on the street. Don't forget to be humble! As the saying goes, be nice to people you meet on the way up, because you might meet them again on the way down.

How Do You Know When You're Ready?

When you start filling the house, on a regular basis, and the audience cheers like crazy—perhaps even hollering out specific song titles—you may have "maxed out" in the small clubs and theaters of your hometown. You've probably exhausted all the local outlets, and it's time to graduate to a bigger level.

How do you do all this? You'd be surprised. So far, you've had to push for every opportunity, from auditions to newspaper reviews. With large numbers of fans, radio play, and perhaps CD sales on your side, it's likely the influential people will start coming to you. Maybe the concert promoter of the local basketball arena will ask if you're available to open for Incubus in a few weeks. Maybe the record-label A&R person will approach you after a show. Answer your phones. Now's the time to talk to people.

On a more practical level, the process of expanding the band may be as simple as moving from the 100-seat club you've been packing to the 500-seat theater down the block. It can also be as complicated as hiring new people, including business managers, lighting technicians, and bigger-time booking agents, and arranging a tour of larger venues around the country.

Preparing for the Bigger Venues

Everything blows up when your gigs expand from small clubs to theaters and arenas. To name one example, the physical stage itself will become wider and deeper, so the singer will have (and should use) more room to move around, and the guitarist will be able to move to the lip of the stage for solos.

More generally, your band will have to expand its *infrastructure* in order to accommodate the larger venues. To begin with, you'll probably have to buy more gear—larger amplifiers, more microphones, and perhaps even a more elaborate lighting or sound system. The complexities of live sound will grow, which means you'll need to "mike" acoustic instruments such as drums and pianos. In small clubs, the drums' natural sounds probably carried to the back of the room; in arenas, people in the upper deck can't possibly hear your snare if you don't amplify it.

This additional equipment may also require more people to take care of it. If the band is accustomed to loading its own gear in and out of the venue, it will almost certainly have to hire at least one roadie (we describe roadies in more detail later in this chapter) to handle everything. And while the guitarists may change strings themselves during smaller shows, the stakes are higher at an expensive arena show, so an instrument technician may have to hand them freshly tuned and strung guitars in midsong.

Small clubs probably provided you with a sound person, but you'll probably have to hire such a person for your touring crew.

If you haven't used a personal manager at this point, this is almost certainly the time to hire one. Deals with arenas are more complex, financially, than deals with mom-and-pop-style club owners, and unless somebody in the band has an M.B.A. degree, the musicians will want to focus on music rather than business.

The economics of your band change, too, as you expand to larger venues. More roadies, technicians, and managers mean paying for more hotel rooms—plus "per diem" allowances so these people can afford to eat a few meals a day in between gigs, not to mention a host of other expenses. You're no longer just Fabulous Dogs. You're Fabulous Dogs Inc., and the band is responsible for the salaries and livelihoods of many touring employees.

Making More of the Music Conventions

As we've mentioned, the big music conventions are South by Southwest in Austin, Texas, and *College Music Journal*'s New Music Marathon in New York City. You've probably played showcases at these confabs already. So far, you've had to apply for the conference, pay the required fee, and (if you're lucky to get in) accept whatever venue and time slot the organizers give you. But if you have a huge fan base and sell records, you may have more influence in the negotiations—instead of accepting the 1 A.M. Thursday gig, ask for the central city theater at 11 P.M. on a Friday. It's time to turn your performance slot into an *event*.

Aim slightly higher and try to book one of the larger theaters in town, rather than the small clubs you may have played in previous years. And continue the press-networking efforts we described in Chapter 14, only more intensely. Your hired publicist may want to set up interviews with newspaper and magazine reporters attending the conventions; accept these graciously and enthusiastically, as press on this level can be crucial for your career.

> **Backstage Insights**
>
> Consider designating a *schmoozer* in your band. The friendliest, most charming "people person" will be your front-person when making contact with important record-label executives, radio programmers, or media reporters. When the stakes get high, it's time to stop letting the guitarist, who sweats through every interview, handle this task.

Big-Time Record Labels

Why do you even need a big record label? Good question. Many artists on various levels, from veteran singer-songwriter Tom Waits to the Seattle punk-rock trio Sleater-Kinney, have shunned the majors in favor of smaller labels that pay them more attention. But it's generally true that you can't sell 15 million copies of a record and get on the cover of *Entertainment Weekly* without a major-label deal.

Getting A&R Scouts to Your Gigs

In Chapter 22, we talk about A&R, or artist and repertoire, scouts who search for new talent. If you aspire to be signed to a major label, the most direct and effective way is to impress an A&R executive. At first, it's not easy, and few bands can lure these busy scouts to their gigs. But you may be in the position by now to lure A&R people to your gigs.

If you've successfully built a huge base, you might find making contact with a record label surprisingly easy. All you have to do, in many cases, is report the number of people in attendance at each of your shows. Talent scouts know each of these loyal fans represents a potential CD sale.

> **Backstage Insights** _____
>
> If you're big enough, you may wind up the subject of a "bidding war" between several different major labels. Bidding wars are infrequent, but if you're lucky enough to be involved in one, be sure to have a lawyer or manager who's adept at negotiation and scrutinizing contracts. There's an art to playing big companies off each other to make yourself look attractive, and it's often best left to negotiators with experience and finesse.

If an A&R scout does wind up in the crowd, just perform really well. You'll want to do your best material. And if you get advance warning of a potential Very Important Audience Member, pack the crowd with as many friends, family members, and loyal, enthusiastic fans as you can find.

Sending Out the Demo

Before sending your demo to big record companies—see Chapter 19 for details about demos—make sure the band is ready. That means in addition to being good, and confident of your music-making abilities, you'll need a track record of filling concert halls and, possibly, selling your own self-produced discs to fans.

For years, record labels practiced something called *artist development*, and spent tons of money to "season" young, talented bands before they hit it big with their second, third, or even fourth records. (The Red Hot Chili Peppers and Neil Young are successful examples of this approach.) Note that in almost every case, bands who follow this career outline have to pay back the label's money. If they hit it big on their second or third record, it's easier to do so. If not, many bands wind up leaving the label in massive debt.

Words to Rock By

Artist development refers to a long-standing record-label process of signing a new band and waiting patiently for it to grow into a moneymaking act. This process happens far less frequently these days than it used to, as most of the big labels seek instant financial gratification.

So make sure you have some self-generated commercial clout—in other words, a solid base—before sending your demo to a record label. If you have even an inkling of doubt about whether you're ready, wait six months. Once you've gone to a label and its A&R executives have turned you down, it's tough to get them to flip-flop later and pay attention to you. Of course, no matter how good you are and how solid your base, much of this decision is out of your hands.

Using Your Newfound Clout with the Record Label

Once you've signed with a record label, and start to sell records, you may no longer be at the mercy of the company. You're no longer a developing artist; you have clout. Rather than sending demos and praying for an A&R representative to get back to you, you may find people happily returning your calls. At this point, you almost certainly need a manager, as label reps prefer not to have separate dealings with three or four different band members.

Since record labels first began, artists have complained that their companies don't pay nearly enough attention to them. But maybe you'll be lucky and find yourself a priority artist, which means respect, attention, and money allocations when you ask for them. Just remember to scrutinize—or have your manager scrutinize—the financial records. Labels are infamous for spending large sums of money without informing their artists. Remember, the more frugal your operation, the more money you'll take home. Try to train your label according to this philosophy.

Radio Stations

Radio is another example of the classic music-industry catch-22. You can only get on the air if programmers have heard of you. But they'll have heard of you only if you've been on the air. So how do you get on? It's possible, as we've discussed in previous chapters, to latch on to radio stations via local-band contests and weekly programs. But a much more effective way, if you have the opportunity, is to sign with a major label and benefit from its marketing and independent-radio promotion resources.

Reality TV Shows

There are shortcuts to the building-your-touring-base, climbing-slowly-up-the-music-industry-ladder approach we've discussed so far. The reality-television craze, in the form of Fox's *American Idol*, made a star of unknown singer Kelly Clarkson. The next year, winner Ruben Studdard and runner-up Clay Aiken landed major record sales and magazine covers.

Alas, not many reality-television outlets are available to bands—unless you count VH1's 2001 series *Bands on the Run*, which followed several (realistically) impoverished bands through various cities attempting to draw crowds to their shows. The winning band was Flickerstick, which earned a record deal and put out a debut, *Welcome Home the Astronauts*.

Nonetheless, even if you're not interested in singing Simon and Garfunkel's "Bridge Over Troubled Water" in a slick falsetto before millions of television viewers, reality television may offer opportunities for your band. Certain rapping and country-singing characters on MTV's long-running *The Real World*, for example, have sustained mildly successful music careers. (Keep in mind, though, this route leads you to becoming famous as "that dude from *The Real World* instead of "that dude who makes really good music.")

If you're really aggressive—or shameless, some might say—it might be worth trying for exposure opportunities on other reality shows. They're hard to get onto, of course, but hits such as *Cupid*, *High School Reunion*, *Dismissed*, and other non-music-oriented shows might help one of the band members become a minor celebrity. And this can be a marketing or publicity angle to advertise your band. Then again, a game show like *The Price Is Right* or a talk show like *Jerry Springer* may have the same effect. Television is an exposure machine. Use it wisely.

Can You Work in the Music Business?

If you're in a band because you think it's a savvy career decision and a ticket to riches and stardom, you're probably in the wrong business. Most bands won't "make it." Most won't even stay together long enough to become a solid attraction on the local club or wedding circuit.

But if you're not successful even after coming this far—you've gone through the hard times, developed thick skin, dealt with rejection, played dinky, smoky clubs, and hit the road in a van—the experience hasn't been wasted time. It could lead you to a job in the *music business.*

If you're in a band for the other reason—the music is inside you and it just has to come out—try to stave off the 9-to-5 job for as long as you can. The band you're in may not function perfectly, or it may have structural problems that need to be worked out, but making music is your thing, so stick with it as long as you can afford to.

Words to Rock By

When most people refer to the **music business,** they mean record labels—specifically the big ones in New York, Los Angeles, and Nashville, like Sony, Warner Bros., and EMI. But music is a decentralized business, with career opportunities in management, publicity, radio programming, concert promotion, road-crew work, merchandise sales, rock journalism, tour work, and many more.

Getting a Record Company Job

Do you need a college degree to get a record company job? Fortunately, no. It can help in some areas, including management, but while you're toiling away for four years learning the academics of contracts and negotiation, some kid in a band is (perhaps unknowingly) spending the same time getting hands-on experience. What you learn as a performing musician, from management to guerrilla marketing, can be directly applied to a record-company position.

"Everything I do these days as a music-business consultant and personal manager had its beginnings in the years I spent dragging my drums around the road," Mark says.

What record-label positions are available to you? As we mention in Chapter 22, they include publicist, promotions director (for radio and video), A&R, and, if you have some retail experience, sales. After years or months of band experience, if you learn from the band business, you may have enough know-how to handle one of these jobs. But to land one, you'll have to go through the usual travails of connections and job interviews. Although the labels go through tough times like any other industry, it's easier and perhaps more comfortable to sit behind an L.A. desk than to endure endless nights of tour-van trips, smoky clubs, and lugging amps around.

Note, also, that you may not have to move to L.A. or the other big music-industry towns to work at a record label. Independent labels are everywhere, from Chicago's Bloodshot Records to Boulder, Colorado's, What Are? Records. The pay may not match that of Sony or Warner Bros., but you'll probably have better opportunities to work with artists and move up quickly to influential positions. Many indie-label employees stay in their jobs for years; many also "graduate" to bigger labels after hands-on seasoning.

Working at a Radio Station

A job at a major record label, as we've mentioned, usually means a career in New York, Los Angeles, or Nashville. Radio stations, however, are everywhere.

To work in most high-level radio positions, from engineering to programming to sales, you may need a college degree—and most likely a few years of work at the campus radio station.

Before venturing into a radio career, pay attention to how the industry works. Unless you snag a (probably low-paying) job at a community station or Public Radio International, you'll probably work for one of several huge companies. These include Clear Channel Communications, Cumulus Broadcasting, and Infinity Broadcasting.

Words to Rock By

In the context of radio, a **demographic,** or demo, refers to the ages, genders, and other characteristics of the listening audience. Certain demos— 18- to 34-year-old males, for example—are extremely important because the audience buys lots of advertisers' products.

Commercial radio is great fun—what's not to like about exposing millions of people to songs they like?—but don't expect to be able to play whatever you want. The days of free-form rock DJs have been gone since the mid-1970s. Today, radio stations hew to specific formats (see Chapter 24 for examples) in order to draw the broadest possible *demographic* of listeners.

Radio has developed into a real science over the last few decades. The idea is to find a broad niche, or targeted audience (such as young affluent females), and air a mix of music, news, and talk to catch their attention. Successful radio stations capture big advertisers.

Almost always, major radio stations rely on audience research to determine which listeners like which songs, DJs, or talk-show hosts. Some stations hire pollsters to play snippets of songs to potential listeners over the phone; listeners rate the songs. The resulting data is often influential in deciding which songs get on the radio.

In most major markets, radio stations are incredibly competitive with each other. Station managers pay close attention to the quarterly *ratings*, which help advertisers choose which stations to patronize. Stations with consistently low ratings often have to make abrupt changes—anything from replacing key members of the staff to shutting down one format and starting up another.

Although there are stable stations in the United States where the same employees have worked for years and years, radio tends to be a volatile industry with a high turnover rate. You can establish yourself as a talent and have an excellent chance of "hopping" from one station to another depending on market trends. But don't count on job stability.

Managers, Agents, and Entertainment Lawyers

Mark's career took him from band drummer to newspaper rock critic to publicist. Then, in the mid-1980s, a long-time colleague, concert promoter Chuck Morris, approached Mark to co-manage a young Texas singer-songwriter named Lyle Lovett.

Mark and Chuck traveled to Houston for Lovett's first record-release party. (The singer had pulled off the difficult trick of signing with a major label, MCA Records, on the strength of his demo tape.) At the party, Lovett's father cooked barbecue and the singer did a few of his early songs. "I remember specifically hearing 'This Old Porch' and going, 'Whoa!'" Mark says. "That's how I got into personal management." Lovett became his first client.

In Mark's experience, his background as a member of bands has been crucial to his managerial instincts. "I have certain empathy for what musicians go through on the road that maybe some other managers don't," he says. "It's hard to understand how much hard work goes into it if you haven't done it."

Like managers, *agents* (see Chapter 8 for the definition of an agent) tend to fall into their jobs after years in bands or working at other levels of the music industry.

But music attorneys require a different kind of experience. For one thing, they have to go to college and then law school, and then pass the bar in their respective states. Still, any kind of band background will serve a music lawyer well.

"Chill for a little bit after law school," Josh Grier, a lawyer who represents rockers Wilco, Bob Mould, and many others, told Steve in an interview for *Request*. "You don't have to come roaring out of the gate and get a job representing Madonna. It's probably better if you don't."

Studio Musicians

Although they rarely get the superstar glory, musicians who are lucky enough to find solid studio work tend to have more stable lives than members of touring bands. They don't have to travel all the time, for one thing, and can raise a family in one place. They also don't have to worry about the politics of being in a band—see Chapter 6—and can simply make money by following other people's musical direction.

Some notable, influential studio bands:

♦ The Funk Brothers, a rotating amalgamation of jazz, R&B, and funk musicians that backed almost every major Motown artist, from Stevie Wonder to Michael Jackson. They're the subject of the superb documentary *Standing in the Shadows of Motown* (2002).

♦ Booker T. & the MG's, the house band at Memphis's Stax Records in the 1960s, backing such stars as Sam and Dave, Otis Redding, and Isaac Hayes. They had instrumental hits of their own, too, notably "Green Onions."

♦ The Chess Records band, led by the great songwriter Willie Dixon, was a crucial but unsung part of 1950s Chicago blues classics by Muddy Waters, Sonny Boy Williamson, Buddy Guy, Koko Taylor, and many others.

Hired-hand musicians aren't limited to work in studios. They can also serve in clubs' house bands, or major artists' touring bands. Most of the best-known "working musicians"—drummer Jim Keltner, keyboardist Al Kooper, guitarists Steuart Smith and Eric Ambel, and others you may have heard introduced at many different concerts—began their careers as members of other bands. Kooper, for example, played the famous organ part on Bob Dylan's rock classic "Like a Rolling Stone" and was a member of the funky blues collective Blood, Sweat & Tears, among other things.

What makes a good studio musician? Talent, of course. But also reliability. Stars can occasionally get away with erratic behavior, but studio musicians absolutely, positively have to show up on time and prepared. Once you get a reputation for doing this, more work follows.

Roadies

Generally speaking, band members rarely become roadies. The path usually goes in the opposite direction—Brian Henneman was a roadie for the alternative-country band Uncle Tupelo in the early 1990s before forming his own band, the Bottle Rockets, which wound up making critically acclaimed records and developing a national reputation.

That's not to say you can't become a roadie. The job is strenuous, usually with a lot of heavy lifting, and much travel is involved. It can be exciting, though, with direct access to stars and moments of tuning guitars or making emergency repairs in front of thousands of people.

"Grunt" roadies load the heavy stuff from the trucks to the stage and vice versa. "Specialist" roadies, such as lighting and sound technicians, have technical expertise and operate high-tech equipment during the show. Salaries vary widely, depending on your experience and the level of performer you work with.

Rock Critics

If you can string a sentence together and have an opinion about music, a career as a *rock critic* may be worth pursuing. As Steve can attest, it's a fun job in which you get to listen to CDs all day and review concerts. To be successful, you should probably learn something about music history, interviewing people, and taking fast notes.

The career isn't especially high-paying, and in order to land at a prominent publication you'll almost certainly have to climb up the ladder from small alt-weeklies or daily newspapers. Director Cameron Crowe's experience of being a 15-year-old cover-story writer for *Rolling Stone*—as documented in the movie *Almost Famous*—is rare indeed.

Rock critics, also known as music journalists, are often dismissed for back-talking rather than creating art themselves. Some say they're just frustrated musicians. That may be true, but many prominent critics, such as the late Lester Bangs, former *New York Times* writer Ann Powers, and *Fargo Rock City* author Chuck Klosterman, have put out influential works of their own.

Avoiding Bad Notes

Writing about music is like dancing about architecture.

—Quote generally attributed to rocker Elvis Costello

You may need a college degree and some level of journalism experience in order to land a job as a rock critic. But plenty of critics, especially freelancers, came to the profession as band members or other music experts. It works both ways, too, occasionally: Ira Kaplan, singer for the veteran trio Yo La Tengo, is a recovering rock critic.

The Least You Need to Know

◆ If your band regularly sells out small clubs, attracts a consistently large following, and even has some record-sales successes, it may be time to graduate to bigger concert venues—and, in general, the big time.

◆ Once you expand from small clubs to large theaters and even concert arenas, you'll have to hire additional help and build a larger infrastructure. Suddenly, your band is a business, with employees and responsibilities.

- To break into the music business—which is to say, become a star—you may have to hook up with a major record label.

- Reality TV shows like *American Idol* are geared more toward pop singers than traditional bands, but some shows may present potential exposure or marketing opportunities.

- Your band experience can serve you well for a record-label or studio-musician career—and maybe a job in radio or other media.

Glossary

A&R Short for "artists and repertoire," it generally refers to record-label scouts.

artist development A long-standing record-label process of signing a new band and waiting patiently for it to grow into a moneymaking act.

burning Slang expression for copying a computer music file (*see* MP3) to a blank, rewritable compact disc.

buzz Slang expression for a mixture of aggressive media coverage and word of mouth

charisma A certain magnetism that makes a musician attractive to the public.

club Short for *nightclub*, this is a facility that usually features live music at least one or two nights a week.

cover songs Tunes artists perform that are widely associated with other artists.

demo Short for *demonstration*. It's a homemade recording usually used for noncommercial purposes, like "pitching" your music to club promoters, radio stations, or record labels.

demographic Used frequently in radio, the term refers to ages, genders, and other characteristics of the listening audience.

distribution Industry of "middleman" companies that receive CDs from the artist or record label, then ship them for a fee to retail outlets.

DJ Short for *disc jockey*. A performer responsible for electronically stringing funk and dance songs together at a nightclub. Alternatively, it's a radio-station "personality" who talks on the air and plays records.

electronic press kit An electronic version of the *press kit*. Often reproduced on DVD or VHS.

fake book A thick collection of popular songs, from jazz to standards to folk to rock, printed in rough, easy-to-follow sheet-music form.

feedback A jarring electronic nuisance that comes from positioning your electric instrument or microphone too close to an amp; it's mostly to be avoided, although performers such as Jimi Hendrix have turned it into an art form.

format Narrowly defined type of music a radio station plays all the time.

gig A live performance, after which (usually) the band gets paid.

group dynamics The personal interrelationships among members of a small group—in this case, a band formed to create music.

groupie A super-fan who follows around a particular rock group in order to make a personal backstage connection (often sexual) with the star.

guerrilla marketing Untraditional means of gaining business exposure, like sticking fliers under windshield wipers

guitar tab Short for "tablature," it's a style of writing down music for guitar and bass.

head arrangement The opposite of writing out a piece of music on paper, it means a band verbally agrees on chord changes, basic orders, and solos.

hook Usually part of the chorus, a hook is whatever makes a song stand out and appeal to people—for example, a melody or a catchy guitar riff.

HTML Hypertext markup language, which uses text commands to tell Internet web browsers like Netscape or Explorer how to display a file online.

hype Like buzz, only less intense.

link Core concept on the World Wide Web, in which the owner of one web page refers a reader to another web page.

MIDI Short for Musical Instrument Digital Interface, this is a type of computer file enabling musical instruments to "talk to" each other (and to computers).

miking   Shorthand term for setting up microphones next to drums and other acoustic instruments.

mixer   An electronic gadget that combines different instruments together on tape.

MP3   Short for MPEG Audio Layer 3, it's an audio compression technology many people use to distribute digital songs over the Internet.

music business   Usually used in the context of big record labels, but actually a decentralized industry incorporating management, publicity, radio programming, concert promotion, road-crew work, merchandise sales, and all other areas.

networking   The art of making contact with important people who can help your career.

overdub   A recording-studio term for adding new sounds onto the tape after the band has completed its basic tracks.

press kit   A package of promotional materials, usually including *bio, press release*, and photo, which bands send to media outlets such as newspapers and television stations.

publicist   A record-label employee or independent professional hired to help entertainers get free media coverage.

publicity   Free media coverage.

publishing rights   What you automatically hold, in the legal sense, whenever you write a song.

rider   A general business term meaning "addendum to any contract specifying extra details," it has evolved in the music industry to represent special backstage requests for star performers.

ripping   Slang expression for transferring a song from a compact disc to a computer hard drive.

royalties   Payments a songwriter receives whenever his or her song winds up in a television show, film, or on the radio or compact disc.

schmoozing   Like networking, only less formal.

set list   The band's master list of songs, negotiated long in advance and affixed to the stage so everyone can refer to it.

shredding   A metal or hard-rock guitarist's slang term for playing a really excellent, fast, rocking solo during a song.

singer-songwriter   An artist who writes and sings his or her own songs.

sound check   The performer's preconcert rehearsal, usually at the venue a few hours before the show.

stage presence   Charisma that comes across while a musician performs.

tablature   *See* guitar tab.

Publications of Special Interest

Acoustic Guitar
PO Box 767
San Anselmo, CA 94979
415-485-6946

Billboard
770 Broadway, 6th Floor
New York, NY 10003
646-654-4400

Blender
1040 Avenue of the Americas
New York, NY 10018
212-302-2626

Blues Revue
Route 1, Box 75
Salem, WV 26426-9604
304-782-1971

College Music Journal
151 W. 25th Street
New York, NY 10001
917-606-1908

Country Music Today
3113 S. University Drive,
Suite 202
Fort Worth, TX 76109
615-298-3718

Dirty Linen
PO Box 66600
Baltimore, MD 21239-6600
410-583-7973

DownBeat
102 N. Haven Road
Elmhurst, IL 60126
800-535-7496

Guitar One
6 East 32nd Street, 11th Floor
New York, NY 10016
212-561-3000

Guitar World
1115 Broadway
New York, NY 10010
212-807-7100

Harp
8737 Colesville Road, Ninth Floor
Silver Spring, MD 20910-3921
866-427-7624

Keyboard
2800 Campus Drive
San Mateo, CA 94403
650-513-4400

Living Blues
PO Box 1848, 301 Hill Hall
University, MS 38677
800-390-3527

Modern Drummer
12 Old Bridge Road
Cedar Grove, NJ 07009
973-239-4140

MOJO
Mappin House, 4 Winsley Street
London, England W1W8HF
020-7436-1515

No Depression
2 Morse Circle
Durham, NC 27713
peter@nodepression.net

Q
Mappin House, 4 Winsley Street
London, England W1W 8HF
020-7436-1515

Radio & Records
10100 Santa Monica Boulevard,
Third Floor
Los Angeles, CA 90067
310-553-4330

Relix
180 Varick Street, Fourth Floor
New York, NY 10014
646-230-0100

Rolling Stone
1290 Avenue of the Americas
New York, NY 10018
212-484-1616

SPIN
205 Lexington Avenue, Third Floor
New York, NY 10016
212-231-7400

Sample Performance Contracts

We've included two extremely simple performance contracts bands can use before playing professional gigs. The first is between the band and the gig organizer, whether it's a club owner or wedding planner. The second is for when the band hires a booking agent as a middleman.

Contract Between Band and Gig Organizer

THIS CONTRACT, entered into on this _____ day of _____, 200___, is for the services of the (band name) for the performance described in the following sections. The undersigned employer and the undersigned musician(s) agree as follows:

  1. NAME OF BAND _____

  2. NAME AND ADDRESS OF PLACE OF PERFORMANCE

       _____

  3. DATE OF PERFORMANCE _____

  4. TIME OF PERFORMANCE _____

  5. PAY AGREED UPON _____

  6. DEPOSIT (if applicable) _____

  7. PAYMENT OF BALANCE OF _____ TO BE PAID IN CASH OR CERTIFIED CHECK AT THE END OF PERFORMANCE.

  8. ANY ADDITIONAL TERMS/SPECIFICATIONS

       _____

  9. This contract constitutes a complete and binding agreement between the employer and the (band name).

10. The persons signing for Employer and the Musician(s) agree to be personally, jointly, and severally liable for the terms of this contract.

_____ for [band name]

_____ for Employer

Contract Between Band and Booking Agent

THIS CONTRACT for the services of the musicians described below made this _____ day of _____, 200___, between the undersigned Purchaser of music (hereinafter referred to as Purchaser) and the undersigned Musicians (hereinafter referred to as "Artist"). Agent refers to the booking Agent who secures the engagement on behalf of the Artist.

The Purchaser hereby engages the Artist. Artist hereby agrees to perform the engagement with all of the terms and conditions herein set forth including those entitled "Additional Terms and Conditions":

1. **NAME OF BAND** _____

2. **PLACE OF ENGAGEMENT** _____

3. **ADDRESS OF ENGAGEMENT** _____

4. **DATE(S) OF ENGAGEMENT** _____

5. **HOURS OF ENGAGEMENT** _____

   TIME VENUE AVAILABLE FOR LOAD IN _____

6. **TYPE OF ENGAGEMENT** _____

   DRESS CODE _____

7. **PRICE** _____

METHOD OF PAYMENT:

DEPOSIT $ _____, Payable to Agent upon return of contract.

BALANCE $ _____, Payable to (band name) in cash or certified check immediately upon conclusion of engagement.

IN CASE OF DEFAULT BY PURCHASER: Liquidated damages of the Artist will be the amount stated in BALANCE in Section 7, plus reasonable attorney's fees and court costs. Deposit will be retained by Agent for services performed.

8. **SOUND PROVIDED BY** _____

   LIGHTS PROVIDED BY _____

9. **BREAKS:** Only one 15-minute break for each hour of performance is allowed unless other arrangements are made with Purchaser.

10. **GUIDELINES FOR PRIVATE PARTIES:** Band members and personnel should refrain from eating or drinking on the premises of all private parties unless invited to do so by Purchaser. No guests of Artist(s) are permitted without the consent of the Purchaser.

11. **THE PURCHASER** shall at all times have complete supervision, direction, and control over the services of Artist(s) and all details of the performance by Artist. The leader shall enforce disciplinary measures for just cause, and

carry out instructions of the Purchaser as to the selection and manner of performance.

12. **THE ARTIST** _____ agrees and guarantees to pay ____ % percent of the agreed price $ _____ for personal services, booking fee, and contract fee to the booking Agent. This commission is due and payable when all parties have signed this Contract and must be paid within five days after the date that the Artist(s) is to perform for the Purchaser except where Agent has already retained said commission from the deposit already paid by Purchaser. Additional postage and telephone fees may be added by Agent, not to exceed $100.00 within any one month period without prior consultation between Agent and Artist. If leader or key personnel of this musical group is rebooked into this or any establishment represented by the Purchaser within 12 months from the termination of this Agreement, Purchaser and leader shall be jointly and severally liable for payment to AGENT for commission in the rate set forth in this engagement.

13. **THE AGREEMENT** of the Artist to perform is subject to proven detention by sickness, accidents, riots, strikes, epidemics, acts of God, or any other legitimate conditions beyond their control. If artist is unable to perform, Agent will take reasonable measures to provide a suitable alternate Artist.

14. **THIS CONTRACT** constitutes the sole, complete, and binding agreement between the Artist(s) and the Purchaser. Agent and its employees act only as Agent and assumes no responsibility or liability as between the Purchaser and the Artist(s). Covenants herein contained between said Artist(s), their leader, manager, or representative and Agent are intended to be binding as between said Artist(s), their leader, manager, or representative and Agent.

15. **MEMBERS OF UNIONS OR GUILDS,** which may include leader and members of this unit, agree to accept sole responsibility for complying with the rules and regulations of said unions or guilds of which they may be members.

16. **ADDITIONAL TERMS AND CONDITIONS**

See Attached Rider if any.

_____

For Purchaser

(Street address)

(SS# or Federal Tax ID#)

(City, state, ZIP)

(Telephone)

For Artist

(Street address)

(SS# or Federal Tax ID#)

(City, state, ZIP)

(Telephone)

(Contract #)

For Artist

(Print street address)

(SS# or Federal Tax ID#)

(City, state, ZIP)

(Telephone)

(Contract #)

Sample Tour Itineraries

Here are sample tour itineraries from bands of various levels. Note the dates and locations. The San Francisco underground-rock quartet Erase Errata has a particularly grueling schedule, with few days off and long driving distances every day. Jam band O.A.R.'s strategy is to play mostly colleges—in the band's brief, heavy-touring career, it has graduated from small campus clubs to large fieldhouses, theaters, and even arenas.

Established rockers Neil Young and Crazy Horse leave five days to travel between Manchester, Tennessee, and Milwaukee, Wisconsin, and leave eight days for five New York gigs. If you're serious about building a tour base, you'll have to take the Erase Errata approach, possibly for years, until you can coast, Young-style.

Erase Errata (Underground Rock Quartet from San Francisco)

August 2003

29	San Francisco, California—Verdi Club

September 2003

3	Omaha, Nebraska—Sokol Underground
4	Minneapolis, Minnesota—Triple Rock
5	Chicago, Illinois—Abbey Pub
6	Chicago, Illinois—Hideout

7	Detroit, Michigan—Magic Stick
8	Oberlin, Ohio—Oberlin College
9–10	Montreal, Quebec, Canada—La Salla Rosa
11	Cambridge, Massachussetts—Middle East Downstairs
12	New York, New York—Bowery Ballroom
13	Washington, D.C.—Black Cat
14	Philadelphia, Pennsylvania—First Unitarian Church
16	Carrboro, North Carolina—Cat's Cradle
17	Charleston, South Carolina—Village Tavern
18	Orlando, Florida—Will's Pub
19	Tampa, Florida—Orpheum
20	Atlanta, Georgia—Echo Lounge
21	Knoxville, Tennessee—Pilot Light
23	Memphis, Tennessee—Hi Tone
24	Lawrence, Kansas—Bottleneck
25	Denver, Colorado—Climax Lounge
26	Salt Lake City, Utah—Kilby Court
27	Reno, Nevada—The Arkaik

Centro-Matic (Improvisational Folk-Rock Band from Texas)

September 2003

12	Fort Worth, Texas—The Aardvark
13	Austin, Texas—Mercury Lounge
15	Albuquerque, New Mexico—Launchpad
16	Phoenix, Arizona—Modified
17	San Diego, California—Casbah
18	Los Angeles, California—Spaceland
19	San Francisco, California—Café du Nord
20	Sacramento, California—Capitol Garage
22	Portland, Oregon—The Tonic Lounge
23	Seattle, Washington—Tractor Tavern
24	Boise, Idaho—Neurolux
25	Salt Lake City, Utah—Kilby Court
26	Denver, Colorado—Larimer Lounge

27   Kansas City, Missouri—The Brick

28   Lincoln, Nebraska—Duffy's

29   Iowa City, Iowa—Gabe's Oasis

30   Des Moines, Iowa—Vaudeville Mews

October 2003

2   Minneapolis, Minnesota—400 Bar

3   Madison, Wisconsin—Toronto Club

4   Chicago, Illinois—Subterranean

5   St. Louis, Missouri—Hi-Pointe

O.A.R. (New York City Jam-Rock Band)

October 2003

9   Lancaster, Pennsylvania—The Chameleon Club

17   New Orleans, Louisiana—Tipitina's

18   Austin, Texas—Austin Music Hall

20   Morgantown, West Virginia—West Virginia University

22   Huntington, West Virginia—Marshall University

23   Blacksburg, Virginia—Virginia Polytechnic Institute

24   Bloomsburg, Pennsylvania—Bloomsburg University

25   Storrs, Connecticut—University of Connecticut

26   Wheaton, Maryland—Wheaton's Fall Music Festival

28   St. Louis, Missouri—Saint Louis University

29   Lawrence, Kansas—Liberty Hall

31   Cincinnati, Ohio—Xavier University

November 2003

1   Waukesha, Wisconsin—Carroll College

2   Charleston, Illinois—Eastern Illinois University

6   Winston-Salem, North Carolina—Ziggy's

7   Athens, Georgia—Georgia Theater

9   Ypsilanti, Michigan—Eastern Michigan University

10   Cleveland, Ohio—Case Western Reserve University

12   Boston, Massachusetts—Boston College

13	Providence, Rhode Island—Dunkin' Donuts Center
14	State College, Pennsylvania—Pennsylvania State University
15	Hanover, New Hampshire—Dartmouth College
17	Durham, New Hampshire—University of New Hampshire
19	Elmira, New York—Elmira College
20	Geneseo, New York—State University of New York-Geneseo
21	Bethlehem, Pennsylvania—Moravian College
22	West Point, New York—West Point Military Academy
24	Worcester, Massachusetts—The Palladium
25	Annapolis, Maryland—Armadillo's
28–29	New York, New York—Hammerstein Ballroom

Neil Young and Crazy Horse

June 2003

8	West Palm Beach, Florida—Coral Sky Amphitheater
9	Tampa, Florida—St. Pete Times Forum
13	Manchester, Tennessee—Bonnaroo Festival
19	Milwaukee, Wisconsin—Marcus Amphitheater
22	Clarkston, Michigan—DTE Energy Music Theater
23	Toronto, Ontario—Air Canada Centre
25	Columbia, Maryland—Merriweather Post Pavilion
26	New York, New York—Madison Square Garden
28	Uncasville, Connecticut—Mohegan Sun Arena
29	Wantagh, New York—Jones Beach

July 2003

2	Camden, New Jersey—Tweeter Center
4	Saratoga Springs, New York—SPAC
16	Auburn, Washington—White River Amphitheater
18	Mountain View, California—Shoreline Amphitheater
20	Concord, California—Chronicle Pavilion
22–23	Los Angeles, California—Greek Theater

August 2003

5	Dallas, Texas—Smirnoff Music Centre

Sample Tour Budget

The following is a sample budget for a typical band's tour. Note that budget items often differ from tour to tour; a superstar artist, for example, may have to budget for the artist's jet or a traveling golf pro. Also, a band just starting out probably won't have a crew, other than a friend or two to help carry the amplifiers in and out of the van.

Tour Budget Worksheet

Crew salaries (if any): _____

Band salaries: _____

Band/crew per diems (daily "allowances" for food and so forth): _____

Transportation costs including gas/maintenance/rental: _____

Hotels: _____

Phone/fax/Internet access: _____

Postage/overnight pkgs.: _____

Tolls/parking: _____

Equipment rental/repair: _____

Other out of pocket expenses: _____

Totals: _____

Income (total of what band will make from gigs): _____

Expenses (total of all expenses on the road): _____

Profit/shortfall (subtract expenses from income to get this figure): _____

Sample Press Kit, Including Press Release and Bio

A press kit, as we mention in Chapter 14, should contain a band photo (with all the musicians' names printed clearly and spelled correctly), a bio, and a press release about an upcoming event. Following, from the Ataris, a young band signed to Columbia Records, are examples of the bio and press release.

Bio

The Ataris are …

>Kris Roe: Lead Vocals/Guitar
>
>Mike Davenport: Bass/Vocals
>
>John Collura: Guitar/Vocals
>
>Chris "Kid" Knapp: Drums

The Ataris, one of the most successful independent rock bands of recent years, have a brand new album, *so long, astoria*, the group's eagerly-awaited major label debut on Columbia Records. *so long, astoria* is the first full-length Ataris album in nearly two years.

"Musically," says Ataris front man Kris Roe, "we took a back-to-basics straightforward rock approach. There's no novelty, no silly aspects to this record at all. It's a serious story-telling record. Everything is really personal, every song is about something different, each song is like a page in the scrapbook of memories, but it's not a dark record at all."

"In a lot of my lyrics," Kris reveals, "I like to encode a lot of hidden messages and whatnot. I like our fans to read into things. I feel that our fans are smart and I don't want to give them just a bunch of surface lyrics that you can take at face value."

Conceptually, *so long, astoria* takes its inspiration from a concept expressed in punk pioneer Richard Hell's novel, *Go Now* (which also exists as a spoken word album): that memory can transcend the experience that generated the memory. "That really hit home with me," Kris points out. "That's how I try and structure my life: to try to do what will produce the best memories for later. When we're traveling on tour, there are a lot of things that you let go of and leave behind, but, at the end of the day, even if you didn't accomplish anything, you'll have these great memories of all the people you've met and all the places you've been and all these things that you've done and all this time that you've shared with your friends."

The primacy of memory is a theme that runs through the songs on *so long, astoria*. When writing for the new album, Kris Roe got in his car and drove around to "places where I grew up, places where I used to live, my old school, all these places. At two in the morning, I'd sit in my car and I'd just write. I'd take all these Polaroids of where I grew up. I went back and stole back these memories that were once mine by taking all these Polaroids. At this point in my life and career, I can't very well go back to the house where I used to live and say to the people that live there now, 'Can I sit in my old bedroom?' But I could take photographs in the f***ing window. I tried to do anything I could to make this record more vivid and detailed, even going to stalker limits."

The album's title track encapsulates the idea of memory being a kind of buried treasure: "Life is only as good as the memories we make/and I'm taking back what belongs to me/Polaroids of classrooms unattended/These relics of remembrance are just like shipwrecks/only they're gone faster than the smell after it rains …./And when this hourglass has filtered out its final grain of sand/I'll raise my glass to the memories we had/This is my wish and I'm taking it back, I'm taking 'em all back."

"In This Diary," the album's first single, has been slated to be lensed as a video by cutting edge director Steven Murashige, whose resumé includes clips for Incubus and Rage Against The Machine. The song itself finds Kris admitting that "Being grown up isn't half as fun as growing up" before offering up the hope that "… eventually you'll finally get it right."

For Kris, getting it right means connecting in a real way with the band's audience and the Ataris are ferociously dedicated to their fans. "We are a very personal band with our fans," Kris is eager to stress. "We definitely go out of our way. We take it an extra mile. We write all our fans back personally, we run our own website personally. We have a kid from the audience get on stage and play guitar on a song with us every night. We opened up a record store in Santa Barbara, where we live, so that when we're off tour, people can come visit us. We even rehearse and practice there so when kids come, we'll let them jam with us. We listen to the demos kids give us and we've helped a few bands get signed to indie labels. We want this to be known about our band: all we are is a bunch of music fans who got lucky and happen to be living our dream. We are a band that exists solely for the purpose of our fans."

But this kind of 24-7 attention to fans can create conflicts with other real-world responsibilities. In "The Saddest Song," Kris writes a heartfelt apologia to his daughter, hoping that she'll grow up to understand why her father's work took him away from home so often. "I'm trying to tell my daughter that I know what it's like to be without your father," he confesses, "because I was without my dad for about five years after my parents got divorced." "I pray I get the chance to make it up to you," he sings to her. "We've got a lot of catching up to do."

Kris extends both identification and empathy to the poet Emily Dickinson in "Unopened Letter," tracing a spiritual kinship between the Belle of Amherst and Kurt Cobain, two great poetic souls who live on in a "posthumous life." "It's about how a lot of artists never get the credit they deserve," Kris offers, "until they pass away." Visiting the Dickinson Homestead while collecting the stories and images for *so long, astoria*, Kris was inspired to ask "If I died tomorrow, would this song live on forever?"

When the Ataris received a fan letter written to the band by a young girl confined to a hospital bed with a life-threatening illness, Kris was moved to write "My Reply," one of the most emotionally powerful songs on *so long, astoria*. "I want to make sure that everything I say is something that is really from my heart, something really personal, and something positive," Kris says about writing this song. "I want to know that if I'm reaching kids, I'm reaching them in a way that's really helping them. I know what it's like to be a kid that's totally down, that grew up in a small town and doesn't have many friends, that doesn't feel like he or she fits in or belongs. If I'm speaking to somebody in that way, I want to make sure that I let them know that 'Hey, man, there's hope out there. There's a lot more beyond this life and you need to look for it.'"

When it came time to find a producer for *so long, astoria*, the Ataris chose Lou Giordano (Goo Goo Dolls, Sunny Day Real Estate, Samiam, Paul Westerberg, Hüsker Dü, Sugar). "I wanted this album to possess this kind of straightforward powerpop rock vibe," Kris admits, "kind of what the Replacements always did. I wanted to make a record that spoke to a wide audience. Lou had worked with a lot of bands outside of just our scene."

The result is a dream come true for fans of this high-energy modern rock combo, with the new original songs showcasing the emotionally charged Ataris sound while a revved-up rendition of Don Henley's "Boys of Summer" gives a full-on jolt of the band's spirited fun.

The Ataris are: Kris Roe (lead vocals/guitar), Johnny Collura (guitar/vocals), Mike Davenport (bass/vocals), and Chris "Kid" Knapp (drums). The group was first discovered in 1997 when songwriter Kris Roe passed along his demo tape to Joe Escalante, bassist for the Vandals and owner of Kung Fu Records. Moving from Anderson, Indiana, to Santa Barbara, California, Roe assembled The Ataris' line-up and recorded the group's first full-length offering, *Anywhere But Here*, for Kung Fu. The Ataris subsequently recorded an EP, *Look Forward To Failure* (1998—Fat Wreck Chords), as well as the additional Kung Fu albums: *Blue Skies, Broken Hearts ... Next 12 Exits* (1999) and *End Is Forever* (2001), each of which has sold more than 100,000 copies in the United States and has achieved similar sales successes around the world.

A virtual touring machine since the band's inception, the Ataris have shared bills with Jimmy Eat World, Social Distortion, Blink 182, the Hives, 311, and others. The group has been a main stage attraction on the Van's Warped Tour and has sold out tours in Japan, Australia, New Zealand, and Europe.

"After months of writing and recording our new album, we are very excited to be getting back on the road to see all of our loyal fans again," said the Ataris' Kris Roe. Following the release of *so long, astoria*, the band intends on touring for at least a year with shows including performances on the main stage of the 2003 Warped Tour.

With the release of *so long, astoria*, the promise of the Ataris' early indie roots is fulfilled with some of the most provocative and emotionally powerful rock sounds this continually-evolving group has ever made.

Press Release

July 1, 2003

FOR IMMEDIATE RELEASE

COLUMBIA MUSIC VIDEO RELEASES LIVE AT CAPITOL MILLING, A BRAND-NEW DVD FROM THE ATARIS

In Stores Today

(dateline—New York—Columbia Records—July 1, 2003)

Columbia Music Video has just released *Live at Capitol Milling*, the eagerly awaited DVD video from the Ataris, one of the most successful independent rock bands of recent years. The release of *Live At Capitol Milling* comes in the midst of the band's current series of main stage performances on the 2003 Van's Warped Tour (see itinerary following).

When it came time for the Ataris to film the video for "In This Diary," the first single from the group's Columbia Records debut *so long, astoria*, the adventurous indie rock band invited a few hundred of the group's biggest fans to Capitol Milling, a cavernous warehouse space in downtown Los Angeles, to appear in the shoot.

Shot over the course of two days—January 16–17, 2003—the "In This Diary" video captured an intense live performance by the Ataris. As a special treat for the fans at the Capitol Milling video shoot, the Ataris performed a high-spirited mini-concert of songs from *so long, astoria* and crowd-pleasing classic tracks from the group's catalog.

With the release of *Live At Capitol Milling*, Ataris fans can experience first-hand the excitement and emotional power of the filming of "In This Diary" and the subsequent exclusive for-fans-only Ataris concert.

Live at Capitol Milling includes the finished version of the "In This Diary" video, directed by Steven Murashige (Incubus, Rage Against The Machine), as well as exclusive behind-the-scenes footage of the making of "In This Diary."

Rounding out *Live at Capitol Milling* are scorching live performances of "Takeoffs and Landings," "Teenage Riot," "My Reply," "Unopened Letter To The World," and "Song #13."

Released on March 4, 2003, *so long, astoria* debuted at #24 on the Top 200 Album Sales and has sold close to 400,000 copies to-date. The Ataris rendition of "The Boys of Summer" is Top 10 on the Modern Rock charts while a companion video clip, also directed by Steven Murashige, will be released to MTV. The album is produced by Lou Giordano (Sunny Day Real Estate, Samiam, Paul Westerberg, Hüsker Dü, Sugar).

A virtual touring machine since the band's inception, the Ataris have shared bills with Jimmy Eat World, Alkaline Trio, Social Distortion, Blink 182, the Hives, 311, and many others. The group has been onboard on the Van's Warped Tour since 2000, graduating to the status of main stage attraction in 2001. The Ataris have sold out tours in the United Kingdom, Japan, Australia, New Zealand, and Europe.

Index

A Little Knowledge Goes a Long Way ...

Check Out These
Best-Selling
COMPLETE IDIOT'S GUIDES

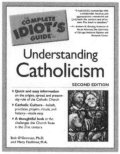

Understanding Catholicism
SECOND EDITION

1-59257-085-2
$18.95

Learning Spanish
THIRD EDITION

0-02-864451-4
$18.95

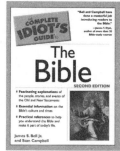

The Bible
SECOND EDITION

0-02-864382-8
$18.95

Grammar and Style
SECOND EDITION

1-59257-115-8
$16.95

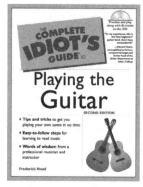

Playing the Guitar
SECOND EDITION

0-02-864244-9
$21.95 w/CD

Personal Finance in Your 20s & 30s
SECOND EDITION

0-02-864374-7
$19.95

The Perfect Resume
THIRD EDITION

0-02-864440-9
$14.95

Buying and Selling a Home
FOURTH EDITION

1-59257-120-4
$18.95

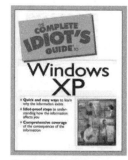

Windows XP

0-02-864232-5
$19.95

More than *400 titles* in *30 different categories*
Available at booksellers everywhere

ALPH